On Becoming
an Innovative
University Teacher

2nd edition

Birmingham • Bristol • Chester • Guildford • London • Manchester • York

SRHE and Open University Press Imprint

Current titles include:

On Becoming
an Innovative
University Teacher

Reflection in Action

2nd edition

John Cowan

Society for Research into Higher Education
& Open University Press

Open University Press
McGraw-Hill Education
McGraw-Hill House
Shoppenhangers Road
Maidenhead
Berkshire
England
SL6 2QL

email: enquiries@openup.co.uk
world wide web: www.openup.co.uk

and Two Penn Plaza, New York, NY 10121–2289, USA

First published 2006

A catalogue record of this book is available from the British Library

ISBN-10: 0 335 21992 6 (pb)
ISBN-13: 978 0335 21992 6 (pb)

Library of Congress Cataloging-in-Publication Data
CIP data applied for

Typeset by YHT Ltd, London
Printed and bound by CPI Group (U) Ltd, Croydon, CR0 4YY

Contents

Preface: Why did I write this book?

Just as the second edition of this book is rather different from the first, so this Preface is very different from its predecessor. The first version of the rewritten preface provoked my good friend Alan Harding to comment helpfully that I had explained *how* the book came to be written, but not *why* it had been written. He urged me to concentrate upon two obvious questions which I had not considered explicitly. These were why I had written a book, after all these years without so doing; and why someone who is starting out on a teaching career should buy or borrow this volume, and take time to read it. Both questions troubled me considerably. I did not have a ready answer for either, but I saw the need to focus this Preface upon them.

Why *did* I decide to write a book? Come to think of it, why had I accepted invitations over the years to speak at staff development events in Britain, and to work, usually unpaid, on educational development abroad? Why had I even agreed in later years to write chapters for other writers' books, on specific topics? I couldn't immediately pinpoint an answer which convinced me, but I knew the answers I could reject. For a start, I haven't ever had it in mind to have an improving impact on higher education in general. Indeed, Graham Gibbs described me recently (Gibbs, 2004) as someone paddling energetically in his own idiosyncratic canoe, trying to pull the supertanker of higher education on to a different course, without any discernable effect on the progress of that juggernaut. Equally, I have never seen myself as an educational evangelist, charged to persuade colleagues to sign up to the pedagogical banner to which I adhere; for I have always simply regarded it as my primary function to provide the best possible education for the students entrusted directly to my care. Certainly I am not a seeker of professional advancement; even when Napier University awarded me an honorary degree, the citation accurately recognized me as someone who preferred the anorak to the suit, who was more at home and effective at the grass roots than in the corridors of power. So I feel fairly comfortable with my self-judgement that I have not written a book to change higher education, nor to promote my pedagogical philosophy, nor for vainglory. Why *did* I do it, then?

I suppose the wish to pass on good ideas began in my childhood. My father was a kindly man. He took joy in offering help to complete strangers, whose needs he had noticed. In that wartime era, he would offer strangers a meal, accommodation, a lift in his car, even some financial support. He would shrug off their thanks by explaining that he saw goodwill as a kind of pond or reservoir, from which we each at times have needed to draw and to which, at other times, we can each contribute and thus make repayment. Seldom, in his view, did it happen that we were able to repay directly those who had helped us along our way. However, we could all contribute to the pool of goodwill as our response; and that was what *he* chose to do, as *his* response to the kindliness which had been his good fortune in the past.

I suppose some of that rationale rubbed off on his young son. I have usually tried, for much the same reason, to repay the pool of educational wisdom and advice from which I have taken so much, so often. I am always very conscious of the debt I owe to those men and women of great educational stature who have helped me along my way, and inspired me to be what I could never have managed on my own. These are not people whom I could ever have meaningfully repaid directly, for I have had little to offer that would have been of worth to them. Even thanking them has usually proved almost impossible. So, in my efforts to pay something back and to pass something on, I have accepted invitations from academics who seemed to think I might have something to share, from which they too could benefit. These prospective hosts seemingly knew of me and of my efforts, but were generally strangers to me at the time I received their invitations. I often took up the opportunities they provided for me to engage in my form of repayment. Their requests for help have taken me to places like Colombia, the Dominican Republic, Mexico, Syria and Sri Lanka. In so doing, I have had the joy of working with some wonderful, motivated teachers. In many cases we took risks together and consequently enjoyed exhilarating successes and built enduring relationships. This usually left me feeling that I had indeed been fortunate in acquiring yet more new experience, which should again be repaid and passed on. And so there has ever been occasion for me to contribute to that pool of wisdom and of good experiences.

Why, then, this book? In 1986, while I was laid up in Sri Lanka with a serious illness, my thoughts turned to reviewing what I had done, in a thesis for a higher doctorate (Cowan, 1986a). I could see advantage in bringing together papers I had written for educational journals, whose editors and readers did not want to know about engineering, and in linking these to my papers written for engineering journals, whose editors and readers likewise had not wanted to hear about educational concepts and arguments. Finishing that thesis pushed my thinking forward and helped me to consolidate it. A new model for reflective development of abilities emerged for me. And, at that time, I ceased to be a professor of engineering education and moved to become Scottish Director of the Open University (OU).

Now I was mainly a manager and partly an experienced senior colleague, expected (at least by me) to exercise academic leadership. I was only sometimes a teacher, with a slight teaching workload. My way of leading academically was to encourage teachers who showed potential and eagerness to develop and progress in partnership with me. I encouraged them to join me in exploring and drawing from that worldwide pool of educational wisdom and all that it contained. I aired innovative suggestions which they might wish to take up in their own teaching, made myself available to assist or advise if they so wished and provided modest resources where that was possible and appropriate. We worked together as peers, with a common purpose and in shared fellowship. Above all, I believe, I helped them to find, as I myself had done, the fulfilment, satisfaction and particularly the great fun of working together with like-minded colleagues and students, to bring about noteworthy educational development. These were fruitful and very happy years.

So it was that, when I retired, I had the notion of assembling as much as I could of the ideas and thinking which seemed to have been welcomed and adopted to good effect by these OU colleagues and by those with whom I had worked in developing countries. I wished to make such a useful resource available to the current generation of teachers, amongst whom I still practised my former trade, albeit now simply as a part-time colleague.

That, I suppose, was why I wrote this book. This answer takes me on to Alan's second question. Why should *you* go on to read what I have written? I picture you as a university teacher who has a concern for teaching and for your students' learning, which has brought you this far; and I imagine that you are wondering what you might get from the pages that follow. I hope that you will find some suggestions which you would like to try out or explore, some ways of thinking which you find helpful, and some questions which have not hitherto occurred to you, but which will profitably raise issues for you when you read them. I hope you will not find yourself meeting a writer who thinks he knows what you should do and how you should do it. On the contrary, I hope you will regard me as an older colleague into whose somewhat avuncular experience you can usefully tap, and with whom you would have liked to team teach had that been a possibility.

I trust you will be reassured that I describe and commend only what has been successful relatively recently – either for me or for someone with whom I have been collaborating. I can also assure you that I suggest nothing which is beyond the competence of readers like yourself. I therefore hope that, if you read on, you will want to take up some of my ideas and adapt them to your own talents and situation. If you do so, my last wish is that you will find the results effective, and so will be ready in your turn to share that experience with other colleagues. Above all, I trust that you find reflective engagement in educational development to be as rewarding, fulfilling and joyful an experience as it has always been for me.

John Cowan
May 2005

1

Introduction

On the structure of this text

I set out originally to write something practical on the topic of reflection in adult learning. I wanted to offer to my colleagues ideas which would be relevant to their work as ordinary teachers. I yearned to avoid the use of jargon and specialized vocabulary which needs time to explain, to master and to assimilate. I have never wished to dwell on theories and pedagogies unless they are directly and almost immediately useful. So I wanted to deal with theory or abstraction only as much as is necessary, and to do so as succinctly as possible. That was my starting point.

With these aspirations in mind, I decided to approach the chapters which follow in a somewhat unconventional style. I have generally:

- used (admittedly fabricated) questions to focus my inputs;
- set out examples which contain answers to these questions;
- generalized from the examples;
- employed everyday language as much as possible.

That style and sequence were deliberately chosen. I ask you to bear with me for the next few pages, while I take each of these features in turn and explain why I have judged them to be important.

Using questions to focus my inputs

In my work for the Open University, I concentrated on trying to help new students to become effective learners. In so doing, I set out to encourage them to adopt a way of studying in which they would notice questions that it would be worth their while to ask. In addition, I tried to help them to formulate such questions in terms which – if posed to the right person – would generate answers that would be useful to them as learners and would lead to progress as far as their learning was concerned.

I am now writing for readers who, I assume, are hoping to develop further as teachers. I wish to ensure that my text will be something which will facilitate that development, and do so directly. I would like to support you in making changes in your practice which will respond effectively – in *your* judgement – to needs that you may have identified, and which will bring about developments that will be valued by you and by your students. In other words, I'd like to help you to be innovative. I also wish to assist you to advance in your understanding of what reflection in higher education can mean and can achieve, and in your appreciation of how you can harness that potential in your own situation and subject area.

So I have chosen to avoid simply communicating information which matters to me and which *I* want to pass on to *you*. Instead, I have done my best to identify or predict questions which could have been asked by the type of person for whom I believe I am writing. I have posed them starkly at the head of most chapters; and I have disciplined myself, as far as I am able, to keep the question at the front of my mind as I have been writing. I hope the questions I have chosen are ones with which you can identify, and that they will cover the range of your interests in this subject area.

Working from examples and generalizing

Conceptual understanding generally begins from examples. Skemp, who was a mathematician turned educationist, argued this point with delightful effectiveness in a popular textbook (Skemp, 1971). He convinced me that, as a child, I was probably shown some items like a red car, a red book, a red pencil and a red traffic light, and hence acquired an understanding of the idea of 'red', which is a concrete concept. Then, sometime later, I would have encountered the abstract concept of 'colour', by being told, and by learning (again from examples), that red, blue and green are colours.

Skemp argued for the teaching of mathematics according to a similar approach. He believed that it is essential that a concept is first encountered in the form of examples which establish the beginnings of understanding. And he maintained that it is only when an initial understanding has been acquired, through the use and consideration of examples, that any abstract generalization or refinement of definition is then possible or meaningful. For only at that point, he asserted, has the learner developed sufficient understanding of the underlying concept to be able to build thereon the theories and understanding which use and consolidate that concept.

In Berlin, in 1972, I attended an elegant demonstration of this approach at an international conference on higher education. In her keynote address on the acquisition of concepts, Susan Meyer Markle (for whom I have no reference, only a vivid memory) taught her audience, as she had taught her research subjects, the grammatical concept of a 'morpheme'. First, she provided an assortment of examples, all of which were undoubtedly morphemes, and so this concept was established in the minds of her listeners – including me – who had not hitherto encountered it. Then she quickly tabled a similar set of examples, all of which, she told us, were definitely *not* morphemes – although I might a little earlier have classified them as such, while I was still somewhat uncertain about what a morpheme was. Thus the concept was yet more firmly developed in the minds of the learners like me in her audience, as it had been for the subjects in her research study. As her next step, and in refinement of our understanding, she gave us some borderline examples which were just morphemes and no more. Finally, she gave us other borderline examples, which were marginally *not* morphemes. By this point, we had well and truly mastered the concept of morpheme – from examples. Notice, of course, that the presenter had (and needed) a sound grasp of the concept in order to make effective choices of examples. We, the learners, had not had any such understanding, until we worked with the examples as she arranged for us to do.

Conceptual understanding thus appears to begin from examples (of increasing subtlety), although it is undoubtedly refined subsequently through the consideration and formulation of definitions, models, abstract approaches and theories. I would argue that, even in the case of fuzzy concepts which lack well-defined boundaries, we can only move towards the definitions from which we then define boundaries when we have some idea – from examples – of the concept. We will then wrestle to define and redefine it, refining our understanding in so doing.

In this text, I have therefore answered each of the questions set for me by my imaginary reader, by presenting examples. If I have been successful, you will be able to establish your own personal understanding in your own way, and thence move towards your own generalizations and abstractions. However, I am aware that examples can be like anecdotes. If they are well chosen, they can have the seductive effect that most good anecdotes often have, which is to concentrate attention on the details of the story. They may then divert the reader, and even the writer, from the underlying point or principle. Although I have tried to avoid unhelpful digressions, I may not always have resisted that temptation. As my aim is to make it possible for you to generalize from my examples, you should be accordingly wary of my digressions.

Sometimes generalizing will happen almost subconsciously, and in a distinctly personal and private way. But where situations and principles are rather more complex, and are more encumbered by additional and confusing detail, it is usually helpful if a teaching person prompts the process and facilitates the explicit generalizing. In every chapter after this one, I have therefore followed each of my sets of examples with some thoughts of my own, pointing towards tentative and partly formed generalizations. However, I try to leave you to revise, to redraft or to compose anew – in your own way and for yourself. Learners differ; so learning should never be regarded as a travel down a one-way street. For where there is one way, there must, almost by definition, be another way, or perhaps quite a few other ways. I hope you will look for these other ways for yourself as we progress through my examples. In adopting a facilitative style, I will use my examples to explain the models I offer for you to test. You will also no doubt wish to apply these to the further examples that emerge from your own activity, which will be personal to you and to your students.

Until we reach Chapter 11, you will find that most of my examples are taken from my own first-hand experience. They are therefore inevitably drawn from my activities, mainly at Heriot-Watt University, the Open University, Aalborg University and the UHI Millennium Institute. I have chosen to restrict my coverage in this way because I do not wish to write much from second-hand accounts, since that would entail interpreting someone else's work and their reflective self-evaluation. I attempt to redress that imbalance slightly in Chapter 11, but I do so with grudging acceptance of a commonly expressed need which troubles me. For, as I will argue in Chapter 8, perhaps too much is made, in Britain especially, of the alleged distinctiveness of our disciplines. Some would claim that these are so fundamentally different that we cannot learn much from educational practice outwith our own area. That has not been my experience when I have been pillaging good ideas from other subject areas, and eagerly transferring them with good effect into my own learning and teaching. Neither has it been my experience when I have moved during my lifetime as a student and learner, from engineering to theology, and then to education, and so to social sciences. I have certainly found that disciplines vary in the emphasis which they place on the cognitive and affective abilities demanded of the learner, but not in the general nature or relevance of these abilities. That is one reason why I do all that I can to develop interdisciplinary abilities which will prove profitable to the learner, whatever the next subject of study proves to be. Similarly, as a teacher, I value interdisciplinary transfer and the transferability of good ideas for learning and teaching. I therefore ask you to suspend disbelief on this matter of disciplinary constraints, at least until we have considered it further in Chapter 8. You will then be in a position to decide if significant interdisciplinary differences are a valid obstacle to transfer – or are merely perhaps a frequently quoted form of defence against a perceived challenge from more developed practice elsewhere.

Nevertheless, one rather different matter troubles me about my concentration on the use of examples, and that is their discrete nature. I appreciate that transforming your teaching process is a long and gradual task, which is usually done incrementally. It is probable and natural that you will want to begin tentatively, by using individual ideas in a compartmentalized way, and then will gradually extend your appreciation of the essence of them into a complete process. However, there is a risk in trying out isolated examples of innovation. I caution you that it may prove disturbing if you simply insert into your curricula as individual exercises the strategies which I describe. They may not sit comfortably with the status quo, and the disharmony may be positively unhelpful to you and your students – and your colleagues.

Using everyday language

Researchers have studied adventurers who have sailed solo around the world. These hardy souls have apparently worried on occasions for their mental health because, when acute trouble was at hand, they began to talk to themselves. They are greatly reassured, I am told, to learn that people who talk to themselves at times of trial tend to be more effective in their problem-solving than they would have been if they had not done so.

This finding is certainly consistent with my own modest experience some 20 years ago, when I researched the problem-solving activities of my students, in distinctly less spectacular or demanding circumstances (Cowan, 1977, 1980a). I had persuaded (and paid) some of my undergraduates to talk out their thoughts aloud, as they solved the type of problems which confronted them in their studies with me as their teacher. These reports, or recorded protocols if we use the proper title, were transcribed so that I could analyse them and use the consequent findings about learning difficulties as a basis for curriculum development (Example 3.5). As my research enquiries progressed, and as I encouraged the student subjects to undertake their own initial analyses of what they had recorded, I was surprised but pleased to discover that they were becoming more effective problem-solvers, in this and in other subjects. So, talking out your thoughts aloud, and thinking about what that revealed, seemed to be profitable for my students as well as for their teacher (and round-the-world sailors). The same emerges, in my experience, when you write down a reflective account of your thoughts in what has come to be called a learning journal, as described in Example 2.4. But I suspect there are important differences between the slow reflective nature of writing and the speedier act of talking.

In my recorded protocol studies (Cowan, 1977), I also found that the language the students used to describe their problem-solving was markedly more colloquial than that in which they wrote when they were drafting coursework for submission, or when they were writing examination papers. The vocabulary of their running commentaries was even different from the vocabulary that they used in talking to me, when they asked me for help or tried to tell me what they were doing in their problem-solving. They often favoured a cryptic oral shorthand.

A friend provided for me a delightful example of the fact that we often use private and shared phrases like cryptic code within our personal and shared version of disciplinary thinking. He instanced a school teacher who deliberately used this ploy when bringing out the importance of the sensuous and evocative specificity of good literary writing. He would begin his first year tutorials with a comparison of two passages describing an island – one perhaps from Ballantyne's *Coral Island* and the other from William Golding's *Lord of the Flies*. He would get the students to see that one description was vague and generalized, whereas the other made one feel that the writer had actually been there and had seen things for himself.

After that, the teacher would often activate and then test this critical criterion, which he then generalized, by colloquially – and yet with a shared and understood meaning – asking the students, of some quite different piece of writing, 'Has this author been on the island?' You'll find another example of private and shared meaning in the 'log-jam' example (Example 2.4).

We tend only to use the formal language of our discipline when we communicate punctiliously with others, or record our professional thoughts on paper. Otherwise we do much of our personal thinking within our discipline in colloquial language. That is my reason for trying, initially, to avoid using words which do not already have meaning for you or my other readers. To be sure, as we progress from my examples and from your understanding of them, to our generalizations and abstractions, we will undoubtedly need to make, or will at least profit from, some use of specialized and generally accepted vocabulary. For this will give meaning to new depths of appreciation, or will allow us to make subtle distinctions. That will especially be the case when we wish to explain our thinking to others, or to specify something with precision. It will also be helpful, as we progress, if we employ (which implies that we have been introduced to) words that are commonly used educationally and have a special meaning in that context. Nevertheless, in these pages I have earnestly tried to delay the use of specialized vocabulary for as long as possible, since I am sure that it is in our own everyday language that we should and do first think about any personal understanding which really matters to us. And my commitment to that belief appears so far to have paid off for me and for my students.

I hope I have so far written in a language which we can share and in which we should be able to find shared meanings. I will continue to write as plainly as I can in what follows.

Summary

For the reasons I have explained, the content of this book has been presented in a series of chapters, usually having something of the following structure:

- I will begin with a *question,* written as if addressed by you to me, the reader, or originating from other teachers who have asked me recently about this business of reflection in the education of adults.
- I will next attempt to give a response to that question, within a number of distinct *examples.*
- After each sequence of examples, I will add a *generalization* or two, to prompt (but not, I trust, to direct) the process of assimilation on your part.
- Thereafter, to ensure that I do not have things all my own way, I will generally attempt to prompt your *second thoughts,* by offering an

alternative view or by posing valid questions on which you may wish to ponder. I hope it will be useful for you to have these in mind as you test out, in your own context, what you can take from my examples and your generalizations.

In the next chapter, I set out to help you to reach an understanding, shared with me, of what reflection in higher education can entail. That seems to me a useful starting point. We will then move on to look at what such reflection has to offer in the education of adults, and in particular how it can help when we aspire to develop cognitive and interpersonal abilities. After that, we will consider what you and I can do as teachers to encourage our students to reflect effectively – and the differences in emphasis between reflection which is predominantly analytical and reflection which is mainly evaluative. If the facilitation of reflective learning then seems worthwhile to you, I imagine you will welcome some thoughts about how to get started on the business of being an innovative university teacher in today's context; and after that some ideas for the evaluation of your efforts, again as an innovative teacher. Finally, in a book which is based heavily on the experience of one man and his immediate colleagues, we'll take a look at what others have been doing.

Let's begin, then, almost without further ado, with a thought to prompt your immediate reflection about the topic which brings us together. Pierre Teilhard de Chardin, in *The Phenomenon of Man* (1955: 165), suggested that:

> Reflection is ... the power acquired by a consciousness to turn in upon itself, to take possession of itself as an object endowed by its own particular consistence and value; no longer merely to know, but to know one's self; no longer merely to know, but to know that one knows.

What questions, then, does that prompt you to ask about reflection within higher education?

Dear John

I'm really reading this book because I'm interested in being an innovative university teacher. But it seems fairly clear from your subtitle and preface that you want me to concentrate on this concept of reflection.

I'm not quite sure where that fits in to the educational scene, or to this book. To be frank, although I keep encountering the term nowadays in the context of higher education, I'm far from clear about what it means. I also have a sneaking suspicion that those who use it have a great variety of meanings in mind.

I'd say it makes sense to begin what you have to say, for me at least, by making it quite clear what you and others mean by 'reflecting', in an educational context.

2

What is Meant in Education by 'Reflecting'?

Outline

I will briefly outline the structure of this chapter before you begin to read it, so that you have some notion of where we are heading.

I will try to keep the question at the head of this chapter firmly in mind as I write. I'll use most of the space to provide my answer in seven examples of effective reflection in higher education, taken from six different contexts and subject areas. Some of the examples are quite full, because I will refer back to aspects of them in later chapters. Meanwhile, I hope you will find them of interest in their entirety.

In each example I will finish by identifying those parts of the activity which called on students or teachers to reflect. After that, to help us to tune our use of the word 'reflection' to a shared meaning, I'll offer a few further one-sentence examples of reflection, followed by several non-examples. I will then set out my own generalization about what reflection means to, and for, me when I am learning (not teaching) in ways which depend on reflection. And then, as promised, I'll close with second thoughts on this whole matter – expressed from the standpoint of someone who might critically appraise what they have read in these pages.

Example 2.1: Developing enquiry skills

I begin with an example which was current until the time of writing (Weedon and Cowan, 2002, 2003), the two originators having subsequently moved on to other institutions. It is taken from an online module studied by Scottish students in semester 1 of their third year of study. The module set out to develop and consolidate the skills of enquiry in the social sciences, on which subsequent projects and open-ended assignments would depend. The students were drawn from various of the colleges which comprise the UHI Millennium Institute. Technically they were college-based, but due in many cases to the distance of their home from their college, and their even greater distance from other students, almost all of the work of this module took place in the virtual learning environment (VLE). As a tutor, I did not meet any of my students until the degree ceremony.

Groups of six to eight students collaborated on a project where each group had first to determine a viable research question from within a suggested subject area. They then had to undertake the necessary literature survey, choose the methodology for enquiry, plan their investigation, carry it out, analyse the results and assemble conclusions. They concluded by self-assessing the group project and presenting their substantiated individual claims for the development of enquiry skills during the semester.

Every fortnight, each student was expected to identify the main demand of that stage of the process of the enquiry with which they were engaged. They had to summarize how they had gone about that part of the task, consider how effective they had been and pinpoint any ways for improvement they could see for next time. My task as tutor was to formatively facilitate that analysis and evaluation. I did not offer my own thoughts or suggestions. I gave no mark. I simply attempted to point out unanswered questions, unsubstantiated assertions or conclusions, failure to explore all relevant options and so on. I did also declare my qualitative judgement of particular strengths and weaknesses in the submissions. The rationale and methodology for this approach to facilitation, which I think of as Rogerian (following Carl Rogers – Rogers, 1961), had originated in the (chronologically earlier) innovation described in Example 2.4 and in the experiences which had then followed for me and my various groups of students over the intervening years. I shall expand upon the methodology and its rationale in Model 4.4.

At the end of the semester, groups were marked on their project report and their self-assessment of it. Individuals were marked on their substantiated claims for personal and professional development, which might draw upon the data of their fortnightly submissions to support the claims made. In module evaluations, the students were profusely clear about the value of the facilitative interchanges to them, in respect of the development of their enquiry skills (Weedon and Cowan, 2002, 2003).

These students were reflecting when they asked themselves *and* when they sought answers to the following:

- How they found and refined a viable research question.
- How they planned a literature survey.
- How they chose a methodology, (and so on).
- How well they had carried out each of these stages.
- How they might do them better next time.

Example 2.2: Mastering algorithmic procedures

My second example originated over 30 years ago. I still use it, to good effect. It concerns the provision of remedial tutorial assistance to students who have difficulty in numerate subject areas, from engineering to maths, physics and chemistry. In the early years of study, these are subjects where often the weekly problem sheet centres upon one or a few 'type solutions'.

In my role as personal tutor, I meet individually with students who are having difficulties dealing with the problems on the sheets. I ask them to bring with them their problem sheets for the entire module or course, to date. I select one, almost at random but deliberately featuring only one type solution. I talk the student through how we might tackle one of the problems, which I select for that purpose. I ask step by step questions and only offer suggestions when the student is lost for an answer or gets it wrong. As I ask and the student responds, I build up their solution on a pad. I now take a $6'' \times 4''$ index card and draw a line across it, to allow perhaps three lines of writing between the line and the foot of the card (see Figure 2.1).

I double back over what we did and sum it up above the line, step by numbered step, in general terms, and as far as possible in the student's original words. I explain to the student that this summary of the method should apply to the other problems on the sheet which belong to the same 'family'. We check that, on problems chosen by me so that at first the application of the general method is unquestionable. Sometimes we amend what we have written to make it more general.

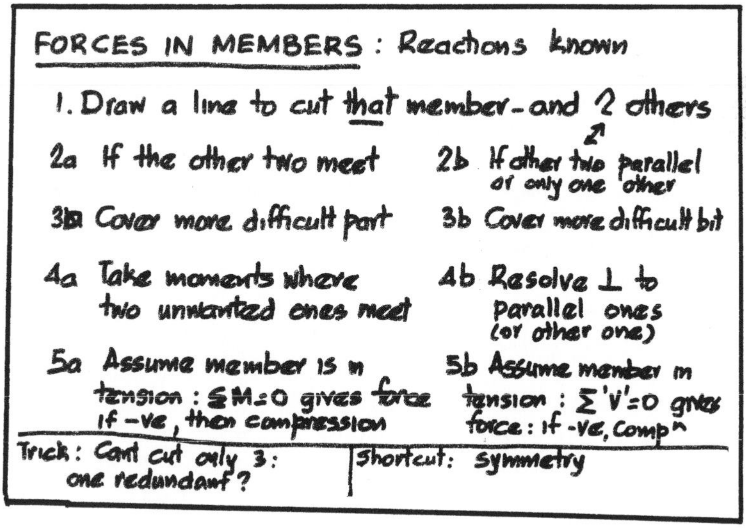

FORCES IN MEMBERS : Reactions known

1. Draw a line to cut **that** member – and 2 others

2a If the other two meet	2b If other two parallel or only one other
3a Cover more difficult part	3b Cover more difficult bit
4a Take moments where two unwanted ones meet	4b Resolve ⊥ to parallel ones (or other one)
5a Assume member is in tension : $\Sigma M = 0$ gives force if –ve, then compression	5b Assume member in tension : $\Sigma 'v' = 0$ gives force: if –ve, Comp^n

Trick: Can't cut only 3: one redundant? | Shortcut: symmetry

Figure 2.1 A 'solution card' for an algorithmic approach

Now I explain the function of the part of the card below the line. I insert a vertical line to give us two small boxes. In the left hand box, I explain, we will make a note of any little dodges the lecturers may adopt to disguise the fact that they are asking what is virtually a standard question with a type solution. I explain that this trick is rather like wrapping up presents, so that the contents of the parcel are not immediately obvious to the recipient. We find one or two such 'wrappings to disguise the problem', and I get the student to summarize them, in their own words, in that box. They should not be caught out next time they meet these tricks. The remaining box we keep for any shortcuts which can sometimes be applied, from familiarity, to speed up the process of solution.

I then select a couple of problem sheets coming from other parts of the programme and ask the student to go away and try to draft two further 'solution cards'. When we next meet, we test out the steps on the new cards, and the 'trick wrappings', on the whole range of relevant problems, amending as necessary. Usually one further such cycling around the process leads to the student thanking me, and saying that they have got the idea and can cope on their own with the other problem sheets and their standard methods. Those who reach that stage have not, in my experience, failed in the subsequent examination.

These students are reflecting when they:

- ask themselves how to tackle *any* of the problems on the sheet;
- think about how to summarize that approach to aid their memory.

Example 2.3: Study skills for isolated and inexperienced students

(This is quite a full description, because I will want to refer back to details of this case study in later chapters.)

If geographically isolated students in the Open University (OU) are to survive and prosper academically in their post-foundation studies, they must learn, one way or another, to be somewhat self-sufficient. Such self-sufficiency calls for the development of study skills which go well beyond the making of notes or the interpreting of graphs and pie charts, or even the routine application of methods outlined in the published study units.

Some years ago I collaborated with Judith George, who was at that time responsible for the academic care of OU students in the sparsely populated south of Scotland. We designed and presented a skills programme at the Dumfries study centre (Cowan and George, 1989). The activities in this programme were planned to help fairly isolated students in what had to be an interdisciplinary group, since its composition was determined by geographical proximity rather than by course of study.

We set out to develop what we described as survival and developmental skills. We began to tackle a new skill in the middle of our activity for a particular evening; and we finished dealing with it some four or five weeks later, in the middle of our next evening with the students. In the interim, we expected the students to engage in 'active experimentation' – actively testing out the ideas from that first half-evening – as they progressed their studies.

We concentrated on skills which we expected to be judged relevant by the students. For one workshop we chose 'Overcoming difficulties you meet in your studies, when you're basically on your own'. We began in that case by getting the students to make up their own personal lists of obstacles (with examples) which they had already encountered in their learning and which had thwarted their progress. In groups of four or five they began by swapping experiences. For example, one of them had had great trouble working out what to concentrate on in the second block of the social sciences foundation course. Another had disagreed with something in the study materials for a Third World course and wasn't sure what to do about handling that.

After the initial exchange of particular experiences, we encouraged the students to try metaphorically to 'pigeonhole' these obstacles, under headings or titles which were meaningful to them and which could encompass several examples under one heading. The entire group of 20 to 25 students now worked together with a tutor as their facilitator. They were able to reach a fair degree of agreement about titles for the various categories of obstacles which had been experienced by one or more in the entire group. These were listed by the tutor on a flipchart. The first problem mentioned above eventually went, with others, under 'How can I tell the difference between need to know and nice to know?' The second figured under 'What if I think the materials say something wrong?'

We next set small groups the task of examining their experiences with obstacles from each of the types listed on the flipchart. We asked them to recall occasions in the past when at least one of them had been successful in overcoming that type of blockage to their learning. And we got them to summarize what these solutions had entailed, again remaining with particular examples only for as long as seemed necessary in that process. The groups now reported back, in plenary. They were assisted as before by the tutor, who was acting as their scribe. She took a generalized problem title from the flipchart sheet, often still in colloquial terms and always using the students' words. As one group or another suggested ways in which that type of obstacle might be overcome, the scribe summarized that method, at first orally and in particular terms, but then more briefly and (skilfully) in *generalized* written terms with which the students could still identify. She took care to use the students' vocabulary, but wherever possible cleverly tried to omit detail which related only to one particular circumstance. For example, in the 'need to know/nice to know' area, she helped the group to the first step in that terse and shared advice: 'Find out what they want in assignments and exams – because that's the pointer to 'need to know'. The note then continued with specific advice about how to do this.

Even after prolonged group discussion and exploration, the workshop might fail to come up with an effective solution to a really difficult obstacle. In that case, a tutor might intervene with a suggestion. This occurred rarely – and with reluctance on the part of the tutors. But when it had happened, the students were then immediately charged to appraise the feasibility of the suggested solution, according to their recent experiences, which featured in the examples which they had already used to describe the obstacle. And then they had to decide whether or not to take the suggested tactic on board.

So it was that, by the end of the second half of that first evening, the plenary group had prepared, virtually on their own, what amounted to their advice to themselves when faced with a possible range of obstacles to their independent learning. They had created a summary of the types of challenge they might expect to encounter in their studies under the chosen heading. More importantly, they had responded to each of these with a constructive and generalized summary of their own ideas about how the challenge might be tackled effectively. This composition of advice, which was now expressed only in general terms, was word-processed for the students on the next working day and immediately posted out to them.

During the next three or four weeks, the students, virtually in isolation, continued with their studies. When they encountered further obstacles in that learning, they were encouraged to attempt to use, test out and maybe even refine the generalized advice which they had generated for themselves. Sometimes they were successful in dealing with the challenges they met; sometimes they were unsuccessful; sometimes they discovered in their struggles how to enrich the advice on the summary sheet; sometimes they encountered a new type of challenge; and sometimes they discovered that the advice on the sheet was oversimplified and needed to be refined. Time, and repeated returning to the generalizations in hand, enhanced their appreciation of the potential of their self-generated advice and their ability to improve on it.

When the group came together again, with the benefit of the intervening period of practical experience, the students exchanged their accounts of what they had been doing. Some reported successes and extensions to the group's methodology; and when they did so (through anecdotal examples), many of the others were able to profit accordingly. Some students reported frustrations, and were assisted by others to see how these might have been overcome – again enhancing the general methodology.

The first part of that second evening was structured so that, from consideration of examples taken from their very recent study experiences, the students worked to improve their own advice to themselves – in this particular case, advice about how to deal with challenges inherent in their studies. As they did this, they were now in a sense amending the word-processed sheets which had been sent out. But they hardly needed these sheets any more, because the methodology had virtually become an integral part of their ways of working and of their thinking.

We could then move on to a different skill and tackle it within much the same structure. It might be, 'How can you assemble a sound argument or proof?' or 'How can you score higher marks in assignments and examinations without working any harder or having brain surgery?' We could set off again in the now familiar pattern of reflective and constructive group and individual working.

Years after that series of workshops was run, grateful messages were still trickling in, with such heartfelt sentiments as, 'I don't think I would ever have got this degree if I hadn't learnt from the workshops how to separate "need to know" and "nice to know".'

On the first half-evening devoted to this type of activity, these students were reflecting when they:

- were thinking about their answers to the question, 'What type of difficulties have we met recently in our studies in relation to the skill the tutor has selected?'
- identified in general terms how such challenges might be overcome, by answering the question, 'What has worked for at least one of us in this type of situation?'
- summarized their advisory methodology in general terms.

During the interim five weeks and in the half-meeting which followed, the students were also reflecting when, having tested out their generalized advice in new situations, they:

- asked themselves how effective their advice had been;
- either confirmed that it worked or decided that it needed to be refined or extended (and explained how).

Notice the scheduling of two half-evenings to the one challenge, with learning experiences intervening so that the new thinking was to be actively tested out. This contributed to the integration with real-life activity and demands which is often lacking, but pedagogically desirable, in developmental learning activities.

Example 2.4: 'Unpicking log-jams'

(This example makes an interesting contrast with the previous one. I'll refer to that contrast in my 'second thoughts' at the end of this chapter. It is also another long example, because I will be building upon it later in Chapter 4.)

In the early 1980s, my first year civil engineering students studied a year-long course called Interdisciplinary Studies (Cowan, 1986a). Three time-tabled hours per week had been found for this course by reducing the allocations of hours which were given to civil engineering subjects from 15 hours per week to 12 hours per week. The remaining nine hours per week were devoted as before to mathematics, physics and chemistry.

Interdisciplinary Studies, titled 'IDS' by the students, set out un-ashamedly to develop core capabilities which really matter when studying in higher education, and in professional life thereafter (Fordyce and Cowan, 1985). Roughly speaking, the first term of the three-term programme concentrated mainly on communication in the broadest sense of that word, including the abilities of listening, empathizing with feelings and so on. The second term concentrated mainly on problem-solving, again in the most liberal sense of that title. Finally, the third term focused on relevant aspects of interpersonal skills, since much of the first year programme in my department depended on a wide range of group activities and project work.

A powerful component in the learning and teaching scheme which I had set up for this course was the weekly writing and submitting for facilitative comment of what we called 'learning journals'. The task featured in the journal (which was a new experience for me as well as for the students) was to think carefully while writing about the answer to the question, 'What have I learned about learning or thought about thinking, as a result of these IDS activities, which should make me more effective next week than I was last week?' Students were encouraged, if they so wished, to rephrase that question, to define 'effective' in their own terms and even to refocus their reflective journal writing, all as they found most useful.

Each learning journal was to be read either by me or by my colleague, Derek Fordyce. We told the students that we already knew in broad outline what they had done in our class that week as well as, or perhaps better than, they themselves did. Consequently, or so we conveniently and emphatically told them, they should avoid recording events. Only then could we all ensure that this would be a journal which concentrated on thinking about thinking, rather than a diary devoted to recording factual detail.

It was a coursework requirement that the learning journals were to be submitted each week. Initially the students had great difficulty with this demand – because it was such an abstract one and called on them to engage in an unfamiliar activity. They struggled with this strange need to write – and to think – about learning. A typical journal, in the beginning, tended to contain a halting entry which was seldom more than half a page long. But, by the middle of the second term, it was not uncommon for someone who had had a 'blue flash' or a Damascus Road experience to wish to write for us at length, sometimes up to ten pages (as in Examples 2.1 and 2.6).

Awareness of the usefulness of the process, linked to appreciation of the confidentiality of the commenting, took some time to develop. We were helped, after the first run, by the presence on campus of second year students who had been through the experience. Some of them (remarkably, and very privately) continued to keep journals after it was no longer a course requirement (Gibbs, 1988). I cannot think of any other coursework requirement with which students persist even after it is no longer expected of them. These students certainly could and did testify sincerely to the eventual impact of the activity on their learning abilities.

The journals came in each Thursday morning. As quickly as possible,

Derek and I commented on them, without offering any judgements or even suggesting where and how to improve. We simply tried to understand and to identify with what was written. Where we didn't understand, we asked a question. However, it was not meant to read as a threatening or critical question, just a question genuinely if bluntly suggesting the need to clarify or amplify. Where there seemed to be a break in the logic, we pointed it out, but without stating criticism or suggesting how the break might be repaired. Where it would have been helpful to test a confident statement against recent experience, we suggested how that might be done, without implying that it *should* be done. Where a success was reported, we shared their enthusiasm. We expected no response. There was seldom any feedback to us, until years after the event.

The journals could be returned by the Monday morning, or sometimes earlier. When they had been sorted out into the students' pigeonholes, they would disappear in about six minutes flat – with students standing around in the lounge area a few metres away, eagerly reading our comments. That behaviour, unusual in respect of returned coursework, suggested to us that the activity, and the comments, were valued – which does not necessarily mean they were valuable.

Now, to the IDS programme itself. What happened in a typical week? I will begin my detailed description at the end of a previous week, and from a journal entry. During one particular second term, a student had volunteered in his learning journal that he had had considerable success as a result of the previous week's activity in IDS, which had been devoted to developing a general problem-solving approach for use in numerate subject areas:

> It was great. I went to my physics problem class the following day. For the first time since I came here, I found I could answer the first three questions on the sheet without help. And I got the correct answers. I moved on to question four. I didn't get the correct answer – but as soon as I looked at the answer on the sheet, I could see where I had made a silly mistake. Then I tried question five, and I didn't know where to start. I looked at my lecture notes, and I couldn't find anything to help me; but I couldn't find anything in the lecture notes that I didn't understand, either. I looked at the set book. I couldn't find anything there to help me. And, again, I couldn't find anything which appeared to be relevant, and which I didn't understand. So I had a log-jam in my problem-solving. It was stuck and wouldn't move. I don't want anyone to show me how to answer question 5. I want someone to help me to unpick log-jams.

I spoke to the class and told them the substance of this account – without, of course, identifying the person who had written it. For those who did not understand, I explained how logs which had been felled in Canadian forests, and sent down to the sea on a strongly flowing river, could 'jam', until a daring lumberjack unpicked the offending log. I asked how many others had encountered a 'log-jam' situation in their recent studies. Some two-thirds of them identified with the description and admitted that it had thwarted them. They had usually only 'dealt' with it by seeking help with the particular problem in which their problem-solving had been blocked. We agreed that developing the ability to overcome this type of blockage would be a useful task for the next week in IDS.

Derek and I undertook to prepare a response to this declared need. We devised a workshop activity accordingly. During the two hours which were timetabled for the class on the Tuesday afternoon, we arranged for the students to explore and analyse successful and unsuccessful methods of unpicking log-jams, taken from their and our experiences. After this structured sequence of activities, each group of students charted on flip-chart sheets their progress with finding an unjamming methodology, noting their outstanding difficulties. (Note the similarities to the, later, Dumfries model in Example 2.3.) They left these sheets for us, in the working area, as informative wallpaper. After that they went off happily (I hope), either to their homes or to their halls of residence.

Derek and I looked at the flipchart sheets and identified the progress (or lack of progress) that the groups had made. We moved on to reconsider the activity which we had tentatively planned and scheduled for the first hour on the Wednesday morning as a form of learning enhancement and consolidation. (In running IDS, we sometimes found that our tentative plans for that follow-on hour had to be radically changed. On this occasion, as I recall it, they only had to be mildly modified.)

On the Wednesday morning, we facilitated a one-hour activity in which the groups tested out a further (constructive) input from us. This incorporated and analysed much that they had assembled in their summaries of the previous afternoon. After that, they went back into their other classes. And on the Wednesday evening, following these experiences of the Tuesday and the whole of Wednesday, they wrote the next entries in their reflective learning journals. It was from one such (earlier) journal entry that I had extracted the suggestion that dealing with log-jams might be useful.

These students were reflecting when they:

- analysed past experiences during the workshop activity in groups on the Tuesday afternoon;
- attempted to generalize from that;
- tried to consolidate and extend the total group experience along similar lines during the Wednesday morning activity;
- individually related the IDS activity to their learning experiences in the remainder of the Wednesday (and thereafter);
- brought that together in a critical and analytical journal entry;
- individually thought forward to their forthcoming needs and ruminated on these privately in their journals.

Example 2.5: Piloting reflective review

In the aftermath of the students' revolts of 1968, a number of universities in northern Europe established courses based on project orientation. These were unlike the traditional British programme in which a project, when it figures in the curriculum, is an extended exercise based on the taught syllabus. The project in project orientation is the origin of learning and teaching; for the students only study what they need to in order to cope with the demands of the problem at the heart of their project. In that sense, project orientation is akin to problem-based learning. The main difference is that in project orientation the students have to select and formulate the problem – as in Example 2.1, which was in a sense derived from the current example.

For many years, the Basic Education Year for students of technology at Aalborg University (formerly Aalborg University Centre) was an example of project-oriented study of this form. Students arrived at the university either directly from school or, more commonly, after a gap year between school and university. They entered a Basic Education Year, in which half of their time was to be spent in groups working on projects and a quarter was given to project-unit courses in which the subject matter arose from their learning needs as occasioned by the project. The remaining time was devoted to study-unit courses in areas such as computing and physics, where it was apparent to all concerned that this instruction would be needed by all students and that there was no point in playing a game of learner-directed learning for this highly predictable part of the syllabus. Group working was central to all of this, with communication skills and reflection on learning expected to feature in assessment and elsewhere.

Project groups had two supervisors, one of whom – the main and technical supervisor – was responsible for the technical content of the project and for the development and assessment of process competencies. The other (assistant) supervisor, who was usually a social scientist, was charged to ensure that the group took due account of the social implications of both their problem and their suggested solution. However, titles and descriptions can create problems for those who often work in what for them is a second language. Shortly after I completed the draft of this text, I happened to meet with another writer, Anette Kolmos, who told me that 'supervisor', the word in English, has unhelpful connotations of direction and management for a Danish speaker. I asked what the Danish word would be, and I was told 'vejleder'. Next day a Danish colleague offered me a helpful, poetic and usefully ambiguous translation of this title – 'a guide for the way'. That delightfully describes for me what I have seen of the best practice of Aalborg supervisors.

A project originates in a problem area. One such problem area, for a first year class (*ca.* 400 students), was the matter of working conditions in industry in Aalborg. Project groups (of five or six students) had first to identify, and then to grapple with, a chosen problem from within that problem area. One group chose to concentrate on what they judged the appalling noise levels in the butcheries. Another concentrated on the fact that EC regulations would shortly render mushroom growing, as practised in Denmark, illegal – and hence would lead to the demise of the mushroom growing industry unless a way could be found to improve working conditions. Consequently, the butchery group found that they needed project-unit courses on acoustics and the biology of the human ear – topics of little relevance or usefulness to those interested in mushroom growing. In contrast, the group focusing on the mushroom growing required instruction in plant biology, respiration, and the effect of spores and the like on human beings.

The project was assessed by a panel at the end of the semester under two headings. One was the success of the group in tackling the problem which they had formulated, while the other began from the group's review of their performance. They were to present a realistic and analytical self-appraisal of the processes they had followed, with perhaps a constructive identification of their learning needs and their aspirations for the (as yet undefined) project they would undertake, possibly in different groups, in the second semester.

I had met Mona Dahms, the then leader for the Basic Education Year, for the first time in Stockholm in 1994, in discussions which followed my keynote paper (Cowan, 1995) at a conference there. She told me that she felt that there was considerable scope for improvement at Aalborg in the process analyses and in the use made of the first semester experience in preparing students for work on a second project in the second semester. Her colleagues, loyal to a format which had proved effective and had been well regarded by industry for almost 20 years, were not all of that mind. Mona recruited about a dozen lecturers who were prepared to suspend disbelief and experiment with 'the Cowan approach'. This was to occur in a pilot activity (Cowan, 1994), which would take place between the two semesters of the first year and would be run with some 25 students. The event would take place in a summer guest house at Slettestrand, in Jutland, in midwinter.

Mona and I planned for an event in which:

- we would not *tell* teachers or students what we wanted them to do in the tasks of the programme – we would *show* them;
- when Danes were working in groups, they would speak in Danish;
- we would repeat the same pattern of activity, in three cycles (of which more below);
- the thinking would focus on the demands of project working and how to meet them more effectively in the second semester than in the first;
- it would then be left to students and teachers to decide what, if anything, this event had offered them which it might be worth pursuing.

The first stage took place in English. The Danish teachers were observers and the Danish students had not yet arrived. My two Scottish colleagues, Helen Wood and Claire Geddes (who are both scientists), joined me in going through a series of activities, in which I questioned, Helen answered and Claire acted as scribe, on a flipchart in full view. The questions at this stage focused on project work in science in a UK university – a situation deliberately distinct from the project-oriented studies in Aalborg. The main questions were:

1. What do supervisors actually do when they are facilitating a project? (General headings.)
2. What does each heading entail? (A step by step description.)
3. How do you judge how well you are doing each part of the job? (Criteria and some notion of scales and method of judgement.)
4. How well did you do it last time? (A judgement, hopefully based upon some data.)
5. How might you improve next time? (Specific suggestions.)

We covered these questions for the situation of the chemist in our number. We did this as quickly as possible, consistent with comprehension by the Danes of the summaries and of the process. The Danish teachers then moved into small groups, facilitated by Mona, with the remit to do what we had done, working as an answering group, providing fragments of analysis as Helen had done (individually) with a questioner (like me) and a scribe (like Claire). Of course, they focused on the supervision by some of their own number of Aalborg technology projects in the semester just completed. Since this was essentially an opportunity for Danish teachers to experience what they would later be asking the students to do, there was no need for reporting back on the answers to the questions. However, we needed a plenary discussion of what they would move on to do with the students.

The students then arrived, and were briefed by Mona on what had happened so far and on the goals of the next stage of the pilot. The Danish teachers 'declared' tasks by exemplifying (as the Scots had done for them) what they wanted the students to do. This was essentially a refined replay of what they had earlier done on their own. They then led as questioners and scribes into a sequence where students in groups considered their answers to similar questions, which were now:

1. What did we have to do, as students, in our semester 1 project? (General headings.)
2. What did each stage in that process entail? (A step by step description.)
3. How can we judge how well we did each part of the job? (Criteria and some notion of scales and method of judgement.)
4. How well did we do it last time? (A judgement, hopefully based upon some data).
5. How might we improve next time? (Specific suggestions.)

Having completed this sequence of tasks, the students then reviewed the experience, distinctly positively, and reported back to the Danish teachers.

It being Burns Night, and Mona having a Scottish partner who could play the bagpipes, we had a Burns Supper – complete with haggis, malt whisky, Tam o' Shanter (in full!) and Scottish Country Dancing – the students departing the next day. Thereafter, the Danish teachers in turn reviewed the experience, rather more cautiously than had the students.

At the end of the second semester, we returned to the student group to ask them if their euphoria at the close of the residential event had proved well founded. A tall, blonde Viking spokeswoman indicated that they had already discussed this. They had come to the stern conclusion that, 'You must never do that again!' Mona thanked them for their frankness and asked if they would mind explaining why we should not repeat the experience. The reply was, 'Because we had *such* an advantage over the other students, that you must *never* do that again, unless you do it for everyone.' And so began a process of curriculum change and enhancement which was not completed in a mere year, and has been reported by Kolmos and Kofoed (2004) to have moved in the interim from project orientation to problem-based learning.

The students and teachers in the pilot were reflecting when they:

- thought out their answers to the questions posed within the task structure, and listed above.

In particular, they were reflecting when they:

- formulated constructive advice to themselves about how they might improve performance in the next project experience;
- evaluated the worth and potential of the pilot.

Example 2.6: Concentrating on one's own priorities

On 12 September 2001, my wife and I set out on a long-planned holiday to Lake Garda. Travel on the day following 9/11 was somewhat tardy. I had more time than I had planned to read the book which I had set aside for the journey. This was Jenny Moon's excellent text, *Learning Journals*, from which I had already taken so much (Moon, 1999b). I had intended to re-read to see if there were any points in there which I had overlooked. There was at least one. At one stage of the long journey, I caught myself thoughtlessly reading past the reference to Gatlin (1987), who had let his students have sight of his own learning journals. Then I doubled back, gulped and thought, 'Why don't *I* do that?' And from that day on, I have not asked anyone to keep a learning journal unless I myself tackle the same task, in my own context, meaningfully – *and* pass on *my* journal to each of *them* when they send theirs to me. This decision has meant additional commitment, but it has brought me great returns, notably in the later years of my tutoring in the VLE.

Six teachers at Napier University had heard (I know not how) of this experience and its impact on my practice in the module described in Example 2.1. They approached me out of the blue to ask if I would work with them in this way, to enable them to experience keeping journals for themselves and to explore the potential of that for our own continuing professional development (CPD). All of these six volunteers were just that – volunteers. All had for some time called upon their students to engage in structured reflection. Our agreement, which is detailed elsewhere (Cowan and Westwood, 2006 – in press), called on all of us, including me, to choose once every two weeks a question of current relevance to us, professionally. We were to try, as we wrote, to find at least part of an answer to that question. The participants were then to pass their journals to me for facilitative comment, and I was to pass mine in return to each of them. Together we would review the intended outcomes at the end of a 12-week period, in terms of our CPD. For various reasons, including the fact that all were very busy senior staff, not all completed the target of five main journals. All completed the review and attended the closing group meeting.

The questions chosen for journaling varied in focus and detail. Participants commented that, '*Deciding what to address was not always easy – some of the day to day worries seemed too insignificant,*' and that, '*Perhaps for me journaling needs to be in relation to critical incidents rather than a regular activity.*' Time commitment was addressed in seven journals, work relationships in four and curriculum design and self-management in three apiece. Other topics ranged from ethical issues to assessment. None focused on a particular module or course.

At the end of this experiment, three had completed all five journals and a review, two had completed three journals and a review, while two had completed one journal and a review. The following outcomes were reported and later confirmed as sustained changes:

- Two had separately decided to make major changes in at least one of their modules.
- One had decided to introduce a new type of activity in their module.
- Two had radically changed the way they managed their time.
- One had wound down a well-established working relationship.

I suggest that these are quite noteworthy outcomes from a relatively brief and voluntary activity of the type I have described.

The participants in this collaboration were reflecting when they:

- decided (as I had done) that it might be a 'good idea' to explore for themselves the experience and potential of keeping a journal, as they asked of their students;
- chose questions for which to seek answers while journaling, these questions being relevant to their ongoing professional development;
- sought their own answers;
- considered the value of the experience to themselves, individually.

Example 2.7: Assessing your own work

I have used this approach in a range of discipline areas and at levels varying from first year undergraduate to postgraduate. In each case, my description here covers a situation where I am introducing a class for the first time to the concept of making judgements according to a systematic and objective procedure, with the intention to move that forward before the end of the event into self-assessment of about to be submitted work.

Here's what I do:

1. I ask the students to bring along the draft of a piece of work which they will shortly have to submit in final form. I promise an activity which will assist them to enhance that draft.
2. I put them into small groups which are as assorted in composition as I can contrive without fuss.
3. I describe a totally imaginary situation, in which they are to imagine that they have won a holiday in a competition. The prize is a choice between six holidays, whose descriptions are contained in six A4 envelopes, which I display. The task is to spell out and commit to paper a method of deciding which holiday will be chosen by one particular member of the group, making it clear what headings they will use to judge the possibilities. Groups have to outline the method, with the help of the one of their number who is the subject, without knowing what is in the envelopes.
4. When the method has been drafted, it is passed to another group.
5. The six possibilities are then displayed. The subject person in each group decides on their choice – privately.
6. Groups then attempt to follow the methodology which has been passed to them, to predict what option the subject in the other group will have chosen.
7. Choices are compared, difficulties with the instructions are aired, discrepancies analysed and lessons learnt.
8. I input brief suggestions regarding methodologies for the making of such judgements objectively.
9. We discuss ways to make headings and instructions more usable and realistic, and especially how to cope with multiple criteria.
10. We now repeat this activity of 'choosing from given options', but this time for the prize of a car and with a different student as subject.
11. I now open the activity to the making of judgements regarding the drafts which students have brought with them to this class. I tell them that they will be required to accompany their final submissions with a self-assessment and that some marks will be available for the soundness of that self-assessment. I leave the students to self-assess and to discuss their judgements (and the making of them) with peers, if they so wish.

Usually, within three days of this activity, at least a quarter of the class group will have approached me by email to ask diffidently whether 'it will be all right if I change my draft' – the draft as yet being unsubmitted. The response is of course affirmative, because I welcome and am actively encouraging self-determined improvement. Word then gets around. The standard of the submitted work is markedly superior to that of similar assignments submitted before the introduction to systematic self-assessment.

These students are reflecting when they:

- confront the challenge to think about how they make judgements;
- choose criteria which are of relevance to them, when judging the quality of their own work;
- think about the strengths and weaknesses of their work in relation to these criteria;
- perceive ways in which that draft work can be improved, in terms of criteria which they have chosen as important.

Other examples

- A student is reflecting when she notes that there is something different about a case that she is considering in comparison with the cases she has encountered in class, and when she then identifies what the difference is and what she should do about it.
- A golfer is reflecting when he notices that, when practising on the driving range, five out of six shots curl away to the right – and when he wonders what the correlation may be between his posture and grip for that type of shot and that type of deflection.
- A student is reflecting when she reads the comments on an assignment and tries to deduce from them some guidelines which can help her produce better work in the next assignment in that discipline, which will be on a different topic.
- A student is reflecting when he looks back on a personal development plan which did not work out as successfully as he had hoped, and tries to identify what it was that he did not anticipate, and how that knowledge should affect his next planning.
- A car driver is reflecting when she begins to assemble a mental list of behaviours by other drivers, which signal that she might well anticipate unpredictable actions on their part when they are near her on the road.

Non-examples

In contrast:

- A student is not reflecting when he rephrases an explanation which has been given to him and passes it on to a fellow student.

- A student is not reflecting when she narrates to herself or others what she did.
- A student is not reflecting when he regurgitates the perceptive views of his teacher or of the writer of a recommended textbook.

Generalization

My way of answering the question at the head of this chapter is to maintain that learners are reflecting, in an educational sense, when they ask themselves relevant questions for which they have not already formulated an answer and then go on to seek at least part of that answer. This may call upon them to analyse or evaluate one or more personal experience or future challenge, and to attempt to generalize from that thinking. Learners can quickly be urged to engage in this kind of thinking about thinking, so that in the future they will be more skilful or better informed or more effective than they have been in the past.

When I searched my experience for examples to illustrate reflection, and went on to ruminate about the common features which they might all share – and which would define what reflection entails – then I was myself reflecting analytically. So reflection often involves me in thinking about *how* I did something – which is analytical. However, it can also involve me in thinking about *how well* I have done something – which is evaluative. (Please remember that distinction: I will develop it in Chapters 5 and 6.)

I picture analytical reflection as being rather like a bridge between particular experiences and generalizations, or as the shared area where practice overlaps with theory. It begins for me in situations where I have thought hard about one or more experiences. Through reflection, I can formulate a personal theory or generalization which attempts to bring together and summarize all that is relevant and evident to me in the examples. This generalization should then usefully inform my actions in future experiences which are similar.

I picture evaluative reflection as a matching or mismatching of my performance and my aspirations. It is undertaken with the intention to formulate a judgement about the accuracy or otherwise of that gap, and perhaps to plan to minimize it by learning from my mistakes, failures and successes.

So what leads us to reflect? I know that I reflect deliberately and usually to good effect when:

- I have *committed myself* to reflect and know how and when I intend to prompt myself to do so (as in Example 2.6).
- I *notice something* which perturbs me, and I reflect in order to find improvement, explanation or understanding (as in my reaction to that line in Moon's book, also in Example 2.6).
- An *intervention* by someone requires me to think reflectively (as when a

student asks, 'Why don't you offer that type of course in Design, JC?' – in Example 6.2).

- *Dialogue or correspondence* with a peer prompts me to engage in reflection, which may be shared (as when Alan Harding prompted me to use my Preface to look at the answers to the two questions which should really matter for readers and so for me).
- I *decide that I should reflect* on my processes of reflection, and determine my own outcomes and my desired standards in that reflection about reflection (as at various stages in the writing of this book!).

What leads *you* to reflect – to good purpose?

Some second thoughts

I have a distinct advantage in this text. For it is I who control the input and direct the thinking. At this point, it is therefore only fair to offer an opportunity for you to look at this first input of mine from a different standpoint. Some second thoughts, then, mostly as valid questions on which you may wish to ponder:

1. Surely thoughtful students from time immemorial have been reflecting almost as described here, without the intervention and structuring provided by zealous teachers. Is the stress on reflection anything more than a remedial operation to cater for students who should be able to engage in this aspect of learning and development, but cannot do so on their own as their predecessors did in the past?
2. I seem to have concentrated on reflection as a distinct activity. Would it not be more accurate to portray reflection as an adjunct to experiencing, which happens even as you experience?
3. Are there really sound reasons for treating reflection as something which happens because we stand outside ourselves and our actions? If so, is it always to be separate, or usually so, or simply sometimes so?
4. Examples 2.3 and 2.4 are rather similar in their purpose, but readers may already have noted that in Example 2.4 inputs were more generously supplied by the tutors than in Example 2.3. Should tutors contribute in this way, rather than facilitate? Or should they strive to restrict themselves to the facilitation of reflection based on the personal experiences of each learner? How should we decide on our answer to that question?
5. The examples I have given describe planned activities. Is the most valuable reflection not something which happens unprompted, like my sudden insight on 9/11?

Dear John

Let's face it, you've chosen to begin with some rather unusual examples. As a result, although I'm quite intrigued by what you've told me so far, I find I've been more interested in the unusual ways in which you have been teaching than in the need to incorporate reflection as a feature in my own learning and teaching situations. I'd still like (and need) to know a whole lot more about why you feel that this reflection business is important.

What's wrong with the well-established teaching methods which have survived the test of time? Surely the traditional seminar is set up to occasion this reflection you instance? Have there not always been forms of teaching which have challenged students to do their own thinking about the content of what they were learning, in ways akin to the examples you've given me in that last chapter?

You've also stressed the contribution which you believe reflection makes to the development of abilities. Do you not acknowledge that abilities have always mattered a great deal in vocational courses, from education for the ministry centuries ago to education for medicine, engineering and law over more than the past hundred years? Surely the graduates of the past developed their abilities fairly well without being reflective practitioners? What was wrong with the approach which led them to these developments, then?

John, if you want me to spend more time on this concept of reflection, and since I see from the table of contents that it is your intention to devote more of your chapters to it, then you need to persuade me that it offers something worthwhile for higher education practice today.

3

What Does Reflection Have to Offer in Higher Education?

Outline

In this chapter, I'll provide six examples which suggest that reflection does indeed have something either new or additional to offer higher education. The first three are short accounts that describe situations, in an assortment of disciplines, where the advent of IT has made reflection possible, and subsequently effective for worthwhile learning. They indicate what reflective learning, when it is possible, can do to enhance curricula. They concentrate upon the potential for learning when the learners are reflective about the course *content* and their use of it, rather than – as in the examples in Chapter 2 – reflective about how they go about the process of *learning*.

Two further examples present the case and the demand for prioritizing those educational outcomes which are best achieved through the use of reflection. Both stem from perceived inadequacies in the status quo. The first centres on a national statement of priorities for UK education in the years following the students' revolts in Europe, and the initiatives by the Nuffield Foundation in Britain under the heading of 'Independence in Learning'. The second is a more specific example, from my own discipline and area of research activity, in which the need to radically enhance curricula features strongly. Finally, the last example describes an institution in which the demand for change has been anticipated and has been met in a manner which has attracted attention and admiration worldwide. Thus the second trio concentrate on the weaknesses of the status quo and the need and possibility of improvement therein.

After that you'll find further short examples and non-examples to clarify where I believe that reflection does, and does not, have something to offer. Then, after some tentative generalizations from me, I finish with a quartet of serious caveats, to stimulate your second thoughts on the questions raised and the answers given.

Example 3.1: Reflective learning activity in mathematics

Some years ago, the Open University (OU) foundation course in mathematics (Open University, 1978–97) contained a summer school activity which dealt with topics drawn from the study of calculus. One half-day of the week-long residential programme was devoted to this part of the syllabus. The activity was designed primarily as revision and consolidation. It took the students over familiar ground, while bringing together one or two topics in a fresh and motivating way. It offered no new content. However, in an attempt to refresh the subject matter and make the agenda a little more attractive and rewarding, the tasks for small groups were shaped so that they pointed forward to a short, potentially interesting but non-examinable closing lecture. In this, the learners were to be shown that what they had been doing, as first year students, could lead on to the development of the (then) relatively new and complex concept of mathematical chaos. The lecturer was well briefed to present this complex theme. However, he or she was fortunate (and extremely competent) if the resultant lecture even managed to persuade the students that what they had been doing had had a relationship to this deep and worthwhile topic. As a tutor in summer school teams at that time, I cannot recall ever forming the impression that the students in these classes had grasped the concept of chaos – nor did I feel any criticism of the lecturers concerned for failing to achieve that outcome.

Six years on from my first encounter with this summer school activity, the OU was able to introduce computers to the group work in this part of the programme. Students were provided with some elementary software and an ingenious adaptation of an otherwise standard spreadsheet. This software enabled small groups to explore questions in the form, 'What would happen if ... ?' They were encouraged, but not directed, to explore what would happen if there were changes in the magnitudes of the populations of rabbits and predatory foxes in an island area with limited potential for the vegetation to grow.

The students had met the software a few days before and were reasonably familiar with it. They were able to use it to investigate in a short time many possibilities which they generated in their own ways. They could thus engage almost automatically in creative reflection, spurred by their curiosity about 'What would happen if ... ?' This query of their own choice and formulation led them to explore and discover what the answer might be. This was followed by another such question, and another answer. This creative reflection and rapid accumulation of results from their further experiments soon led them to deeply perceptive generalizations, which they could then test out and develop further in the study of new examples.

They spent a mere hour in exploring the potential of the learning materials to enable them to discover 'What would happen if ... ?' By that time, most of those in the groups I was tutoring that year had begun to discover for themselves, and to formulate and comprehend – in their own words, of course – the main features of this complex concept of mathematical chaos. Yet this was the concept that lecturers in previous years had struggled in vain to convey in the lecture format, which had been generously supported by a thoroughly planned selection of excellent audio-visual aids and computerized displays.

The availability and structured use of software for direct student engagement in open learning, combined with a task in a form which encouraged creative reflection, had made it a straightforward reality to achieve speedily, through self-directed reflection, the mastery of a concept which had never before been seriously contemplated as an achievable learning outcome.

Example 3.2: Reflective learning activity in economics

I was involved in facilitating the Teaching Quality Improvement Scheme at Salford University (Heywood *et al.*, 2002). In one project, we enabled a lecturer who was teaching business economics to purchase access to a massive data bank which had been prepared for commercial rather than instructional purposes. Ingeniously, he devised some attractive open-ended tasks which invited his students to pursue questions of the 'What if ... ?' variety, addressing possible economic interventions. Within a few hours online, they mastered understanding of certain fundamental principles of macroeconomics, to an extent which had proved unattainable in the old days, when lecturers lectured. In the past, even if students had set out to explore speculative questions, they had needed to slog for so long to obtain (particular) results that they had no energy left to see generalizations. In addition, they may well have generated sufficient errors in their calculations to obscure the generalizations.

With the use of the software and the database, plenty of examples could be rapidly explored and analysed comparatively in richly resourced and carefully facilitated reflection, which led to the desired deep understanding and learning. That valuable learning outcome had not been achieved hitherto, despite the outlay of considerable and committed effort and of learning and teaching time.

Example 3.3: Reflective learning activity in classics

The advent and development of information technology in education has led to many changes in OU courses, including classics (Open University, 1993–2005). For some years now, students have had access on CD-ROM to the full text of the works they are studying, as well as to other learning resource materials. They are also provided with simple software to enable them to carry out searches. The student of Homeric texts, for instance, is thus freed for analysis, rather than being tied down (as in the recent past) to the tedious ingathering of data as the fodder for analytical thinking.

For example, there was a student who wished to test out a suspicion about the contrasting use in the writings of Homer of imagery involving domestic and wild animals and birds. She was able to instruct a computer to search the texts. It found all the relevant examples for her in only a few minutes, rather than her having to devote days to inefficient labour based on incomplete indexes and tedious hand-searching methods. She could thus check the viability of her initial hypothesis quickly – and might perhaps have found the need to abort her enquiry. But in the case in question, the preliminary findings justified further work. Thus she was not merely freed to engage in, and direct, the analysis which led her to a deeper under-standing of Homer's use of imagery. She could also carry out a full study, because the computer could bring together within a short time-scale all the information acquired and required. Of course, this situation also had its demanding flipside. For when the humdrum tasks had been delegated to the new technologies, it only remained for the learner to engage with the demanding development and exercise of higher level cognitive abilities. This in turn inexorably encouraged the devotion of time and effort to reflection on the processes of enquiry and analysis.

The mere transcription of textual material on to a digital record, toge-ther with the availability of fairly straightforward software which enables textual or similar searches through recorded data, has freed students of classics to proceed directly into speculative analysis and reflection – without being hampered by the time demanded for searching, or exhausted by the effort devoted to that menial activity. They can formulate their own spec-ulative and reflective questions in the form, 'I wonder if . . . ?' and then seek out and analyse the answers.

Comment on Examples 3.1–3.3

These three examples featured changes in intended learning outcomes which demand changes in learning and teaching. Students of mathematics no longer need to spend time learning to differentiate and integrate, for calculators, let alone computers, can do all of that for them. Instead, they are freed to become creative problem-solvers. Students of economics can leave routine data-sifting to the computer, and can harness its power to enable them to assimilate and grasp important concepts which could scarce-ly be conveyed in traditional teaching. That understanding is essential for graduates in a world where they must monitor the computers which now do what yesterday's graduates used to try to do (tediously) by hand. Stu-dents of classics are enabled to undertake analysis on a scale and with a thoroughness which was inconceivable half a century ago. Now they are challenged by the march of technology to develop fully, and to use profoundly, abilities which in the past were only marginally developed.

Thus learners in all of these (and other) discipline areas are nowadays freed to move on to higher educational efforts. And they can do so in learning activities where the speed and coverage of the computer makes it fully possible, for the first time. This in turn encourages concentration on learning about the process of learning, by giving the students and their teachers the opportunity and the time to formulate and answer their own reflective questions within the discipline area. They can think about (or rather reflect on) how best to develop understanding, or to analyse, or to find and solve problems, without a heavy demand on them to first carry out tedious and low-level work.

Each of these examples has thus featured three important consequences for higher education of the advent of the new technologies (Cowan, 2004a):

1. Much of what students used to learn and do is obsolete, because the machine now does it, and does it better than humans. Thus students and graduates have to think more deeply and operate more consistently at the higher end of the cognitive continuum than ever in the past.
2. The potential to develop abilities purposefully through planned reflection, which was neglected in the past, is now a meaningful and challenging reality.
3. The technology enables students to pose a barrage of reflective questions concerning their subject area and to seek answers to them – learning deeply accordingly.

In many ways, the advent and impact of the new technologies is fortuitous. For other pressures, national and even institutional, have been encouraging the increased emphasis on the development of capabilities – through reflection – as our best option to date. It is with these general pressures and responses to them that my second three examples are concerned.

Example 3.4: The demand from society for increased capability

In 1980, a number of prominent British personalities came together to formulate the 'Education for Capability' manifesto (Royal Society of Arts, 1980). I leave that document to speak for itself, and simply reproduce here the criteria which it set out for any education that this group felt would satisfactorily develop 'capability'. These criteria were regarded at that time as both radical and controversial, even after making due allowance for the status of the majority of the signatories.

Criteria for Education for Capability

The Committee believe that the following criteria must underpin any programme designed to educate for capability:

1. the demonstrated *competence* of the learners is increased, particularly through active methods of learning which develop the existing interests, skills and experiences of the learners;
2. the capacity to *cope* is developed by encouraging learners to find solutions to problems which they have personally identified, in contexts relevant to their own lives;
3. the *creative* abilities of learners are drawn upon and expanded through doing, making and organizing;
4. learners are encouraged to get on with other people, and to initiate and engage in *co-operative* activity;
5. learners are involved, according to their maturity, in negotiating with their teachers what it is they need to learn;
6. programmes are accessible to a wide range of learners;
7. methods of assessing and giving recognition to successful performance are appropriate to the activity undertaken;
8. the aims and objectives of the programme are understood and accepted by learners and staff; and
9. there is a coherent programme design with effective execution. [My italics]

It is only fair to give due credit to these campaigners for a number of consequent initiatives which were taken up by secondary and tertiary education in Britain in the 1980s. Notably these commenced with the widespread promotion of Education for Capability, through the Royal Society of Arts (RSA) recognition scheme. Later, this trend continued to some extent in universities, through the Enterprise in Higher Education initiative, which was in effect launched by the British government, and funded accordingly. More recently, there has been the move to offer vocational qualifications at sub-degree levels (QAA, 2001a, 2001b). These qualifications specify outcomes of further and higher education which should be able to be applied in a workplace, and which will attempt to assess them accordingly.

None of these developments originated within further or higher education. The original Education for Capability Committee included relatively few academics, yet it powerfully pinpointed what it saw as a fundamental weakness in education which did not develop 'appropriate' abilities. This committee hoped to rectify that omission, on behalf of society and particularly, perhaps, of employers. Its recognition scheme encouraged, approved and commended the purposeful development of capability. In my own case, I found that an RSA award gave my work (Cowan, 1980b) credibility almost overnight, and made it much easier for me to launch my next, similar, innovations (Cowan, 1984b).

The many achievements in Education for Capability which were recognized by the RSA award scheme showed that the most effective programmes attributed a great deal of their success to the encouragement of structured reflection on learning processes and on the use of abilities used to meet the criteria. Those who set out to follow such pioneers naturally judged it worthwhile to adopt similar teaching approaches, as they attempted to repeat and to better their successes. They tended to be successful in their turn, and so – empirically – the need to arrange for the contribution of reflection was endorsed by what Education for Capability programmes had achieved.

You will notice, however, that the manifesto and the criteria did not explicitly call for reflection on the process of learning. That was not to become a distinctive feature of progressive education, other than in the most adventurous innovations, until the 1990s.

Example 3.5: A need for reflective learning and analysis – in a professional curriculum

This specialized example concerns education in civil and structural engineering. However, I've tried to explain it so that non-engineers – who are themselves members of society who live and work in, and travel over, engineering structures – can understand and, I hope, even share my concern.

As a result of my experiences as a section leader in a design office, I have always wanted to turn out graduates who understand how structures behave. I'd like them to be able to look at a loaded bridge, roof truss or building and know which members are being stretched (in tension), which are being squashed (in compression) and which are being bent. I feel that they need that appreciation because they should from the outset consider and choose different shapes for members which are to sustain tension, compression or bending. Of course, I also want my students to be able to determine the magnitude of the force in a member for a given loading arrangement. However, I'm not so worried about that nowadays, because the computer can readily do the calculations for them – provided they feed in the correct data and would notice if there had been any errors.

Way back in my career as a teacher, I began to note that my students might be able, given time, to calculate the forces in members – but they usually had no idea what to expect, in terms of tension, compression or bending. And that worried me, because if they carried out calculations – or nowadays were to get the computer to do so – and if they made a mistake, then they would probably not even notice that the answer was quite wrong. And if a structural engineer gets it wrong, structures may fall down and people could die.

So I devised tests and enquiries to investigate the problem. I showed my own and other students a photograph or a diagram of a bridge or a roof truss, with a real load or loads in position. I asked them merely which members would be in tension (being stretched) and which members would be in compression (being crushed). I usually found that they were incapable of giving me an answer, or of reasoning one out – other than by first carrying out calculations, or by what virtually amounted to guesswork (Cowan, 1981b). They lacked what I came to call 'qualitative understanding' (Cowan, 1980c). I found that students who were able to 'number crunch' accurately (which I called 'quantitative understanding') might nevertheless have no grasp whatsoever of the behaviour of the structures for which they were able to carry out these complex calculations.

I teamed up with David Brohn, who had had similar concerns. He had shown convincingly (Brohn, 1973) that good honours graduates, on entering employment with one of the top consultants in the country, could carry out calculations which produced diagrams showing the amount of bending at different points along beams. Nevertheless, without first carrying out these calculations, they could not anticipate, even approximately, the shape of diagram they were expecting to produce. Thus, if a computer to which they had given incorrect data produced an erroneous diagram for them, they wouldn't notice the error.

Coming from these similar but slightly different starting points (Brohn, 1973; Cowan, 1975, 1977), Brohn and I attempted to demonstrate this weakness in common curricula to those responsible for the education of civil and structural engineers (Brohn and Cowan, 1977). We showed that there were serious weaknesses in course objectives, as well as in the outcomes they were achieving. Practising engineers confirmed our concern over this defect and the grounds for it. They expressed supportive horror at what we had found and described (see various ongoing discussions of Brohn and Cowan, 1977, over 25 years later, in *The Structural Engineer* – Verulam, 2005).

The teaching profession, who had at first expressed frank disbelief at our findings, gradually accepted the importance of qualitative understanding. Some attempted remedial measures within existing curricula. These initiatives have often not been particularly successful – in my opinion because they have depended on didactic instruction ('I'll tell you how to do it' – or rather 'I'll tell you how I think *I* do it'). That is an inappropriate and ineffective approach to developing higher level cognitive abilities.

To rectify the weakness in my own curriculum, I first sought to understand the ways in which my students (albeit ineffectively) handled qualitative analysis, which I researched using recorded protocols (Cowan, 1983). My students talked out their thoughts aloud to a tape recorder while attempting carefully chosen qualitative problems, and I analysed their methodology from the transcripts. I found, significantly, that when the students analysed and understood their own processes became strikingly more effective in carrying out the tasks I was setting. So I built on my initial findings to develop a style of tutorial question (Cowan, 1982) which literally demanded qualitative understanding – and offered no return for quantitative understanding. The solutions could not be obtained merely by applying formulae and carrying out routine calculations. Instead, the questions called, to good effect, for the application of deep conceptual understanding, applied analytically – and developed reflectively (Cowan, 1986b). Demanding stuff! But rightly so. For it had become clear to me that there was a difference akin to an order of magnitude between the two types of 'understanding'. For displaying what is generally called 'quantitative understanding' merely requires the student to be able to apply a standard method to carry out routine calculations in familiar settings. 'Qualitative understanding', in contrast, calls for true analysis based upon a sound grasp of concepts.

Some 30 years after this debate began, the issue is still aired as if it were a new problem (Verulam, 2004). What is called 'qualitative understanding' is clearly a required and valued professional ability in engineering. Yet the profession still bewails the lack of qualitative ability on the part of graduates emerging from the system. I submit that this example shows the continuing importance of deep learning at higher cognitive levels to acceptable and valued professional performance. I do not see how this understanding can be purposefully nurtured in education without arranging for the learner to reflect on both concepts and processes.

Example 3.6: An institutional change towards reflective learning

More than 30 years ago, the Principal of Alverno College in Milwaukee asked her faculty colleagues to pause and to review reflectively their educational activities. She suggested to them that they should reconsider the nature of the higher education which they offered to their students. She questioned the very suitability of that education, in the context of the society from which the students came, to which they would certainly be returning and within which they would be working and living.

The result of these deliberations was a fundamental change in the nature of the higher education programme which was offered at Alverno College. The details of this radical and innovatory institution have been summarized elsewhere (for example, in Heywood, 1989; George, 1992; Mentkowski *et al.*, 2000). Suffice it to say here that, instead of concentrating in the traditional way on subject matter and content coverage, the faculty concentrated on the development of abilities, in the broadest sense of that phrase. They achieved this by encouraging reflective awareness of process, thoroughly integrated with comprehensive coverage and mastery of content. In addition, they set aside the established system in which assessment by teachers alone provided the ultimate judgement on a student's competence and development. The college moved dramatically to a situation in which reflective self-assessment was encouraged and valued from the outset (Loacker *et al.*, 1986; Loacker, 2000).

Having made that change, this relatively small 'girls college' [*sic*] in the Mid-West of the United States soon found itself one of the most described, most visited and most praised institutions of higher education in the English-speaking world. Visitors of high educational status have trekked from all quarters of the globe to Milwaukee, and continue to do so. They thus testify that the world of higher education has judged the Alverno development and has found it valuable. That judgement surely endorses *inter alia* the strong emphasis placed on reflection within the Alverno model of higher education.

I take Alverno College as the supreme example in recent times of the change which can occur, and in their case *did* occur, when an educational programme and its methods are appraised and redesigned in accordance with the abilities which represent the current needs of society – rather than in accordance with the timeworn and outdated priorities of educationists in higher education. For our present purposes, I pinpoint one feature of the Alverno College development and experience which is highly relevant to the question at the head of this chapter. Faced with the challenge from within to create, or recreate, an educational programme suitable for the external society, Alverno came up with something radically different from the status quo. They chose to focus on abilities as heavily as on content mastery – and to develop these abilities through reflective self-assessment and reflective awareness of process. They have reaped a rich reward from that radical change, and continue to do so.

Other examples

- Recent developments in design education at UK secondary school level have produced a generation of school leavers who are accustomed to reflect on the processes they follow when they are engaged in creative design. They expect this pattern of learning and teaching activity, which has proved profitable for their learning, to continue when they move into higher education. They are often disappointed.
- In many current schemes for continuing professional development (CPD), the identification of needs and the planning in lifelong learning of developmental activity accordingly (Garry and Cowan, 1987) rest nowadays with the individual professionals themselves (for example, in the Chartered Institute of Professional Development – see Megginson and Whittaker, 2003). They must increasingly depend on their ability to reflect – analytically – as they plan, manage and monitor their own CPD. They must further reflect evaluatively, when presenting in appraisals and interviews an almost auditable account of what they claim in respect of personal and professional development.
- Such CPD schemes have presumed (often wrongly) that the necessary reflective ability will have been developed before graduation. National pressures, including the demand for Personal Development Planning

(PDP) while a student and for the compilation of a portfolio accordingly, exacerbate this pressure on higher education to cater for the needed development.

- Workplace-based learning, which is nowadays a valued constituent of vocational courses in higher education, depends on the purposeful reflection that deliberately brings about the generalized learning from particular experiences which is desired.

Non-examples

It is neither desirable nor effective to depend primarily on reflective learning when:

- The learners are being helped to master a standard procedure which they will often have to apply as specified.
- Learners are required to acquire and store, and eventually recall, a vast range of facts.
- The objective is for the learner to develop psychomotor skills, such as ten-finger keyboard skills.

Generalization

We now live in an age in which information is generated at a worrying rate, and in which, at the same time, information becomes obsolete at a terrifying rate. It has been stated that the half-life of the education of electronic engineers is about two years (in other words, within two years the relevance of an electronic education has reduced by half). This situation clearly calls for enhancement through further education and CPD. Whatever the truth of that assertion, I suspect that few would disagree with the suggestion that information in all discipline areas is being generated at an ever-increasing rate, is becoming obsolete more and more quickly and is increasingly being handled by telematics rather than by individuals.

Much of the need to devote curriculum time and emphasis to communicating knowledge and developing understanding has now evaporated. This is because today's knowledge goes rapidly out of date, and because, in any case, computers will supply what we need, when we need it. Tomorrow's graduates will be more concerned to use knowledge and understanding than to acquire it. Fortunately, time can now be made available in most course programmes for the development of the abilities which go on speedily to use acquired understanding. New technology also makes possible the development of these abilities which could not be properly exercised and developed previously – either because the preliminaries were so demanding, or because there was not time for their development, or both.

Consequently, educated people no longer need to have an extensive and detailed grasp of long-established and enduring information (Cowan, 1984a). Rather, we require the development of the higher level abilities of being able to *apply* information and even machine-held understanding; of being able to *analyse* situations and see potential for development; of being *creative* in suggesting ways in which development therein should occur and can be supported; and of being *evaluative* – both in formatively judging recent activities and in creatively judging proposals for activities yet to be translated into the reality of action.

Society and the professions also increasingly recognize the importance of the interpersonal skills and the understanding of relationships which have always mattered but have not, until recently, figured prominently in most academic curricula. Unfortunately, however, many teachers in further and higher education are still regrettably ignorant about the choice and use of pedagogical methods that are suitable for an education which should concentrate more and more on interpersonal abilities. Consequently, their immediate challenge to higher education, in particular, is to develop purposefully the interpersonal abilities which society, the professions and our paymasters value – and which they seek as an outcome of our highly expensive arrangements for education.

Unfortunately, there is still at present a regrettable lack of congruence within education between the abilities which matter and the abilities which are purposefully and deliberately developed. Some educationists, and especially those concerned with mature and often graduate learners, have devoted considerable effort in recent years to eradicating this anomaly. They have sought pedagogies and practices for learning and teaching situations which will effectively foster the outcomes that society, mature adults and employers increasingly seek – and indeed expect. In the practices which have to date proved successful in this respect, we find that most innovators have committed themselves to giving a key role to reflection.

In a tentative summary, therefore, I suggest the following:

- There are still apparent mismatches between the abilities and outcomes pursued in traditional further and higher education and those needed in professional life or felt desirable in the interests of society – or both.
- Social and professional pressures have been brought to bear in recent years, to demand changes to make all education more valid and appropriate – and they continue to be a powerful influence on the reshaping of education.
- Institutions which manage to change their curricula to take note of economic or social needs are valued by society and students alike.
- The new technologies render the acquisition of basic knowledge, and the online handling of that knowledge, less and less important. Instead they place more weight on the higher level cognitive and interpersonal abilities, which in turn call for radically different pedagogies – if learning and teaching are to be effective.

- To date, such pedagogies have given reflection a central place in their methodologies.
- The results obtained by those educators who stimulate reflection on the process of learning itself (which is nowadays called 'metacognition') justify a sea change in our approach to the design of much of what is done in education, at least for adults.
- Reflection thus offers real hope of meeting tomorrow's needs and demands in education.

Before you test this, some second thoughts from me

1. Many would argue that we cannot teach communication skills without getting learners to communicate. Similarly, it can be held that we cannot develop creativity unless the students are concurrently engaged in creative activity within their studies; and that we cannot develop analytical powers unless the students are engaged in being analytical, with meaningful subject matter and working on valid analytical tasks. An observer visiting Alverno, for example, could point immediately to the impressive way analytical ability is developed and assessed within the context of the subjects being studied. So is it not artificial, and hence bad pedagogical practice, to attempt to separate out the abilities, and to concentrate separate attention on the reflection or other distinct activity which seeks to develop them?

2. One could further argue that the educational system has always sought – with considerable success – to develop the abilities which have mattered to the society of the time and for the professions, and that it has done so until now without separately concentrating on reflection. Thus it could be held that no fundamental change in the existing system should be necessary to provide what is now apparently needed. Like all processes, the status quo may well offer scope for improvement and refinement. If the abilities now demanded are being emphasized more strongly, surely that does not in itself justify a call for different teaching methods?

3. The Education for Capability manifesto only specifies outcomes; similarly, many educational developments nowadays, such as the vocational ones, concentrate on outcomes and give little guidance on process. However desirable these new outcomes may be, can we give credence to initiatives which (perhaps naively) set out to achieve radically changed outcomes without giving sufficient thought or attention to the means of so doing, and the necessary changes in learning and teaching methods?

4. Is there not a useful parallel here with the enduring example of education in arts and performance skills, or in an artistic discipline

such as architecture? What occurs there is, and always has been, heavily dependent on intuitions and aspirations which are arguably not in the artist's voluntary control, and may not be of a kind that can ever be given explicit verbal utterance. But in all such artistic processes, including those which occur in educational situations, there are critical moments of feedback, of taking stock, of applying general principles (and of deliberately and consciously going against some accepted principles or criteria). All of these involve reflective thought and judgement. This is what the best artists and their pupils have always done in relation to their own work. It is how reflective learning occurs and is promoted in these disciplines – for making art is impossible without analytical and evaluative reflection. This well-established example of professional development and effective education should perhaps act as our model – and perhaps also as a source of shame to the professions and institutions whose education is more pedestrian. Does it prompt us, for example, to accept that important mental processes cannot always be articulated or even internalized, although they can still be judged by their outcomes?

Dear John

You've argued that the world has changed, and that the world of education has already changed in turn. I wouldn't dispute that. I can see how higher level abilities should feature more and more in our curricula, and how circumstances call on teachers to find appropriate, and probably often new, ways of developing these abilities while students are on degree programmes. So I'm beginning to be persuaded that this reflection thing could be something I should try out in my own courses and teaching, amidst the other approaches I use. But at the moment, all that you have given me are examples. And I'm afraid I'm getting a bit swamped with all these examples.

Just as you push your students to find a pattern underlying a range of experiences, so I now need you to find and show me the pattern which underlies all these examples of yours. If I'm going to take this forward, I need a model on which I can base my planning. I need some guiding principles to follow, so that I can work out for myself what to do in my own situation. I need generalizations about approach which cover a range of your examples. If you already have these, I'd like you to share them with me. There's no point I can see in my rediscovering the wheel. But if you cannot offer me an underlying model, then I'm afraid this reader is going to become very sceptical, very soon.

At the moment, to be frank, it all sounds rather like an assortment of intriguing ideas which some innovators like you have taken up with enthusiasm, and from which you have all managed to produce some motivating experiences for your students. But that doesn't mean that the basis is sound; the positive outcomes could be the result of the well-known phenomenon of novelty bringing improved performance – for a short time. That's another reason why I'd like to scrutinize your pedagogical rationale, and your models and theories, which I would hope to be able to understand and see how to follow – after I have critically appraised them.

So what can you offer me in the way of rationale, theory or preferably practical models as a basis for the approach you are suggesting?

4

On What Models Can We Base Reflective Learning and Teaching?

Introduction

It is indeed about time to concentrate on models. Like most engineers, I find it quite difficult to think about plans and concepts without a writing implement in my hand and paper or a board on which to sketch out ideas and relationships. Models for me are helpful representations or simplified descriptions of systems. I will frame this chapter to be mainly about ways in which I find it helpful to describe to myself as well as others what we are doing, or can do, in helping our students to be reflective.

Models are certainly useful when they help us to summarize, so that we can go on to explain to others what we see as the main features of our approaches to education. They do have limitations, however. Since they only attempt to represent main features as we perceive them, and usually do that in relation to a particular context, they do not necessarily embody absolute truths; so they are restricted in their subsequent applications. Consequently, when we generate, apply and quote models, we do well to remember that limitation, and to refrain from applying them beyond their range of validity. You'll find, for example, that I have several models to offer here, since there are several fundamentally different types of idea which I am trying to encapsulate. I don't see these models as competing with each other, but rather as being complementary. That's an important point to me.

Theories give me more difficulty, in this subject area at least. Theories should be founded upon, or confirmed by, data and even evidence. I'm afraid hard data, sound evidence and proven findings of a generalizable nature are hard to come by in this aspect of educational practice. Karl Popper (1963) would, I suppose, advise us that a theory in this or any other area cannot be proven; it can only exist and be accepted while no counter-evidence has yet been discovered. However, Skemp (1979) stoutly endorsed the view that there is nothing as practical as theory. He argues that using theories has three advantages:

- They tell us what is going on, beyond those things which are immediately observable.
- They reduce 'noise' and allow us to concentrate on what is relevant for the task in hand.
- By having a considerable degree of independence from the examples and classes of examples from which they were constructed, they enable us to make new paths outwards from our thinking.

Skemp stated firmly (1979: 182) that:

> a theory is not itself a model for a particular task, but something much more general: namely a schema within which can be conceptualized all the possible states within a particular universe of discourse, and relations between these states.

For the reasons I have given, I do not find it easy to unearth theories of reflective learning which meet that demanding specification. So I have tried to eschew the use of the word 'theory' from now on, in this chapter at least, and will describe the ideas I present as models. I will return in Chapter 11 to suggestions for those who wish to consider in more depth theories and researches in this field.

Outline

As far as possible, I will illustrate the various models that I find helpful by reference to examples of activities which I have already described in the two previous chapters. I will begin from one of these examples which embodies the main features of perhaps the most widely quoted of the models which purport to explain, or at least to represent, how reflection fits into the process of learning. Then, I will amplify that model, to take on board some current thinking and future development. Next, I will summarize a well-known way of describing reflection, which is not so much a model as a collection of basic concepts. After that, I will present my own model, which embodies much of what has gone before. Finally, with a new example, and a different purpose in reflection, I'll suggest an entirely different – if rather simple – model.

I go on to summarize the various types of demand which characterize the promotion of reflection, and the timing and purposes of the various types of 'answer-seeking' that ensue from those initial questions with which reflection begins. I will as usual state generalizations to help you with your reflection. I will attempt to endorse my generalizations – by summarizing the outcomes, for me and close colleagues, of applying the models I have been instancing. Then, since this will have been a chapter with a fair amount of input from me, I will close with rather more than usual in the way of critical second thoughts, on which I hope you will find it productive to ponder.

Model 4.1: The Kolb cycle

The following relates to Example 2.2 – the tale of the students who were helped to produce index cards describing type solutions covering the problem sheets in their courses with which they were having difficulty. This can be linked to the model, shown in Figure 4.1, which is usually attributed to Kolb (1984), although it originated from Lewin (1951). The words which feature on my version of the diagram are my own, and not Kolb's; it seems that those who instance this diagram often choose to paraphrase it, in their own terminology, so I have felt free to permit myself the same licence.

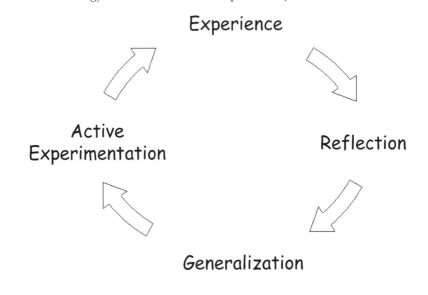

Figure 4.1　The Kolb cycle

The diagram features a cycle which is usually taken to begin at the top, from one or more experiences. There follows reflection on these experiences, out of which the learner should draw a generalization. This should then be tested out in a process of what Kolb called 'active experimentation', when the next similar experiences are encountered by the learner. It is, however, possible to begin the cycle with a generalization provided by the literature or a teacher, which the learner is then immediately expected to test out, in active experimentation (Heywood, 1992).

　　Let's just trace that sequence in my example, working facilitatively with one particular (in this case male) student, to help him to produce cards with 'type solutions':

- Experience: With a little facilitative help or 'nudging' from me, the student managed to solve one of the problems on the sheet.
- Reflection: Together we doubled back, to look at the method which had

led to a successful solution; again, I nudged him, this time to identify its main features.

- Generalization: We now summarized that method on the card, expressing it in general terms which could apply not only to the problem he had just solved, but also to others like it.
- Active experimentation: I encouraged the student to tackle several other problems on the sheet, in order to test out the method we had just formulated in summary. During this phase, he should also have been looking out for places where the summary might be improved.
- Further experience: The student now attempted to apply the method as noted on the card, usually by noting any places where the method did not apply in the general case and so was not as helpful as it might be.
- Further reflection: I prompted the student to see whether there were other ways in which the general statement on the card might be improved – or whether special features needed to be noted in the left hand of the boxes we had provided for this purpose, at the bottom of the card.

Thus this student, during at least the one and a half cycles I have described, was exemplifying the description of how facilitated experiential learning can happen, according to the model which is known as the Kolb cycle (Figure 4.1). He was being taken purposefully round the cycle by following structured activities devised by his facilitative teacher.

In this model and structure, there is a strong concentration on reflection as the bridge from practical experiences to a potentially useful abstract generalization. In my example, there was equally a comparable emphasis on the need to test out the generalization purposefully – through active experimentation. I am afraid that that emphasis is not always evident in other attempts to facilitate or even describe experiential learning. Incidentally, the student's successes in subsequent problem-solving confirmed the usefulness of this model to him – as it did for others – and his ability to progress beyond dependence on facilitation.

I suggest that an important aspect of the tutor's facilitative actions relates to the arrowed arcs *between* the words on the figure – lines which carry no annotation. For much of the task of the facilitative teacher is to encourage movement around the cycle, and hence along these arcs. Teachers can bring this progression about by asking the questions which take the students on from experience to reflection, or by introducing the task which moves them out of reflection into generalizing. At the same time, however, there are naturally occurring events which prompt movement, or lead to flashes of insight or inspiration on the part of the learners. Mismatches between model or generalization and experience are one such stimulus. A student in this example would often notice that a draft of a general method, which had looked feasible for one or two examples, did not work for the next one, and so had to be refined – and improved. Similarly, one problem on the sheet might contain an apparently new feature, which called for reflection to determine how it should be treated.

In this type of approach to learning and development, the learner is assisted or stimulated to construct their own learning, which is eventually summarized internally in their own words. This process is called 'constructivism', since the learners construct their own understanding. And the nudging by which the tutor encourages the learner to dig out all that they can, and to be the best that they can be – and better than they could have managed on their own – is called 'scaffolding'. This supports the learner to move forward into what Vygotsky (1978) referred to as their zone of proximal development, often shortened to ZPD – see Wertsch (1985) for a full explanation of this term. (See further notes on this activity in Examples 7.5–7.8.)

At first sight it might appear that Example 2.3 featured the same model as I have just described, and similarly exemplified constructivism. However, there is an important distinction between the two examples, which it will be profitable for us to explore – and which leads to something more than mere constructivism.

Model 4.2: Socio-constructivist Kolb

The fundamental difference between Examples 2.2 and 2.3 lies in the contribution made to individual learning and development through *planned* interactions with peers. We can confirm that if we summarize the features of the process in the latter example, with a careful eye on what the plan or structure owed to the deliberately arranged involvement of learners with others, in developing the learning for the individuals:

- Experiences: The plan for the first stage of the group work called for a group of students to describe, share and question similar experiences, across a range of disciplines and even levels.
- Reflection: The activity then encouraged group questioning of the accumulation of experiences, successful or otherwise, and hence the beginnings of identification within the group of common features.
- Generalization: From that reflection, there emerged a discursive group activity to assemble the compound lists of problems – and of possible methods of tackling them.
- Active experimentation: The learners were then encouraged – perhaps with less assistance than might have been useful – to follow their normal study programmes, with recourse to the group generated advice list when they encountered difficulties.
- Further experience: The learners now attempted, albeit individually, to follow and if necessary to modify the advice on the sheet, and to note the effectiveness of that for them.
- Further reflection: When the group reconvened, successes, failures and modifications were reported and analysed one by one in the group, with

the individuals then modifying their advice to themselves on this matter, after only informal discussion with peers.

This enhancement of the somewhat individual Kolb experience, where the only interaction is with a facilitator, is important. It expresses the philosophy of the Russian educationist, Vygotsky (Wertsch, 1985), who stressed the important role in learning of interaction with peers.

Notice, then, the types of interaction on Figure 4.2, which shows the extended model:

- Input to Experiences: All learners in the group were able to profit from the tabling of similar or thoughtfully contrasting examples, which had been encountered by their peers.
- Input to Reflection: More pertinent and useful questions emerged from consideration in groups than would have done from isolated reflection.
- Generalization: Group discussion drew upon the perception of all peers in a group, and not merely that of one individual.
- Active experimentation: In planning to undertake active experimentation, the learners were assisted in their planning by the way in which that part of the task had been framed for them, by those who designed the activity.
- Further experience: This was at first individual, but on resumption as a group was quickly to become a shared activity, reporting a useful range of experiences.

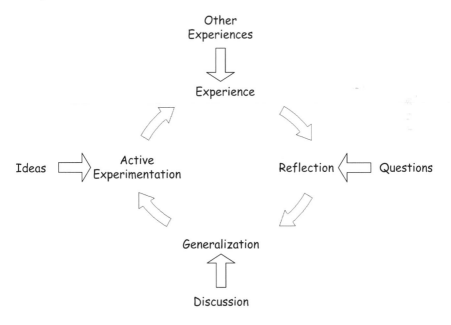

Figure 4.2 The Kolb cycle for socio-constructivist learning

Pavlica and colleagues (1998: 301) have summed this up neatly:

> Kolb tends to over-emphasize the unit of account in learning by concentrating on the individual, and portrays them as a kind of 'intellectual Robinson Crusoe', someone cast away and isolated from their fellow beings. While we feel it is important that learners should be self-directed, we also feel that the social processes involved in learning should not be ignored. Special processes are clearly involved at each stage of the learning cycle. The means by which we experience the world are developed thorough social contact and our actions and experiences are normally shaped through our contact with others.

The issue for the teachers who accept that view is how much effort should be put into structuring tasks and facilitating the activity, to optimize the social interactions.

Model 4.3: The ideas of Schön – and beyond

Schön has written and published a number of popular texts (1983, 1987, 1991) in which he has concentrated on the concept of 'the reflective practitioner'. He identifies this person as someone who engages in reflection related to action – or to experiences, in the vocabulary I have been using so far. He writes sometimes of reflection-in-action, and at other times of reflection-on-action.

Schön (1987) defines reflection-in-action as productive thinking which is generally occasioned by surprise, leading us to question the assumed structure of what he calls knowing-in-action. In this type of reflection we ask ourselves, 'What is this?' or 'How have I been thinking about it?' An example of such reflection-in-action from my own experiences occurred in a workshop for Open University assistant lecturers seeking membership of the Institute for Learning and Teaching. They were to do this through the compilation of a portfolio, in which they should demonstrate their ability to reflect upon their experiences. Despite all my best efforts to explain, the concept and practice of reflection eluded them. Then, almost in exasperation, I urged them to ask themselves how they had tackled the critical aspects of one particular demand. The penny dropped – not just for them but for me. From that instant of reflection-in-action, I stopped talking in workshop activities about 'reflection' until the practice of analysing and evaluating was well established in the minds of those with whom I was working; instead I simply asked questions and encouraged people to think about their answers.

Hirschhorn (1991: 122–3) suggests three different 'moments of experience' which provide him with useful insights of this type. These involve:

- triggers – anomalies, conditions or metaphors;

- patterns – which can emerge when we match an event to our working theory of the situation;
- affirmations – the confirmation of a hypothesis directly, from feelings or from silence.

In the same volume edited by Schön (1991), Russell and Munby (1991: 164) helpfully focus on a pivotal part of Schön's theory, which Schön called 'reframing'. Reframing involves hearing differently or seeing differently, which opens up the possibility of fresh learning for us. I prefer to adopt this broader view of reflection-in-action, without restricting myself to using the term only when the learner is suddenly surprised or prompted to question assumptions.

Sometimes, though not in this example, it can be inappropriate to break away from brisk and thought-provoking action in order to reflect. George Brown (1996) once commented with typical acuity that, when a pilot is landing a light aircraft in a fierce gale, it would hardly be the most suitable occasion for reflection-in-action on how or what he or she is learning best from that experience.

Reflection-on-action, in contrast and as Russell and Munby (1991: 165) remind us, is an 'ordered, deliberate and systematic application of logic to a problem, in order to resolve it'. I find it helpful to restate that description as the considered review of learning taken from an experience, which for the moment has been completed.

However, I suggest that, for our present purposes, we will find it convenient to distinguish between not two but three forms of reflection – depending on their location in the chronology of events. Students often reflect on types of problems which they hope to be able to resolve more effectively in the future than in the past. I therefore propose that this third type of reflection, being anticipatory, is aptly titled reflection-for-action. It is that reflection which establishes goals for subsequent learning or development, by identifying the needs, aspirations and objectives which will subsequently be prominent in the learner's mind.

Lewis Carroll, in *Through the Looking Glass* (1935), has scripted the character Humpty Dumpty to declare arrogantly that, 'When *I* use a word, it means just what I choose it to mean, neither more nor less.' In that spirit, though I trust without that arrogance, I offer these descriptions of terms I will use frequently in the remainder of this book:

- I will take reflection to be a searching for answers to questions about our learning, development or experiences, which we may or may not have posed ourselves.
- I will take reflection-*on*-action to describe the questioning and answering about our learning, development or experiences which occurs once the event which occasioned learning is (for the present) complete.
- I will take reflection-*in*-action to describe relevant perceptions, questioning and answering which occur in the midst of the action, whether very briefly or in a brief withdrawal from the process.

• And (introducing my third category), I will take reflection-*for*-action to describe the questioning and answering about desired learning which occurs before the action in which it is expected, or hoped, that such learning or development may occur.

The types of reflection which Schön describes, and to which I have added my third, can all be found within the experiences of the students working on study skills at Dumfries (Example 2.3). In the first half-evening, they began by drafting an agenda of difficulties which had thwarted past studying, and with which they wished to make progress. That was reflection-for-action. Towards the end of the evening, they generalized, both about the nature of the difficulties they might now encounter and about the style of approach they might pursue in attempting to deal with them. They were then engaging in reflection with hindsight, on recently completed and relatively self-contained activity. This was reflection-on-action – identifying what they now could carry forward, in their intellectual rucksacks, to equip them for the challenges of the coming weeks.

Subsequently, when a student encountered a learning difficulty in the course of their studies, they would try to classify it and relate it to the advice sheet which the group as a whole had assembled. They might go on to respond to, or to modify, the group's advice to its members. At this point they were engaging in reflection-in-action, 'stimulated by triggers, patterns and confirmations within the frame of action itself' (Hirschhorn, 1991: 125). Their classification of the new difficulty, and their identification for immediate use of the corresponding advice they had generated about that type of difficulty, was leading them immediately on from this reflection, to test out and perhaps modify the advice they had helped to set out in the guidance sheet. Reflection-in-action emerges in such ways from immediately past experiences, and points constructively forward to experiences which are imminent. It entails as much anticipative thought and analysis as it does retrospective review. It is a reflection which should, for example, lead to improved or at least carefully premeditated performance.

Model 4.4: The Cowan diagram

Some educationists, in the literature or in conference discussions or elsewhere, have suggested that the endless circling of the Kolb cycle is either depressing or misleading – or both. Some have suggested pulling the coils of the diagram upwards, so that it forms a spiral (Figure 4.3), reaching ever upwards and onwards. Others have chosen a similar spring shape, pulled out horizontally (Figure 4.4). For my own contribution to this debate, I have drawn a somewhat different diagram, though again rather like part of an overstretched spring, with several loops, as in my Figure 4.5. This model, I submit, is radically different in principle from a distorted Kolb cycle, since it features reflection as Schön does, while implicitly embracing Kolbian development (of which more later). It thus highlights and combines the different features of Kolbian and Schönian reflection.

Figure 4.3 The Kolb cycle, as a conical spiral

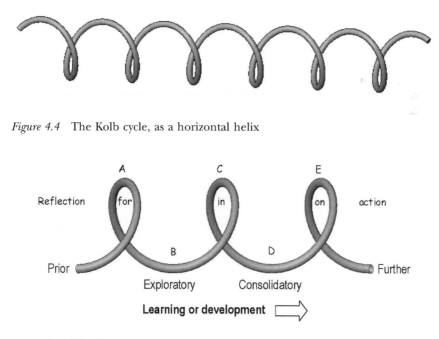

Figure 4.4 The Kolb cycle, as a horizontal helix

Figure 4.5 The Cowan diagram

I will illustrate this model, and that standpoint, by reference to Example 2.4, concerning the Interdisciplinary Studies course, and to the keywords on Figure 4.5. However, it also applies directly to Example 2.1:

- Prior experience: When the students on the IDS course arrived to take part in the workshop programme for a particular week, they knew what skill we were going to tackle, and all brought with them significant prior experience. Part of this came from their relatively common experience as first year students in my department, but a significant part of it came from a wide assortment of previous learning situations.
- Reflection-for-learning: The activity with which a particular Tuesday afternoon was concerned, while it essentially built on prior experience and depended upon it, began with or from declared learning needs with which the majority could identify, or whose potential they saw and could value. An anticipatory reflection-for-action generated a more detailed definition of the diverse needs and goals which were to be relevant to individual students, under the general title which had been declared for the activity that lay ahead.
- Exploratory activity: Having dwelt relatively briefly on reflection-for-action (loop A in Figure 4.5), the students were encouraged to surge forward into an exploratory activity which had been thoughtfully planned for them. In the first burst of that activity (arc B), the students jointly unearthed what they already carried in their intellectual luggage, which might prove useful to them. They also discovered what they could helpfully borrow, or copy, from that which their fellow students were carrying. They were even invited in part of the activity to explore, and to test for feasibility, some possibly useful ideas which were made available to them by their teachers, and which might not have arisen from within the collective experience of that particular group.
- Reflection-in-action: Whatever the progress made on the Tuesday afternoon, students were interrupted ten minutes before the working time elapsed, to 'freeze' their thinking (loop C in Figure 4.5) for an intermediate reflection-in-action. In this they stood back slightly from the action, to take just a little time to reflect on what they had been doing, how they were tackling it and – to some extent – what progress they were making and what remained unresolved on their agenda. This was reflection, occurring in a few minutes which were almost stolen from the action. Such reflection in the midst of action can be immensely valuable, because of that very proximity to action.
- Consolidation: In due course the students moved on to the concentrated activity of the Wednesday morning (arc D in Figure 4.5). There they worked on a consolidating input or plan offered by their teachers. Together, we (students and staff) did everything possible to make good the deficiencies which we had perceived in the learning or development to date, and to build upon the students' reflective analysis of their progress. They completed our Wednesday morning activity without a 'final' reflection.

- Reflection-on-action: This was not to take place until the Wednesday evening, by which time the students had had the experience of returning to take part in more normal student activities. Following that modest opportunity to test out the new development in practice, they were better able to compile their reflective learning journals (loop E in Figure 4.5). You will recall that this reflection was centred on what each had learned about learning or thought about thinking, which should make them more effective in the week ahead than they had been in the week which lay behind. This was therefore a stocktaking activity, and essentially a reflection-on-action. For in it they identified and defined the useful learning and development which had (or had not) taken place in actions completed – learning which was now ready to be carried outwards, and put into service, in everyday studying.

There was always the possibility, of course, that the last loop might swiftly become reflection-for-action, if significant new needs (like the log-jam problem) were identified, or if urgent aspirations emerged. If so, the learners moved into another sequence, in which all of the activities I have just described became the prior experience, feeding into that next learning sequence.

So far we have traced out, in the context of that one example, the components of my model (Figure 4.5) wherein the emphasis is on reflections and experiential actions of particular types. You may have noted that, in my zeal to convey the importance of the three types of reflection, which call for three types of activity by the learner and therefore three forms of facilitation by the teacher, I seem to have lost by the wayside the other three elements in the Kolb diagram, and the subtle transitions between them.

All of this, I assure you, must still be included, even if the figure does not explicitly describe it. Examine, for instance, one of those sections between reflective loops, and consider what I have already described to be happening there. Refer, for example, to the IDS programme described in Example 2.4. In the exploratory activity marked by arc B, the groups followed much the same outline of activity as did the Dumfries students in Example 2.2. They began from familiar examples of their own experience, reflected quickly on the general features of these experiences and attempted to classify them in a generalization. Then they did the same for methods of response which had, or had not, proved effective for one member at least of the group on one occasion in the past. These entail, in effect, at least two cycles around the Kolb diagram, perhaps adequately if unattractively represented by inserting coils in the arc B between the first two major reflective loops of the Cowan diagram, as in Figure 4.6. Notice that the learner is entering the Kolbian loop at the top – from experiences.

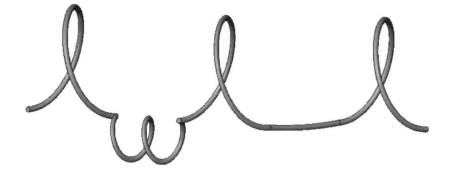

Figure 4.6   The Cowan diagram, with Kolbian detail

Now consider the second section between loops – at D in Figure 4.5. For here something rather different was occurring. The facilitators had provided one or two generalized inputs, which were intended to be of use to the learners. They were offered as something which the learners should test out – and this initial testing by them was the focus for this period of activity. Thus this section of the model covered input of one or more generalizations, planning to test them and then the experience of testing – after which the students were left to reflect on what the proffered suggestions had offered them, overall. This time they had entered the Kolbian loop at the bottom – taking up each input offering a generalization, then to be investigated for its potential, through active experimentation in specific examples (Figure 4.7).

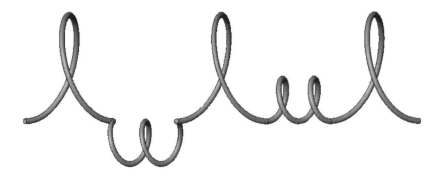

Figure 4.7   The Cowan diagram, with further Kolbian detail

Fortunately, the students were soon in a position to move into the reviewing activity of reflection-on-(the total)-action of the three-hour workshop, unless they had major unresolved needs to figure as reflection-for-(the next needed)-action. This sequence of events might again be represented in a modification to the basic diagram, by adding another coil of Kolbian activity between Schönian reflections. However, this would become so complex as to convey no message.

I therefore prefer to think in terms of the basic Cowan diagram for the overall outline, and then to expand parts of it using other models, as we have just done in words, when the detail of parts of a programme are being considered – or planned.

Model 4.5: Self-assessment

Unfortunately, many people in the academic world tend to think of eva-luation simply as a *declared* judgement, rather than as the process of *reaching* a judgement. That misunderstanding is as likely to be held by students as by their teachers. If self-assessment, which is the evaluation of our learning and development, is to earn respect as a systematic, objective and defensible process, then surely it must be both systematic and objective. One way to make that happen is to follow a simple sequence:

1. Define the criteria against which judgements will be made.
2. Describe performance in the same terms.
3. Compare performance with criteria.
4. Use a predefined scale with which to arrive from that comparison at an objective judgement.
5. Formulate and declare the judgement, whether qualitative or quanti-tative. (See Figure 4.8.)

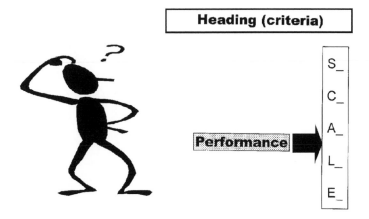

Figure 4.8 The elements of self-assessment

This approach is exemplified by Example 2.7, which describes a process wherein students are introduced to the above method of reaching an evaluative judgement, and are then encouraged to apply it, with formative intent. First they meet the process, with its distinct steps. They should twice try to follow the steps bulleted above, although first time round most definitions of criteria will be particular and vague, and 'performance' may usefully be rewritten as 'characteristics of options'; the comparison step will be largely neglected, and the final outcome of the process will depend on who is following it.

Interactive discussions of the process, rather than the decisions, should sharpen up the approach. Students then go on to try to follow the five steps above when they each apply it to the draft of an open-ended assignment which they will shortly have to submit. They discover, unprompted, discrepancies between their own performance and their own criteria – mismatches which prompt them to see scope for enhancement, and even how to bring that about.

Different purposes, questions and approaches to reflection

I hope that what I have written here so far has shown that there are a range of different questions which may prompt reflection; and hence that there are a range of different purposes for reflective processes, which presumably are best described by different models, and not within one omnibus model. At this point, I hope it will help us both if I summarize the different types of question in common use:

- In reflecting, we may ask ourselves HOW? How do I do something, or how should I do something?

  How did I go about identifying a suitable research question?

  How should I go about planning the process of this enquiry, especially since it is an enquiry which involves searches on the internet?

  How can I stimulate my creativity, to generate more ideas when I am asked to design?

- We may also ask ourselves HOW WELL? How well did I do something, or how well could I do something like that, next time?

  How well did I plan my personal and professional development over the past six months?

  How well did I contribute to resolving the interpersonal problems in our project group?

  How well could I question to good effect the texts and papers which I study in my discipline?

- If we focus upon critical incidents, we may well find ourselves asking WHAT? What happened in that situation, and what should I have done about it?

I disagreed on ethical grounds with the decision they made, and which I nevertheless had to follow. What should I have done?

She did that splendidly – much better than I would have done. What were the secrets of her success, and what can I learn from them?

- There is also another group of questions, often of great importance to our learning and development, which I cannot readily classify. Often they entail a puzzled WHY?

   I had a much better idea than the others in the group, and I explained it clearly – but I couldn't persuade them to adopt it. Why can I not get them to agree with a sound and well-presented suggestion?

   Why should I not go straight to a judgement, instead of following the complex systematic process, as he has described?

We have seen that at least two of these demands – the analysis prompted by 'How?' and the evaluation prompted by 'How well?' – call for different approaches and models. We have seen (at least implicitly) that different purposes and timings for reflection – before, during or after an activity – also call for important differences in approaches, and presumably at least different variants in the model in use. I hope this explains why I have not offered, nor would I seek, one model to serve in our various engagements with reflection.

Generalizations

I feel reasonably confident in offering a list of principles which I believe have been endorsed, over many years now, by the reported experiences not only of myself but, more importantly, of many others. I suggest that you can be confident that:

- Developing the ability to do something begins from examples, including our own experiences, and uses common language, at least initially. My favourite example of this is seen when children teach other children to play chess, or Monopoly. It begins with demonstrations of moves, explained in the examples which occur as a first game quickly begins and proceeds. In contrast, watch adults, who will laboriously spell out rules and the purpose of the game. Children learn much more quickly from other children, whose language is simple and who teach through experiences and examples. For a second example, eavesdrop on a student explaining to a fellow student what they missed in a lecture they could not attend. Note that a student who has grasped the subject matter will give a terse summary, in everyday language, probably with examples of how this is to be applied, and consequently does so remarkably effectively.
- People who think about how they do 'it', and in so doing consider the data available to them, will improve at doing 'it' – whatever ability this features. For example, most students who surf the Web for study

purposes do so with enthusiasm, but little skill. Their searches generate excesses of material, much of which is of no use to them. I have found that a short workshop in which they think about how to plan and carry out effective searches leads to a clear improvement in both their effectiveness and their efficiency – which are different criteria, of course. My enquiry skills students, featured in Example 2.1, regularly claim with persuasive support data that their thinking about enquiry skills in their process analyses has enhanced core abilities which spill over in their use to other modules, and even into employment situations.

- People who think about how well they do things, and how well they could do them, are more effective self-directed and self-managed learners. Witness simply the testimony of the Danish students in Example 2.5. This is endorsed by the paper which one of my first self-assessing students wrote with my assistance, the content being hers (Boyd and Cowan, 1986).

Testing my own generalizations

Do I use the models and principles I have described, and do they work for me and for my students' learning? Unless these two questions can be answered satisfactorily, the generalizations I have attempted to encapsulate here are immediately suspect.

I'll begin with the Cowan diagram. For three years, Derek Fordyce and I designed virtually all our IDS activities with this model much in our minds, as guidance rather than as a prescription. We planned our component activities with different purposes, and hence in different forms, according to which of the three reflections we hoped to facilitate.

In the first loop, we felt that we had to provide an effective activity which would help students to define their needs and aspirations specifically, as their reflection-for-action. The second loop had to feature a brisk part-activity to round off the work of the Tuesday afternoon, when we (and they) needed a snapshot of the current state of their learning. So for that loop Derek and I had to conceive an activity which encouraged and enabled students to stand apart from, or above, the action in which they had already been immersed for 90 minutes or so. Only thus could they effectively summarize what they were doing, how they were doing that, how successful and unsuccessful it was being, and whether they had made progress with their needs or now wished to redefine them with more clarity – all as reflection-in-action.

For the final reflection-on-action we had to facilitate a different type of activity again, in which the students, individually, would be helped to summarize succinctly what they were taking from the activity and would hope to put to later use. They would also, if appropriate, pinpoint what issues remained unresolved, which then became a potential need, leading into reflection-for-further-action.

In the surges of activity between loops, which were the main part of our programme, we planned for testing, for generalizing and for new experiences. This was to provoke reflection on process, with an awareness of the need for coverage at these times of the entire Kolb cycle, which is not, as I have already admitted, explicitly conveyed in my diagram.

User evaluations

Since my time working with Derek Fordyce, I have adopted this framework on many occasions, in differing settings and with various disciplinary groups – with positive evaluations from learners. Importantly, they have always readily grasped the model and its rationale when I have presented and explained them, and they have often referred to them subsequently. We did not make a point of presenting it overtly to students, but we freely explained it to them, if they enquired about the unusual sequence of workshop activities which they were going through. We soon found that, in their learning journals, students would relate their thinking to particular points on the 'loopy diagram', as they called it. A journal might, for example, contain the statement that, 'What I've just written in some ways makes up for the fact that our group didn't manage to get over the top in the middle loop, on Tuesday afternoon.'

In the evaluation of IDS, I systematically examined the impact of the programme on the performance of our students in the subjects where Derek and I were not their teachers (Cowan, 1986a). This evaluation showed that the programme had had an impact on their entire first year learning and performance – although I admit that this does not confirm the model as the cause of that. Still, there is a close correlation between my use of the model in planning and presentation and our effect (through IDS) on the development of the students' interdisciplinary abilities. Accordingly I judge this adapted Schönian model, and its various ramifications into Kolb and socio-constructivist Kolb (Weedon and Cowan, 2003), to be effective.

Before you test this, some second thoughts from me

1. I feel it vital to point out at this stage that the use of the same word by Kolb and Schön does not imply that they seek to convey similar meaning. Kolbian reflection is a component in a sequence, the bridge to be crossed between particular experience and consequent generalization, an activity carried out with that one, almost closed-ended, purpose in mind. Schönian reflection, in contrast, and whichever variant we consider, is an open-ended activity detached to some extent, however briefly, from the action. Its outcomes are not predetermined,

but are rather determined within the process; and their occurrence is not absolutely necessary in order for the action to proceed. How much do these processes have in common – and how significant are their differences?

2. None of the thinking I have summarized in this chapter says anything to us, directly, about the role of the teacher as facilitator. Yet this is obviously of paramount importance, if reflective learning is to occur other than by chance or good fortune. What advice do the models offer us about this role?

3. None of the models which I have described offer guidance about the times when it will be useful for teachers to provide inputs which draw on their accumulated knowledge of the discipline. Nor do they assist us in determining the border line between effective inputs and authoritarian interference with individualized learning. These issues remain to be addressed.

4. I have made no mention yet of well-regarded models by Boud, Keogh and Walker (1985) and Race (2005) – which do not sit comfortably with the contents of this chapter. I will return to these and try to outline what they may offer to you in Chapter 11.

5. If learners are to engage in active experimentation, and if teachers are to carry out and build upon formative and summative evaluations, then more thought needs to be given to bringing about a change in which all will become action researchers of their own practices (Bhattacharya *et al.*, 2000; George and Cowan, 1999a).

6. One of the major challenges in evaluation is that of coping with multiple criteria – a topic which has not been recognized in the simplified model in this chapter. That complication needs to be addressed – by learners, hence by teachers, but, I am afraid, not in this book.

7. In an early version of the Cowan diagram, I included a mirror image above the diagram, rather as if two series of loops and arcs had been sketched on two adjoining faces of a Toblerone packet, which could then be flattened out, although it would have lost something in so doing. What I had in mind to convey was that the two loopings, bolder for student, weaker for tutor, tended to touch or be very close when tutor and learner were in close contact, but ran away from each other – especially in the three dimensions of the Toblerone packet (Figure 4.9) – when the learner was active and the tutor was 'in reserve', observing or merely available. It is perhaps unfortunate that I dropped this version, which I merely did because some people found it an unwelcome complication. For it tried to describe a missing and important element, which is the essentially varying relationship between tutor and student in this process of facilitated learning or development.

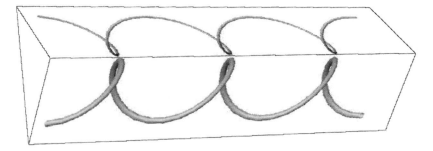

Figure 4.9 The Cowan diagram, with tutor's role incorporated

8. We must beware of the assumption of linear progress in all of the models I have described. In Chapter 2 alone, each of the examples I have given reminds me that I have found that learners may take one particular experience, reflect on it and hence assemble a fragment of generalization. They may then return to another particular experience, reflecting and again partially generalizing. And so they can go on, oscillating between these points on the diagram perhaps four or five times. Only then are they eventually ready (or prompted) to move on to the next stage, that of testing – or what Kolb calls active experimentation. It may take repeated oscillations over this part of the cycle before learners are prepared to test out their now fairly complete and considered generalization on new examples and in new experiences. There would appear to be a tendency for some progress within the Kolb cycle to be an erratically incomplete and repetitive use of only part of the diagram, as I have symbolized in Figure 4.10.

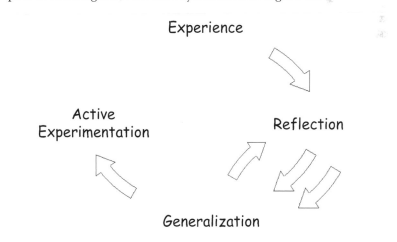

Figure 4.10 The Kolb cycle, with doubling back

9. Evaluative reflection is often an extremely powerful component of development, especially insofar as it identifies needs, aspirations and objectives. But can evaluative reflection, of the type I encapsulated in reflection-for-action (as well as in part of reflection-in-action), lead to a generalization (or a theory or an abstraction) in the way that Kolb describes? How does it relate to Kolbian reflection, in other words?

10. Each interaction, between student and student, or between student and teacher, is a vital element in the process of reflective learning. There are, however, important pedagogical differences between situations which involve synchronous and asynchronous contact between tutor and learner. The pause which allows a little time for thought between question and formulation of response, and between response and further question from the learner, can entirely change the nature of interaction and hence of active learning. This was noted in the use of fax machines at the Open University in Scotland for what were called 'fax tutorials' (Rosier, 1998). In that study, the potential of asynchronous communication for reflection was deliberately harnessed – eight years before it emerged as a feature and much studied aspect of discussion board activity in the VLE (Cole, 2000).

11. There may well be significant differences between the person to person interactions which facilitate reflection and the interaction with oneself in private reflection. Thinking processes in each case must presumably interact with linguistic processes, in order for learning and development to occur. Is there not also a difference between reflection which takes place in spoken or in written words? If so, then in given situations where we set out to structure reflection with a chosen purpose, we as teachers must decide which of these it is best to encourage, in terms of their potential for our students.

12. This chapter has not addressed theoretical understanding of the processes we are trying to harness. It has merely concentrated on empirically justified and reasonably popular models chosen to describe or advocate effective practice. How, then, shall we progress to a sound theoretical basis for the use of reflection in the development of learners? A theory can be regarded as a network of concepts, which are linked together in a coherent framework which allows for testing against evidence and the prediction or planning of action. I hope you may have found it useful to accumulate some concepts from this chapter on which to found the beginnings of your own network and theory of reflective learning.

Dear John

Your models, linked to your examples, have made it clear to me, for the moment at least, what you mean by both analytical and evaluative reflection. I believe I can see what is involved – which in some cases appears to be a fairly convoluted process for both learner and teacher. And so I have a fresh and important question in my mind – which I will express in deliberately ambiguous terms. How does all of this reflective activity affect learning?

I want you to interpret that question in two different ways. The first arises from the fact that I need to be persuaded that reflection is worthwhile for the learner, and for the teacher who cares about promoting learning. How, then, and to what extent, is the consequent learning affected when learners engage in reflective activity as part of their programme? The second way I'd like you to look at my question seeks to move me on from the models to an understanding of the process and its impact on learning. How is it that this reflective activity brings about the effects which I'm sure you will claim?

One question, then, with a double thrust. To make the answering easier for you, and the assimilation easier for me, could you maybe split it under the two types of reflection that you have identified – analytical and evaluative. Let's begin by my asking you – How does analytical reflection affect learning and development?

5

How Does Analytical Reflection
Affect Learning?

Outline

In this chapter, I offer six examples, which I hope are of some intrinsic interest in their own right as modest innovations in higher education. They also exemplify, I believe, reflection which leads to learning and development, and is analytic. For further examples I leave you to refer back to earlier chapters in this book; I quote no non-examples, though the evaluative ones in Chapter 6 should offer the contrast you may seek. My generalizations and second thoughts are included, but are rather shorter than usual.

Most of the examples are written in the first person. These are loosely paraphrased statements rather than direct quotations, and are presented this way to convey rather than record precisely the student voice. One of the students is, of course, me!

Example 5.1: Reflective analysis emphasizes processes rather than content

This example comes from a first year student, describing something that happened some five weeks into the first term:

> We had been given a report to write, for Properties and Use of Materials. We had to find an example of something which had been built by a civil engineer, and which was damaged – in a way which didn't make it immediately obvious what had caused the damage. A crumpled building with a double-decker bus embedded in the front wall wouldn't do. In our report, we had to describe both the building and the damage we had seen in it. Finally, we had to present our diagnosis of the cause of damage, and justify that judgement. The report had to be

written in two sections, which were to be on separate pieces of paper, for some reason which we didn't follow straightaway.

We were offered the opportunity of what our lecturer called a co-operative workshop. We were told that we would only be admitted to this workshop if we had completed a reasonably thorough draft of our report. If we hadn't done that properly, or if we hadn't even started it, we were turned back at the door of the seminar room – and sent to the library, to use our time sensibly, in catching up. I was all right, though; I could show that I had a complete report in draft, so I was welcomed to the workshop.

We were put into groups of five or six students. The lecturer collected our reports, and passed them to another group, some distance away. Our group got the bundle of reports from a group at the other side of the room – we weren't quite sure which group that was, but it didn't matter anyway. We read each draft in our bundle quickly, and we each chose one of them to work on. We had to suggest ways in which each report could be improved. The plan for the activity helped us to do that. This scheme told us that we should first look only at the descriptions, and work out what we ourselves thought was the cause of the damage, and also note any information which we thought we lacked. Sometimes we felt, and would advise, that the writer could usefully have told us more. **This part of the activity made us think about how best to describe things.** [author's bold]

We were encouraged to consult others in our group. We often disagreed amongst ourselves about what we thought had happened to cause damage. We had to discuss our various possible diagnoses thoroughly, but we didn't have to reach agreement. After that discussion, we were asked to check over the writer's diagnosis on their second sheet – and often we found that we disagreed with that as well. This made us examine our reasoning. Often we found weaknesses in it, or in the writer's diagnosis. **This part of the exercise made us think about how to put together a good argument.** [again, author's bold]

The lecturer also told us that, when we had read the writer's diagnosis, we should next try to predict all the consequences which *should* be seen in the building, if that diagnosis was correct. Often we didn't find all of the outcomes that we predicted. **Again, that made us rethink and reconsider – about the writer's diagnosis, and about ours, and about how we had reached our one.** [author's bold]

For instance, our group was given a description of a large house with a whole lot of cracks in it, in one wall which faced a garden area. There were a number of rapidly growing trees in the garden. Some of these were quite near the house. Three of us in the group thought that the cracks were due to the growth of the larger trees in the garden area. Two others noticed, from a photograph in the report, that there was a lot of staining and mould on the face of the wall. They felt that there must have been some chemical action, which had maybe made parts of the wall swell or shrink, while other parts hadn't been affected. But the writer of the report put it all down to subsidence – without saying what had caused the subsidence. When we thought about the effects which subsidence would have had on this house, one of our group pointed out that, if you looked along the brick wall of the building, the horizontal bed lines shouldn't be straight and level any more. We looked at another photograph which was in the report, and the lines seemed to be straight. That made it difficult to agree with the diagnosis of subsidence as the cause of cracking. It also made us more critical of our own diagnoses of the cause of cracking, and so we asked ourselves more questions about our conclusions. **Now we were having to think generally about everything that can go wrong when you make up a diagnosis – and, the other way round, about what *we* should do in order to diagnose soundly.** [author's bold]

We weren't supposed to do the job of the writer of the report for him or her. We didn't have to find or justify our own diagnosis of the cause of failure. We just had to point out ways in which the report, and especially the reasoning in it, if it was unconvincing or incomplete, might be improved. Sometimes, for instance, the description didn't tell us all that we had wanted to know, or the diagnosis seemed to be illogical. In either case, that was worth reporting back. The writer could stick to the original diagnosis, improve the description, or even change the argument for the diagnosis. That was *their* decision.

After all of this, I didn't really need to get my own report back in order to appreciate what had to be done to improve it. I had already seen lots of things wrong with the reports that we worked on, when they were discussed in our group. And I had often found myself thinking immediately that the same criticism would apply to my own report. So I knew what I was going to be told before my draft came back to me. In fact, I had one or two extra suggestions of my own, which the group who looked at my report didn't pick up.

Next time I have to write a report of this type, I'll be better able to put my argument together – and to present it. Because, by looking at reports that weren't well enough done, this activity made me think. **I thought about how to describe building structures, and how to put together convincing arguments, and how to get to a diagnosis. I'll do all of these things better next time, whatever they ask me to do.** [author's bold]

That last paragraph sums it up, doesn't it? The nature of the open-ended task and the demand of the co-operative activity called on these students to scrutinize descriptions, to analyse the coherence of the descriptions and arguments presented by their fellow students, to reflect on these analyses and to learn from them about how to carry out these tasks. From working on the particular examples before them, they moved through their analytical reflection to a developing and generalized appreciation of what makes for adequate describing, and diagnosis, and satisfactory explaining.

Example 5.2: Reflective analysis prompts thinking about thinking – and thinking about thinking about thinking!

(From the context of Example 2.4.) The following description is from a student who is finishing his first year of studies in civil engineering, and discovered for himself what Pask (1975) had discovered many years ago:

> I was writing in my learning journal, near the end of my first year of studies in IDS. This made me look back over the year. I found myself thinking what a change there had been in me as a result of keeping a learning journal.
>
> Mind you, I hated doing it at first. I didn't see the point, I couldn't write anything sensible, and I was really worried about what the lecturer would comment when my dreadful mess of a journal entry went in each week. But, as the weeks have gone past, I have found to my relief that the lecturer doesn't criticize what I've written. I've also begun to acquire the habit of mulling over the week that is past. So it's easier to write nowadays – and more useful, too.
>
> Do you know, it's curious. Sometimes when I sit at my desk at home, either working on course materials or writing up my journals, it's as if a ghost came out of me, and stood behind my shoulder, and offered me advice about how to be more effective in the things I have to do in my studies. If I'm working on engineering or science subjects, it could be advice about how to tackle the studying or the problems on the tutorial sheets. If I'm writing my journal, it could be prompting my thoughts – before I write anything down – about what I should be saying in it, or thinking about.
>
> And sometimes, though it makes me feel foolish to admit this, it's almost as if a second ghost came out of the first ghost and offered advice to the first ghost about how to offer me advice. Can you understand what I mean by that?

When I received a journal entry on these lines, I could certainly warm to the student's account. It reminded me powerfully of a paper by the Cambridge researcher, Pask (1975). He presented a delightful image of the thinking about thinking which educationists call metacognition. He pictured the student, or anyone else who is tackling a problem or a challenge, as being like an animal in a maze, seeking the best way out. Somehow, from that busy little animal, there emerges a thoughtful part – which climbs up a ladder near the maze, to an observation platform. Sitting on the platform, the thoughtful part of the problem-solving animal watches what is happening down in the maze, sees where it is going wrong and how it might be improved, and offers advice to the problem-solving part of the animal down in the maze – advice about how to do better, and indeed about what to do.

And sometimes, Pask told us, there can be another thoughtful part which emerges in turn from the observer on the platform. This one climbs up a further stage of the ladder to a higher platform, to offer advice to the observer on the first platform about how to be a more purposeful and useful observer.

At no time in his studies, or from his contacts with me and my colleagues, did the student whose account we have just read encounter Pask's wonderful picture of metacognition, and certainly not of that meta-metacognition which occurs when the observer on the second platform (or the second ghost) is proactively involved. The week by week experience of reflective and analytical journaling, coupled with the facilitative comments from a tutor, had led a relatively undistinguished first year student of civil engineering to this rather splendid journal entry – which I still keep, and still treasure. I would argue that two and a half terms of facilitated self-analysis and reflection led him to this discovery which, being new for him, was a great achievement, and represented truly deep metacognitive learning and development.

Example 5.3: Using time out – for reflective analysis of process-in-action

In 1991, my colleague Judith George went to Alverno College in Milwaukee as a student. She lived as a student, socialized little with the staff and took part as a student in all the classes where she participated (George, 1992). After one such class, she described her experience along these lines:

> The tutor wished the students to explore four different ways of analysing a piece of literature. She divided the class into four similar groups. She explained to each group an emphasis on which she wished us to concentrate in our literary analysis. It was her intention that, in due course, each group would report back in plenary to the other three groups, with both their findings and their thoughts about their assigned analytical emphasis. Even at that point, I noticed that – typically for Alverno – there was as much emphasis on process awareness and development as on rigorous content coverage.
>
> The small-group activities began, and went well for a while – or, at least, they went well for three of the groups, including the one of which I was a member. The fourth group, however, encountered considerable difficulties. They just weren't able to get going, and none of them could put a finger on what had gone wrong. In characteristically supportive Alverno fashion, someone in one of the other groups noticed this and quickly enquired what was happening, or rather what was not happening. When she confirmed that the fourth group were having difficulties, she called 'Time out!' to the rest of the class.

We reconvened in plenary, with the group tasks set aside for the moment. The entire class, without the involvement of the tutor, began to address the problem of the group with difficulties. We didn't try to work on the task which the struggling group had been given. What we did do was to try to find out why that group was having difficulty with a task of this type, when the rest of us in the room had managed to cope with our own particular emphasis in analysis, in our particular situations. The whole class spent some time on constructive discussion, suggestions, questions and, above all, analytical sharing of experiences – which were experiences of process, and not yet of outcomes. Soon the group with difficulties felt sufficiently in command of the processes which had been shared with them to propose that the other three groups should return to their own tasks, leaving the fourth group, who were now able to proceed, to do so on their own.

This is an interesting example, which arose because there were four similar, but distinct, experiences progressing within one class at the same time. When one of these groups encountered difficulties, the students from the other three groups volunteered to pool their (analysed) experiences of process. Clearly, from the way this was decided by the 'time out' call, and by what happened thereafter, this was by no means a unique experience for the students. Through analytical reflection on the processes being followed, the class as a whole attempted to distil that which was common to the three successful groups, for the benefit of the fourth group. The fourth group, in turn, detached themselves from the immediate frustrations of a process which was not going well for them, and attempted in their own way to analyse what it was that they had been doing. It was by comparing that experience in the full class with what the others had been doing that the students in the fourth group found enough of a solution from the analytical generalization which thereby emerged, and felt confident to test this out on returning to their own particular task.

Comment

Tasks, once understood and mastered, tend to be perceived and summarized by competent learners in generalized terms (as in Examples 2.2 and 2.3). But before mastery is achieved, and especially where a generalized method or process is not yet grasped, learners or problem-solvers tend to see a particular task only as a particular challenge. Through analytical reflection which concentrates on (and brings out and reinforces) the generalities, learners can be enabled to proceed from a tentative and particular experience to the generalized grasp which is associated with the ability to tackle effectively a range of further tasks of a given type.

Example 5.4: Reflective analysis leads to more purposeful reactions to tuition

The following description comes from an Open University student, studying the foundation level course in social sciences. She didn't know anything about Kelly's Repertory Grid. She was told, but only after the event, that it was the research method used in the experience she reports. The enquiry in which she was involved took place when Open University students still posted their assignments, as hard copy, to the university:

> I am an Open University student. In the year I've been asked to tell you about, I was studying the foundation course in social sciences. My tutor approached all of the students in her group, asking us if we would take part in a study which she hoped would enable her to offer us better correspondence tuition. She told us what she wanted us to do – which sounded fairly straightforward. So I agreed to co-operate.
>
> In the Open University, when we send in assignments, the tutor marks these and sends them to Milton Keynes. They are posted back to us a few days later. In this project, it was to be rather different. The tutor had arranged for a colleague to bring my assignment, when she had marked it, straight back to me – like a postman. This man phoned to tell me when he would be coming to see me. He told me that I was to open the envelope, read the comments and think about them, in just the same way as I usually do when the real postman pops a letter from Milton Keynes through my letter box.
>
> The assignment came back to me somewhat earlier than usual. After I had read it, the postman-tutor explained in detail what I had to do. He gave me an example of three types of 'street furniture', as he called it – traffic lights, a bus stop and a lamp post. He asked me to divide these into a pair and a singleton, in a way that seemed meaningful to me, according to the fact that they were items of street furniture. In other words, he explained, I wasn't just to say that the bus stop and the lamp post had a lot in common, because in each case the second word began with the last letter of the first word. That wasn't really an important distinction for street furniture, he said. I agreed.
>
> I chose to go for the two which stopped vehicles – the bus stop and the traffic lights. He said that this was a good response. He told me that it would have been equally valid to separate out the two which required electricity. For, he explained, in each case we would have found out something important about street furniture. The effect that something has on the flow of traffic is important, and the need (or not) for a supply of electricity is also relevant.
>
> He then took me to the comments on my assignment, which I had been warned would have been numbered by my tutor. He told me that he wanted me to divide groups of three comments into a pair and a singleton. He asked me to look at comments 1, 2 and 3 – and to remind

myself of what they said and of how I had reacted when I had read them. He asked me to divide them into a pair and a singleton, according to a category or feature which was meaningful to me. It could be meaningful in terms of either the type of comments that I thought they were or my reactions to them. I chose to separate out comment 2 from comments 1 and 3. Comments 1 and 3 told me that I had done something well, while comment 2 told me that I had missed something out. He now asked me to go through all the other comments, picking out those that told me I had done something well. He ticked these on his sheet, and crossed the others.

When I had done that, he picked a further three numbers, for comments which had all told me I had done well – and again asked me to subdivide. That was more difficult. However in the trio that he chose, one comment explained what it was that I had done well, in detail which was useful – and I was glad to be told what was good. The other two didn't explain, so I had felt a bit frustrated, even though I had apparently written something which was OK. So I divided them on that basis.

We went on doing this several times, always starting with a trio which I had categorized in the same way up till then – until he ran out of available trios. At that point, he checked out with me the various features or characteristics that I had been telling him about. He asked me if there were any other features of the comments on my assignments which had mattered to me. I thought of two more to mention. One of them, I remember, was whether or not the comment was a surprise to me. We went down the list of comments and categorized them again, according to each of my two additional headings.

Finally, he asked me to tell my tutor, through him, about what type of comment I found most useful, and why. I chose the type of comment which told me that I had 'done something well because ... '. I had realized from the activity that I find this more helpful than simply being told what it is that I have done well, because I need to know what it was that made it a good part of the assignment. It's also more useful to me than being told what I've done wrong, and why it was weak.

I found this a surprisingly interesting and useful experience. It made me think about what it is that I am doing and what I'm afraid of not doing, and especially what I should hope to unearth, when I read my tutor's comments on my assignment. The piece of specific learning in the assignment is by then away in the past. By the time the assignment comes back, I'm usually about three weeks further on in my studies than I was when I wrote it – or at least when I began to write it. So I'm on to something new, as far as course content is concerned. That's why the comments that will be most useful to me (at least until we get to exam revision time!) are those which give me an idea about the kind of thing that they want me to do in these assignments, and about how they want me to do it. Now I can see clearly that I can make really constructive use of comments about the things I do which work well, and why; and about the things that matter in this subject I am studying, as I can plan to improve what I do next time. I can't get all of that from the marks and the general comments on the cover note on their own, but I can by analysing the comments and digging out their messages, the way this activity made me do. Since this visit and the messenger's questions, I've found myself spending a lot more time on the tutor's detailed comments, looking for the general messages that they convey, rather than the judgements they make on that particular assignment.

Through an analytical activity which had primarily been planned to provide information for the tutor (Weedon, 1994) about the effect and effectiveness of her comments on assignments, this student (and others) developed a better awareness of how to use, and respond to, tutorial comments. This happened partly because she was urged to differentiate between comments in an analytical way, with the result that she could reflect on what mattered to her in them; and partly because she had the real opportunity to send back an informative message to her tutor, and influence the tutor–learner relationship and her subsequent correspondence tuition accordingly.

Perhaps we leave too much responsibility with the teaching person for the nature and quality of the teacher–learner exchange. Perhaps this should be a joint responsibility, just as it is a joint relationship. If so, an analytical reflection of the type described (Weedon, 1994) can lead to an informed communication from the learner to the tutor. That can be a valuable part of the discharge of the learner's responsibility, and may lead constructively to improvement in the learning experience.

Example 5.5: Reflective analysis deepens understanding of values in a discipline

This example is derived from my own experience as a student:

After years of studying in the social sciences, I decided to study the Open University course A295: *Homer – Poetry and Society* (Open University, 1993–2005). This was an intriguing multidisciplinary course, which provided a mass of fascinating resource material and ideas. It also offered a difficult challenge when, after two fairly standard essay-type assignments, the pattern changed. The third assignment called on me to design my own assignment question and to plan the way I would tackle it. The fourth would expect me to respond accordingly, and then to review the process and the final plan that I had actually followed.

I had been intrigued by a suggestion in one of the papers given in the course reader. The writer argued that peasant societies have behaved similarly throughout the ages in encouraging their members to tell lies, and he maintained that they have all regarded dishonesty as normal, and even praiseworthy, behaviour. This key paper developed that argument, relating it to the lying tales told by Odysseus, and justifying it by reference to a number of research papers about ethnographic studies of Greek peasant village cultures of the twentieth century. These papers appeared to have been translated into English.

I already knew of the existence of highly rated peasant literature from the Irish-speaking community and oral tradition of the Blasket Islands, off the south-west coast of Ireland. This was a community where, from my vague memories of the English version of the texts, I recalled no evidence of the dishonesty associated with Odysseus, and attributed to all peasant societies by the writer whom I felt I might wish to challenge. In addition, I found the argument in the paper in the reader somewhat ragged – and I wondered how sound I would find it, if I went back to the original sources.

I tried to formulate an assignment task based on these vague worries. I had to carry out a great deal of carefully directed searching and reading, linked to an ongoing analysis of what was emerging from these tentative explorations. I found that I now knew my subject matter better, and more deeply, than when I had started out on this assignment task.

Or did I? The more I wrestled with the designing of my final assignment question, the more I realized that I had to think through what 'satisfactory' would mean in this strange new discipline of arts. If I didn't sort that one out, how could I produce a satisfactory piece of work, or better? I went back to analyse the mention of values in the course units, the study guide and the assignment notes – and to my tutor's comments on those first two assignments. It became apparent to me that what they had valued in the course units and in my previous studies in social sciences was not the same as what they valued here, in arts. Having come recently from that social sciences background, I felt like a stranger trying to be accepted in a different cultural village. So, in order to design an adequate task and answer it 'satisfactorily' or better, I first had to analyse what I believe some people have called the 'nature of discourse' in this discipline of arts and, in particular, in classical studies.

In other words, starting from a point of interest, and one or two ideas for reading, I found myself pushed by the task which had been set for me to reflect analytically on the type of enquiry question and the style of response which would be regarded as sound work in this discipline. And then I had to work out how I myself could study, think and write with such goals, while answering that question. In the final assignment, I then had to review the process I had followed to get through the formulation of a question, the assembling of an answer and the judging of what would make a good answer. It was only at that point that I began to realize that this assignment hadn't only been about Homer; it had also been about learning to learn in classical studies.

There are strong echoes here of a declaration by Carl Rogers (1969), who maintained that 'the most socially useful learning in the modern world is the learning of the process of learning, a continuing openness to experience and incorporation into oneself of the process of change.' This student, admittedly me, has described how the structure of the task encouraged him to reflect analytically and searchingly on what he calls the 'nature of discourse' and on the way of thinking characteristic of a discipline. As a result of his reflective analysis, he developed a deeper appreciation of the value framework of the discipline he was studying, and hence an ability to work and study more meaningfully and effectively within that framework.

Example 5.6: Analysing a tutorial experience focuses subsequent participation

This example, like Example 5.4, emerged from what was an action research enquiry, planned to provide helpful information for a tutor, but which branched out into byproducts which enhanced student learning. It is assembled from answers taken from a telephone interview with a mature and very remote student of science at the Open University in Scotland:

> I live a long way from the nearest Open University Study Centre. I'm not on the phone; I stay in a caravan, in a field near the local pub. My only contact with my tutor, other than through the comments on my assignments, comes when I use the pub telephone to join in an audio-conference call, with my tutor and five or six other students.
>
> Once, last year, I was asked if I would take part in an experiment with my tutor. She told me that someone would phone me, after a conference call, and play a bit of it back to me from a recording, and would ask me questions about that. I agreed – and it worked out all right, because the bar was fairly quiet that evening.
>
> The man who phoned me had the tape recording of the telephone conference call. He played back little snatches of it, and asked me if it reminded me of what I was thinking or feeling at the time the call took place. I didn't remember many feelings. But I found that the recording brought back clearly some of what I had been thinking, some 30 minutes or so earlier. Whenever the tape stopped, I tried to tell the person on the phone about this. I hope I did that reasonably well. He seemed pleased enough.
>
> When the phone call had finished, he asked me to summarize what I thought I had learned during the conference call. I could recall that there had been a few points which had been cleared up, and one or two extra ideas which I had added to my notes. But, to be honest, there wasn't much. He asked me if the call had mattered to me – and I said frankly that, yes, it certainly had. He asked me why – and immediately I

reminded him of things I had been telling him about, as he talked to me about what I had been thinking.

First and foremost, it had been enormously important to me to realize that the bits I found difficult were proving difficult for the other people in the group as well. Before the conference call started, I had had that sinking feeling, which I have so often. I was sure that I was the only person who was being stupid, or the only one who hadn't worked hard enough, or the only one who didn't really have the brains to pass this particular course. As the call went on, I realized that we were all in the same boat. That made a tremendous difference to me. I stopped feeling so worried about how I was getting on in my studies. That made me feel better about pressing on with my reading in this block of the course.

The other thing that came across in the call was an appreciation of how well I still needed to understand the various parts of the material in the units, and what I would need to do to show that understanding. I hadn't really been clear about that as I studied the unit – which was probably part of the reason why I was worried.

It's interesting, you know. As a result of talking to that man on the phone, I came to see more clearly why these conference calls matter to me, and how I can get more from them by being upfront with myself about what I'm looking for. So, next time we have one, I think I'll be listening to the discussion with my ear more firmly tuned in to what it is that I want from the call. And I'll feel OK next time about wondering how the others in the group are getting on, instead of hoping that the agenda chosen by the tutor will help me with my own difficulties. After all, the conference call isn't the best way to clear up my individual difficulties. The best way to do that is by an individual call from me to her, or by writing her a wee note. Anyway, when she was replying to individual difficulties, and even when it was something that I had mentioned, I was really listening to find out how the others were reacting to this, more than to her assistance to another student or to me.

We have met here another student who is concerned about the standard of his performance, and about identifying a value framework in the subject which he is studying. Interestingly, as a result of participating in what was actually an action research enquiry on behalf of the tutor, he became more aware of his learning and of how to improve it. The structure of the activity prompted his analysis of the usefulness of the audio-conference tutorial to him, and of what he should seek out in the next one. Hence he was more likely – as a result of that analysis – to profit from conference calls in the future.

This example again raises the issue of the responsibility of the learner for part of the learning and teaching relationship. It also highlights the possibility that a learner's reflective and analytical awareness of what is happening in a learning process can lead to a more effective process then or subsequently, as well as to a more successful outcome, for that learner.

Generalization

I take analysis to be a cognitive process in which we find it useful to look for patterns and generalities, and for noteworthy exceptions – as the students in the examples in this chapter have done. We have visited six examples here, in each of which students reflected on one or more particular experience. Through their analyses, as a bridge between a particular experience and a generalization, they came to an understanding. This summarized, in generic or transferable terms, what they could learn from these experiences and from their analyses of them. In some cases it was the environment which prompted or encouraged that reflection, as in the Alverno example. In others, such as the Kelly enquiry or the review of the learning journal, I suggest that it was the task itself, coupled with the actions of the tutor, which acted as the catalyst for moving learning and learners through analytical reflection into generalization.

I find little or nothing in these examples to suggest (for the meantime) that Kolbian reflection is, or should be, other than analytical. Do you? Please give a little thought to that question before embarking on Chapter 6.

Before you test this, some second thoughts from me

This time I have only one theme for my second thoughts. I will concentrate on the somewhat neglected matter of active experimentation, which I have mentioned already (page 46).

If it is indeed an analytical reflection which takes the learner from particular examples or experiences to the generalization of understanding and competence, must and should there not be a comparable (and reverse) process to complete the cycle? Would this not cover the proactive thinking needed to take the learner back – purposefully – from the generalization into the application and testing of that in the next particular examples, thus widening the learning in new situations? That process seems to have been somewhat neglected in some of the examples I have presented of learning and teaching which follows the Kolb cycle, although not according to my formulation and presentation of this model in Model 4.1, and certainly not in Examples 2.2, 2.3 and 2.4. Would the examples in this chapter have been strengthened, or confused, by building in more structuring for active experimentation?

What does this process of testing, or active experimentation, entail anyway? Can we indeed conceive it as the reverse of reflection, moving from the general to the particular instead of from the particular to the general? And why (other than in the elegant Example 7.5 yet to come) is it apparently neglected in both practice and pedagogy? If it has as much potential to expedite progress around the cycle as does reflection, is the Kolbian approach not seriously incomplete until this, too, is equally developed and understood?

So should we not consider and plan just as deeply for the testing process which takes us from a newly formed generalization to the next experience, as we do for reflection? If so, would this be a form of falsification activity derived from the thinking of Popper (1962, 1963), encouraging the somewhat negative search for counter-examples and disproof? Or should it be a different type of testing, positively seeking confirmation and refinement?

Dear John

Now we come to your second type of reflection, to which I would again like you to apply my two-pronged question.

I can see that analytical reflection concentrates, in the main, on the analysis of processes which should be used to good effect in learning, or in applying learning. I'm less clear about the relationship of self-assessment or evaluation to the achievement of desired learning and development. It sounds almost as if you are getting the learners to do what teachers are paid, and nowadays trained, to do for them. How can passing this responsibility to the student be justified? Can it be justified pedagogically?

Once again, but this time in relation to evaluative reflection, I need to be persuaded that such reflection is worthwhile for the learner, and for the teacher who cares about promoting learning. How, then, and to what extent, is the consequent learning affected when learners engage as part of their programme in reflective activity with an evaluative emphasis? And, again, how is it that this reflective activity brings about the effects which I'm sure you will claim?

6

How Does Evaluative Reflection Affect Learning?

Outline

Before we get on to the purpose of this chapter – and, incidentally, that of Chapter 10 – I feel it will be helpful again to devote a little time to confirming that we are using certain familiar words with the same meaning. In so doing, I'll make my usual use of examples, but this time, for the next few pages, they'll be embedded within my paragraphs. Please forgive me if I am covering ground with which you are familiar and comfortable.

After that, I will then have only three further specific examples to present in response to the question at the head of this chapter. One is simple and short, although it includes three stages of development of an approach. The other two, in contrast, are long. I have dwelt upon them because I feel they offer exemplars and also much food for thought, despite their age. Finally, to compensate for being somewhat short on further examples in this chapter, there will be quite a lot to think about under the headings of generalizations and second thoughts.

Confirming vocabulary

As I have already explained (page 24), l see **evaluation** as a process which leads to the making of a judgement in relation to a set of values or criteria, and one in which the judgement often leads to a consequent decision. When I go out for a meal, I evaluate the items on the menu and make a judgement about which is most attractive to me as my choice for the main course, according to the criteria for selection which matter to me on that particular evening. When the chosen dish has arrived and I have consumed it, I may evaluate what I was given and decide if I made a good choice. In much the same way, when I study a course as a student, I may evaluate in advance the usefulness of the texts which are recommended – and decide which I will use most heavily in my studies. Or when I write an assignment in draft, I may evaluate my hard copy of that, identify where it falls short of my aspirations and decide what to do about these discerned weaknesses.

The evaluative judgements which teachers make may lead to an input in the form of a qualitative grade, or a mark, or a decision on a binary scale such as pass/fail. We tend to label this special case of evaluation as **assessment**. An undergraduate examination which yields a marks list for a class group is such an assessment; and an assignment is similarly an assessed piece of work if it is given a mark (78 per cent) or a grade (B+). Equally, the quality of research in an academic department is assessed when it is rated 4 or 5 on a nationally recognized scale; and when subject reviews were carried out in my country in the recent past, the teaching in a department was assessed when it was judged 'highly satisfactory' by the Scottish Higher Education Funding Council.

The distinguishing feature of assessment, as I use that word here, is that a person or a person's work (or the work of a team) is evaluated in such a way that one of the outcomes is a mark, grade or rating, on some known scale. That scale can be either norm-referenced or criterion-referenced. In **norm-referencing**, that which is assessed is judged against the performances of other similar people or items in the same group. The recipient of an Olympic gold medal gains a norm-referenced award, just as the person who is selected by an interview panel to be offered a particular post would emerge as 'preferred candidate' as a result of norm-referenced assessment. However, candidates who, in the process of interview, are deemed to be 'not appointable' will probably have failed a criterion-referenced assessment, and those who pass the British driving test will have satisfied a requirement which is criterion-referenced. A **criterion-referenced judgement** is made by comparing a particular performance with chosen and objective criteria, and not with the performances of others in the same category.

The evaluation process, which includes assessment as a particular case, certainly requires that there is or should be a fairly clear mutual under-standing of that which is deemed of value, and that which is deemed to be otherwise. But an evaluation does not always result in an **outcome judgement**, which can be described on a scale or profile of judgements, as would be a feature of most of those evaluations which are also assessments. A newspaper column from a music critic, describing a concert which excited and disappointed in parts, would be one such evaluation.

There is a further complication, in that both assessment and evaluation may have two purposes, and hence may take two forms. An assessment, for instance, may qualify or recognize the assessed person in some way, as the driving test entitles the recipient to gain a full driving licence, and as a first class honours degree entitles someone to be considered for postgraduate research work. In that case, it is usually described as a **summative** assess-ment. It sums up where that individual has got to, in respect of the assessed learning or ability. Alternatively, an assessment may be primarily regarded as an important step in the educational process. If so, it is intended to help the learner to identify the current standard of their work, and/or to identify need and potential for improvement. In that case, the assessment is usually called **formative**. It should set out to assist in the subsequent formation of something which will meet up to the desired values or criteria. It helps to form, reform or inform improvement. But we need to be wary of many of the so-called systems of 'formative assessment', for this has become a somewhat slippery concept. Too often an assignment scheme, although called formative assessment, reduces to a collection of summative assessments. They are described and titled as if their main function was feedback, but they have a considerable direct influence on the final outcome – and the students know that and work on them accordingly. In such cases, they are really components of a subdivided scheme for summative assessment, and should be honestly so described. Furthermore, as Taras (2005) has stressed, no formative judgement can be made without being preceded by some form of summative judgement, even if covert and undeclared.

Evaluation, like assessment, may also be either formative or summative. When I first prepared learning resource materials for open learning, I offered them to students as an 'extra' on a Wednesday afternoon (which was otherwise free), for remedial and consolidation learning. I made this additional support available on the understanding that the students, in return, would provide me with an informed judgement on the usefulness of my draft materials, so that I could improve them if necessary and only then decide whether or not to incorporate them in the formal programme of my department. That was a formative evaluation, for its primary purpose was to identify the need and potential for improvement. In one such case, I laboured hard and long to devise a more effective way to teach a particularly awkward topic. I began by subjecting my materials to this type of formative evaluation, so that I could refine and improve them iteratively. Then I carried out comparative experiments on what I hoped was the final version, using pre-tests and post-tests with matched groups of students, to find out if my alternative approach was indeed more effective than the status quo. That was then a **summative evaluation** of the learning in the new approach. It yielded information, in the form of magnitudes of learning gain, which enabled me and my colleagues – by comparison with what we were then achieving – to make an objective judgement about the usefulness of my alternative approach.

One style of educational evaluation that I find methodologically attractive, and tactically effective, is the approach which has been called '**illuminative**' (Parlett and Hamilton, 1972). It seeks to illuminate the situation being described, for the benefit of those who read or hear the reported data. This is an anthropological model, in which the evaluators – as a result of their enquiries – are able to present a thought-provoking but descriptive account of process and outcomes. They do not explicitly judge or assess, although some value framework, even if covert, will undoubtedly have influenced the observations which they have chosen to make, record, analyse and present. Nevertheless, they restrict themselves to assembling and analysing data – and then reporting to others, whose task it is to make their own evaluation based on what they judge the data tells them, in relation to their own criteria.

Please bear with me as I give a detailed, if harrowing, example of illuminative evaluation and its effectiveness. I once carried out an illuminative evaluation of a laboratory programme in a developing country. When I observed the laboratory sessions, I found that graduate teaching assistants from an ethnic majority were teaching students in English, in classes which included many from an ethnic minority, The minority students were treated with what I can only describe as calculated brutality – according to the values which matter to me. Their command of English was pathetically poor, yet they were judged stupid when they did not understand the instructions given to them in English. They were abused verbally, and often hit with sticks and rods, which drew blood. They learnt by trial, error, punishment and humiliation. They learnt what not to do with the equipment before them, and naturally progressed slowly and ineffectively to learning what they should do with it. The same style of authoritative teaching, though with little physical punishment, was given to the students from the ethnic majority, who had little difficulty following the instructions in English on the lab sheets and from the assistants. The suicide rate among the ethnic minority students was alarmingly high.

When I described what I had seen, in an illuminative report presented to the professor and his ethnic majority colleagues, they seemed to swell with pride. 'That's the way these damned —s should be treated,' one declared – literally. I asked them to tell me what the 'good' students, from their ethnic majority, were learning that was of significance, in contrast to the learning of these allegedly stupid ones. They told me, and I noted down their claim. I devised a simple way of checking the learning and progress of the ethnic majority students, without intrusive testing. I reported the (predictably) depressing findings of that enquiry in my next meeting with the staff. This data had admittedly been gathered and selected by me. However, the lecturers now had to confront the objective evidence of ineffective learning and teaching, and compare it with their claim. My results showed beyond question (and believe me, they tried to question) that all was not as they believed and as they wished, even with their ethnic majority students. They now sought my advice and assistance to improve the learning and teaching situation. Needless to say, the improvements which I proposed benefited both those from the majority and from the minority. That had been an effective illuminative evaluation, with a formative intent.

Illuminative evaluations inform and influence. They depend on leaving listeners and readers to formulate their own judgements, and then to respond by making their own decisions for action. The recipients do that in the context of their own value frameworks, of which, however, the evaluator is aware. For that reason, such evaluations are often more effective in the long run than those where it is the evaluator who decides what is right and what is wrong and where changes should be made. Many of the assessments

I describe in this book (and especially in Chapter 8) illuminated for students the progress of their learning, but left them to decide how they felt about that – as did the experience described in Example 7.1, which illuminated for students their lack of ability to describe apparatus.

One last distinction is important in the context of this chapter. It relates almost exclusively to assessment, and to the choice of the person who formulates the judgement. In the traditional British setting, the mark or grade for an examination or an assignment is usually decided by one or more academics, and is ratified by an examination board. However, in recent years it has increasingly become the practice to involve learners in the process of assessment (Knight, 1995; Boud, 1995; Brown and Glasner, 1999). In **peer assessment**, it is the peer group of fellow students who decide the mark or grade to be awarded to each student, individually. In **self-assessment**, it is the student herself or himself who determines the mark or grade, whether or not that is taken into account when the institutional examination boards reach their decisions about awards. Self-assessment, in particular, has served me well since I first committed myself to this approach – with trepidation and with few published experiences of others to draw on (Cowan, 1984b).

Notice, however (and finally in this digression on vocabulary), that we often use both terms, evaluation and assessment, without adjectival qualification. Since the majority of assessments are summative, we assume that to be so unless the term is qualified by the prefix 'formative'. And since most evaluations are formative, or are at least delivered in circumstances where the recipients hope to be permitted to respond constructively to any criticisms or weaknesses, we take evaluations to be formative unless they are specifically described as summative. This is common usage at the time of writing.

An interim reflection on my text

In Chapter 4, I presented models which described two rather different forms of reflection. One was found in the cycle attributed to Kolb; this includes analytical reflection as a stage in a progression that takes learners from particular experiences to generalizations which are applicable in a wider context. The other, in the Cowan diagram, is built on the distinctions advanced by Schön; it portrays reflection as a standing back from the action, for a short or longer time, to take a detached view of what has been, is, should or may be happening. At the time we met these models, I aired the thought that some of the loops of detached reflection in the Cowan diagram were mainly evaluative. At this point, it is as well to remind ourselves of that distinction between models, as well as between evaluative and analytical. Because, as you will have noticed, I have presented further examples in Chapter 5 in which the Kolb cycle, explicitly or implicitly, has underlain the design of the structure for learning. However, I have mentioned little since Chapter 4 of my own model, which features self-assessment, at least implicitly, in its three loops.

That imbalance I now propose to redress in this and the next chapter, since my experience in higher education has been such that I judge the introduction of self-assessment, compatible with the Cowan model, as the most powerful factor for change and development that I have yet encountered. But I have two problems in presenting that suggestion to you. The first is that I know that self-assessment is a hobby-horse of mine, and so I am reluctant to overstress it. The second and more important is that I am convinced that this experience can transform learning – but I don't yet feel able to explain confidently why and how it does that. Perhaps you will be able to help me with finding an answer to these questions, after you have considered my second thoughts.

Example 6.1: Self-assessing – to the teachers' criteria

I link together here three separate examples and present them as one, since they have so much in common. In effect, they are simply steps in a developmental progression for at least some of the students concerned.

Step 1: Criteria provided as a model answer

Many years ago, when students of civil engineering still drew on drawing boards using T-squares, I provided self-marking materials in the Learning Unit at Heriot-Watt University (Cowan *et al.*, 1973). First year students would come to the unit from the drawing office when they had completed their drawing. There they would uplift an audiotape and accompanying print material, and then sit down with their drawing in a learning booth to mark it, add appropriate comments in pencil, and leave the annotated drawing on the counter for a tutor to confirm the marking, or otherwise. The checking job took little time, and drawings could be back with the students first thing the following morning.

The notable outcomes were that:

- Students had feedback within minutes of completing the task – something that is highly desirable pedagogically, but seldom achieved.
- Most students picked up all the mistakes and omissions, and marked virtually as the tutor would have done, though perhaps wording their comments rather more personally.
- A few students marked extremely high, or low. This signalled the need for a tutor to engage with them as soon as possible, to help them to acquire a more realistic view of what was required and of how some serious mistakes and omissions might be avoided in the next drawing.

Step 2: Criteria taken from the module descriptor

Students submitting open-ended coursework in written form with sketches were given the assessment information contained in the module descriptor, together with a short explanation of this scheme, of which the class could ask questions. Students were asked when submitting work to declare their expected mark, and to accompany it with a note of the strengths and weaknesses which they had perceived and which had contributed to that judgement. Tutors marked in the usual way, but commented as endorsement of, or additions to, the students' comments.

The notable outcomes were that:

- Students' comments and identification of strengths and weaknesses were initially woolly, but soon sharpened up, following the implicit feedback of the tutors' annotations.
- Students' marks were initially all over the place, but soon agreed commendably well with the tutors' marking.
- Performance appeared to improve markedly compared with the standard in recent years when this arrangement had not operated – once the system showed signs of settling down.

Step 3: Criteria as an objective description of 'Sound Standard'

Work of Sound Standard is that which is worth a mark midway between Pass and Distinction. Students were given the criteria for achieving this mark, together with an example of work annotated to show where it had features above and/or below the Sound Standard description.

I have used this approach in various discipline areas and at various levels. In every case I have taken great care to describe the elements of Sound Standard without value words. For example, rather than write of 'adequate coverage of the literature', I have detailed in numbers and types of paper what I would regard as 'adequate'. Students submit their work with a qualitative indication of departures from the Sound Standard description, upwards or downwards. I use their assessment as the base to which I add, or with which I disagree, or modify.

The notable outcomes have been that:

- Students faced with a new type of task have managed to produce adequate work more speedily than in the past.
- The standard of work appears to be better than in the past.
- There is significant dialogue, usually electronic, between tutor and students – not indicating disagreements with marks, but questioning to find out precisely what is required and valued.

In none of these sub-examples did the student's mark contribute to the mark awarded for the work.

Shortage of time made it impossible for me to compare the standard of submitted work before and after my introduction of self-assessment. I was therefore encouraged in my belief that the standard had improved when reading the paper by Rust and colleagues (Rust *et al.*, 2003). This detailed an investigation into the effects of a workshop of less than two hours which aimed to help students understand and apply the criteria by which their work would be assessed. It resulted in a significant improvement in performance, although not, interestingly, in self-assessment.

Example 6.2: Self-assessing to own criteria, following the teacher's method

During the early part of 1983, I received an Education for Capability award from the Royal Society of Arts (RSA). This was for a first year course in which individual students had chosen their own individual syllabuses, as they studied the Properties and Use of Materials (Cowan, 1980b). In the midst of the departmental celebrations which ensued, I was talking to some students who had not been involved in the pilot scheme, and who were now about to pass on from their second year to the third year, where I would be teaching them design. One of them asked me why I didn't now offer a similar open learning option in respect of design. That seemed to me a useful suggestion, and one which I immediately began to negotiate with an enthusiastic group of volunteers, who were prepared to take part in a pilot with me.

The original innovation, which had really begun some eight years earlier, owed much of its inspiration to Carl Rogers' popular book, *Freedom to Learn* (Rogers, 1969). So I thought it appropriate to return to this text for inspiration, before I fleshed out the details of my new student-directed design course. As it happened, I had given away my most recent and much-thumbed copy to a Turkish enthusiast whom I had met while on a staff development visit to the Middle East. I had replaced this with what I thought was the up-to-date edition – but one which turned out to be virtually a new text, as befitted the new title, *Freedom to Learn for the 80s* (Rogers, 1983). In the original book, Rogers had written about what he hoped and believed could be achieved by schemes which offered autonomous and student-centred learning. In this new version, I was to find that he had written with hindsight – informed by many reports from his readers and disciples, so that he now felt able to describe confidently what he knew could certainly be done. That confidence influenced me in turn to rethink the provisional commitment I had made to my pilot group.

In their negotiations with me, my students had been clear that they were keen to take responsibility for their learning outcomes (called objectives at that point in time), for the methods by which they would achieve their objectives and for the pace of their studies. But they still wanted me to undertake the assessment. Initially I had agreed, but while I was reading this new book by Rogers, my conscience began to nag me. In less than 24 months' time, I told myself, these students would be engaged in professional work and, to a great extent, would be responsible for their ongoing professional development. This would mean that, if they were to continue to develop, they would have to formatively assess their capabilities, their needs and their achievements. So was it right, I wondered, that the development of the critical ability of being self-assessing people should be postponed until after these students had graduated? I couldn't believe that the Rogers of the second text would endorse such continuing paternalism on my part. Consequently, I decided that it was not acceptable to offer open learning at third year level with this constraint. I went back to my dozen volunteers to explain to them that I was unwilling to accept responsibility for their assessment. This was a unilateral decision which they eventually accepted, though with considerable reservations. (One of my Swedish colleagues once pointed out to me that the most authoritative thing a teacher can do is to decide to pass authority to the student!)

Our final agreement, for what we called 'Learning Contract Design' (Cowan, 1988), was a relatively straightforward one. Each week, each student would prepare on a summary sheet a list of personal learning objectives for that week. These should relate to their studies in the field of design – but it was understood between us that the students would have freedom to interpret that descriptive title across a wide range of possibilities. On the same summary sheet, each learner would outline the approaches they proposed to follow to achieve their objectives. Each student was to ask a fellow to comment on their objectives and plan, choosing to do that someone who had not provided such a commentary in the previous weeks. The learner was committed to consider the comments carefully, but was not obliged to agree with them, or even to satisfy their author, if the learner disagreed with and proposed to disregard the comments. The objectives and methods, and the comments together with the learner's responses, were to be posted on a notice-board which was open to inspection by all in the pilot group.

The time allocated to design was about a quarter of the working week; this was now entirely at the learner's disposal. It was agreed that I would facilitate development if so requested, but that I would not instruct, direct or guide, even if asked to do so. In the context of a particular request for assistance, I would at the most outline several viable competitive and contrasting learning activities which offered the possibility of being effective – thus leaving it to the learners to choose between, or to adapt or reject, my suggestions.

At the end of the week, each learner was contracted to produce something which demonstrated what had been learned, the extent to which the learning objectives had been achieved and the learner's qualitative assessment of that progress against the declared objectives. The tangible outcomes and the assessment of them, briefly summarized on the same sheet, were now shown to a second commenting student, who provided feedback on the outcomes and on the assessment of them, as they felt appropriate. This summary was also posted on the (semi-public) notice-board. The learner, again, was contracted to consider, but not necessarily to accept or respond in person to, the peer judgement.

At the end of each of the three terms in the academic year, the students individually assessed their work quantitatively by:

- summarizing the standards and criteria which they had been striving to achieve;
- describing their performance in comparable terms;
- reporting the process of judgement by which they compared their performance with their criteria and standards.

In this way, they determined their reasoned award of a mark. Their mark, which was the outcome of their personal judgement, came to me in a sealed envelope, because it was a separate matter. This mark went straight into the departmental records – provided these three conditions for the process of assessment, which we had defined and agreed in advance, had been satisfied. My role in assessment was simply to confirm that the conditions had been met.

(All of this took place in a vocational course where a professional body accredited the degree. Obviously, I had to go to considerable lengths to anticipate the inevitable criticisms by incredulous visiting moderators, and to be ready to provide them with sufficient evaluative information – derived from professional peers whose judgement would be respected – to satisfy them that our standards were indeed adequate, and were rigorously maintained. How I did that is a different story which would contribute little, if anything, to the answer that I now offer to the question at the head of this chapter. Suffice it to say that Machiavelli has much to offer those who engage in educational innovation, and have need to ward off their critics.)

The pilot I have described was, for its time, both innovative and unusual. It excited considerable interest from an assortment of educational visitors, the rigour of whose questioning and comments was in accordance with their academic reputations. As a result, some of the students were prompted to reflect deeply and extensively on their year-long experience, particularly after it had concluded. Three of them even opted to prepare a paper on the subject, which they presented to a conference on the Development of Professional Competence, run by the Society for Research into Higher Education. Some months later I was invited by the RSA to write a response to that paper, which was published together with the students' original, in an occasional publication (Boyd *et al.*, 1984; Cowan, 1984b).

I hope it will be acceptable to the students, and to you, to summarize in my own words what they extracted from their experience. Some of the students were encountering truly open learning for the first time, but some of the pilot scheme students had, two years earlier, taken the Alternative Syllabus course (actually the 'Course without a Syllabus') which had gained the RSA award (Cowan, 1980b). This subset of the group were now able to compare open learning which featured self-assessment according to criteria selected by the learners with open learning which had been teacher-assessed and was criterion-referenced. The student paper and review were prepared by three members of this subset, who stated firmly that they perceived self-assessment to have had a significant formative impact on their (open) learning. They felt able to make justifiable comparisons, describing changes in what they had concentrated on in their learning (the actual syllabus), changes in how they had studied (the depth of their learning) and changes in how they had tried to develop personally.

I will first summarize their accounts of what I prefer nowadays to call the learning outcomes. I draw on a visit to the Civil Engineering Learning Unit by David Boud, who is an internationally recognized authority in the field of self-assessment (Boud, 1995). He was able to cross-examine some of the pilot scheme students after it was all over, and when they had just entered the final (fourth) year of their studies. They had now rejoined the students who had been taught [*sic*] design conventionally. All had just been engaged in a design project in the opening fortnight of their final year, wherein the members of the experimental group (like their teachers) had encountered startling differences between the students from the pilot study group and those who had been conventionally taught.

A student from the pilot group told Boud:

> They had been taught so much in their lecture classes, about all sorts of detailed aspects of design. They all had piles of notes that would have choked a horse. *We* had very little, and we were conscious that there were many of the topics which *they* had studied, which *we* hadn't covered at all. But *they* had forgotten most of it – and when they went back to their notes, they found it difficult to make sense of them. On the other hand, *we* had learned how to learn and read to good effect in books and journals, and how to use people. *We* knew how to find what we wanted, and we had developed the ability to understand things on our own, even if we had never encountered them before. And we had effective techniques for revising, and for everything else that was asked of us.

The others present concurred wholeheartedly. Boud then asked this student about the traditional fourth year lecture classes which the students had all attended, and was told of the differences they had found in that situation, as well:

> I used to make notes of what the lecturers wrote on the board, or showed us on the overhead projector, or – if there was nothing written down – of what they said. I don't do that any more. I listen carefully to

what they are actually speaking about, and I make notes of what they are really trying to say, which is often hidden away inside all of that.

The students in the self-assessing group devoted care, thought and purposefulness to considering what would matter to them in their learning and development – and to pursuing that, above all else. Rather like the Alverno students in Example 5.3, they set process on a par with content in their integrated goals for undergraduate learning and development. They decided again and again that they needed to concentrate on how to do things. And, because they did that, and because they were themselves frequently assessing their progress towards such (process) goals, they were constantly thinking about how well they were doing whatever it was, and constructively and effectively considering how they might do it better.

Boyd (Boyd and Cowan, 1986) summed up all of this by saying that being involved with the formulation and setting of criteria gave her ownership and intimate understanding of her goals. That meant that her learning and development were always purposefully directed towards her goals. She also maintained that she frequently had to identify the detail of her performance, so that she could compare it with her goals and standards, and monitor her progress. In consequence, she became, in effect, an active manager of her own learning and development, seeing at the time what needed to be done, and acting accordingly. Her learning profited, she maintained, since she was confident that she knew herself and her thinking better than anyone else could ever do.

I submit that this pilot (Cowan, 1988) was a year-long experience structured by evaluative reflection-for-action and reflection-in-action, although Kolbian analytical reflection featured during the activities of each working week. The end-of-term self-assessments, and one or two crisis sessions in mid-term, occasioned evaluative reflection-on-action. The end-of-term assessments, as they were completed, usually also became evaluative reflection-for-action, leading to marked changes in aspirations, methods and work styles in the following term. Thus, although the individual activities of the learner-directed programme depended on Kolbian (analytical) reflection, the driving force which made this experiment such a success was Schönian (evaluative) reflection.

Example 6.3: Students reflect on the making of judgements about their learning

The Open University (OU) course D300: *Professional Judgment* [sic] *and Decision Making* laid considerable emphasis on the making of professional judgements, and on the sound outcomes which can often emerge. I frankly declare my view that much of the value of this splendid course (in whose conception I played no part) lay in the depth of the readings which had to be studied. These featured in collections of papers drawn particularly from the medical and paramedical professions, and also in key writings from assorted sources on judgemental topics, and in the subsequent application of these concepts and methods in difficult contexts. However, the development of a D300 student's ability to make judgements probably took place most significantly through self-assessment, and in the formulation of student judgements associated with the submission of assignments. These are the aspects of the course which feature in this example (but see also Example 7.2).

Before they began their studies, and indeed before they had read much in the course materials, D300 students were required to submit a 'Prior'. In this, they set out something of their past experiences as students. They identified (from examples they were asked to provide) the qualities which they associated with a praiseworthy course and with a praiseworthy tutor. Their D300 tutor was to comment very little on this prior declaration of values and expectations, merely noting what was said there and expressing interest in the experiences described. Tutors were aware of the danger that any comment might be taken as a judgement, or approval; they attempted to avoid that possibility as far as possible. The Prior was returned to the student with the comments, for use at the end of the course, as I will describe shortly.

Each time students submitted an assignment, they had to self-assess it; they were also required to estimate their probabilities for the mark which would be awarded by their tutor. Note that it was not unusual for tutor and student to differ in the marks awarded. Students consequently came to discover that there are admissible and respectable differences between sound but different judgements, according to the use of different but acceptable criteria, weightings and processes – as well as different perceptions of performance. By the very nature of a course which wrestled with uncertainty, students were also expected to appreciate and anticipate that little in this world is certain, and that this is particularly so in respect of professional judgements.

Early self-assessments were usually fairly primitive and incomplete. There was a tendency for students simply to present a description of part (and perhaps not all) of what they had done, and to do so in terms which were more narrative than evaluative. The mark (from the student, for the student) similarly often merely appeared on paper, without any explanation or justification being given – or, I suspect, having been considered. (The parallel with the weaknesses of institutional self-evaluations prepared in the early days for UK Academic Audit is striking.)

After the third assignment (of eight), the tutors not only declared their mark as usual, but they also described the way in which they had reached it. Tutors were encouraged, although not actually required, to prepare both a decomposed assessment (assembled under a number of subheadings, each with a 'pocket' of marks allocated to it) and a composed assessment (assembled in a holistic way, as a single mark which described the student's overall performance). Most tutors preferred to make the composed judgement first, and then almost to rationalize it by going through the fine detail of the decomposed judgement. The reverse order was recommended by the Course Team Chair, and was the one which I myself eventually came to favour when I was tutoring this course. The two judgements were then more distinct, thus offering some opportunity for triangulation and hence increased reliability.

Once the tutors had begun to reveal the making of their assessments, it became apparent to the students from this modelling that they, too, should be providing a more detailed account of their attempts to specify levels or standards within their composed or decomposed frameworks. They also began to comprehend that their performance should be described in terms compatible with their criteria – because it must be related to these standards or levels, if their judgement based on that comparison was to be formulated objectively. Students did not find it easy to progress along the learning curve to this advanced stage of judgemental development. Consequently, tutors were advised to award their marks for the process of self-assessment according to the stage which had been reached in the course. The demand in respect of both self-assessments and tutor assessments increased as the course progressed, and that progression was made explicit to students from the outset.

At two stages in their studies, students prepared and submitted their assessments of the course itself. These were expected to cover all the components of the experience, from the materials and television programmes to the prescribed course reader, the administrative arrangements, the tutorials and the correspondence tuition. It was here that they were to refer back to their Prior, which was an early declaration of criteria and standards – which they might have wanted to change, on reflection, for good reasons derived from their course experiences. Since the tutor was normally committed to declare his or her assessment of an assignment before opening the envelope containing the student's self-assessment, it always seemed reasonable to me (as a tutor) to formulate and pass on to my students my own assessment of my tutorial support and of my correspondence tuition. That assessment I always drafted and sent to my students in a sealed envelope at course assessment time. I suggested to them that my self-assessment of my tutoring was something which they should not open or read until after they had completed their own course assessment, including their judgement of my work and our relationship. Interestingly, I received little specific feedback on my assessments of my tutoring. But I received strongly supportive comments about the value which students placed on this reversed and open practice of mine.

In the final course assessments, the students' self-assessments of the learning outcomes they had achieved, and of the personal development which they perceived to have occurred for them in the course experience (again related to criteria and to the Prior), were usually encouraging – and thought-provoking. In 1995, for example, I tutored a group of D300 students for whom self-assessment, or indeed any form of objective judgement, was (as usual) something with which they had struggled and for which they had initially achieved poor outcomes. By the time the course finished, more than half of them had discovered that they could carry out the process thoroughly, objectively and individually, to a commendable standard, and with a profitable effect on self-development. The 'before' and 'after' comparisons which they themselves made of their capabilities, including the ability to formulate judgements, were singularly persuasive and convincing.

For example, one student presented convincing data in her final self-assessments to show that, through being driven by self-assessment, she had studied in depth to an extent and rigour of demand which went far beyond her previous experience. In consequence, she had found that the tasks and standards expected of her appeared easier to achieve than ever before. In this, her first third level course, she went on to gain a (tutor-marked) Distinction grade – something that she had never been awarded in any of her previous OU studies, at whatever level.

A second student progressively immersed himself in what he described as 'an enthralling course experience'. It literally dominated eight months of his life, in which he was employed during working hours as a hospital theatre orderly. He found that his thinking, particularly in the dialogue assignments (see Example 7.2) and his self-assessments of them, had a sharpness and generated constructive outcomes which surprised him, and motivated him intensely. This led him into deep supplementary and enrichment studies of his own choosing, including a hospital report in dialogue form, which was well received after the initial astonishment had subsided. He, too, could point to examples to confirm his claims.

Another student found the methodology testing, demanding – and disturbing. Increasingly, she decided to pursue her own goals to her own standards, which differed from the goals and value framework of the subject. Consequently, while feeling that the course might be validly criticized by others for that reason, she nonetheless described her working on the open-ended and self-assessed D300 assignments as her 'best learning and teaching experience to date', in all of her OU studies.

The last student I will cite tended to assess herself at much the same mark as that awarded by her tutor, but ultimately with rich qualitative judgements in addition. She eventually submitted self-assessments which had developed strikingly from the trivial, incomplete and subjective efforts in her early assignments. In her last assignment, she presented one or two devastatingly accurate and formative self-portrayals, in which she not only identified her outstanding weaknesses, but also discerned where there was scope for improvement and development which it lay within her power to bring about.

External judgements appeared to confirm the reliability of evidence in the testimony and data of the students' summative assessments. I concluded that formative self-assessment had certainly had a significant effect on the learning and performance of more than half of the sample. (In this example, the final marks used to determine awards were, however, all decided by the tutors.)

Other examples

Example 5.1 certainly, and possibly Example 7.1, call for, or prompt, evaluative reflection.

What generalization can be taken from this review?

I have speculated, as have others, about causation in regard to the origins of the notable changes which we have experienced and observed in learning and in the learning experience for self-assessing students, especially when the self-assessment is not carried forward to the awarded mark or grade. We have perhaps attempted this in vain, and certainly with insufficient evidence of our own, although the research evidence from Alverno (Mentkowski and Strait, 1983) on the effect of self-assessment is very persuasive.

In this debate, I suggest we should now focus in on two fairly well-authenticated convictions about self-assessment. The first is that learners who self-assess are constantly and effectively focusing their learning on what are usually learning objectives that would be associated with deep learning. The second is that, from their engagement with objectives and standards, self-assessing learners have a keener appreciation than otherwise of what it is that they are trying to do, of how well they are doing it, and thus of what they could do next to improve their performance. They are formatively self-monitoring their progress, in a directly constructive way, to further and especially to deepen their learning and development. This applies both to the institutionally intended learning outcomes and to what I describe as the process abilities on which are founded, or which constitute, the worthwhile learning and development which the students seek.

So it appears that this evaluative reflection effectively encourages:

- a more focused learning experience, through self-direction;
- constant awareness of objectives and standards, which in turn leads to more purposeful pursuit of learning;
- regular self-monitoring which, through awareness of progress or lack of it, enables learners to direct their learning into activities which will bring about development and improved learning for them;
- deeper and more meaningful learning.

Before you test this, some second thoughts from me

1. The educational literature abounds with enquiries into the work of 'good' and valued university teachers. Most suggest that enthusiasm is

one of the major attributes of such people – whether it is enthusiasm for their work or for their subject, or both. Now, it is probably apparent that the teachers in the examples in this and in the previous chapter were all highly enthusiastic. So you should consider what contribution was made to learning by that enthusiasm, rather than by the introduction of reflection to learning and the learning experience.

2. Furthermore, the well-known Hawthorne effect (Roethlisberger and Dickson, 1939) testifies to the impact of novelty on performance in a range of settings. For all of the students in the examples, the situations described were undoubtedly novel. So what impact did that novelty have on the achieved learning outcomes? Might enthusiasm and novelty not be the main causes of the improved results ascribed to self-assessment?

3. On the other hand, is it necessarily unacceptable to achieve improvements in learning and in the learning experience by teaching with enthusiasm and by introducing novelty and variety? Would you welcome improvements in your own learning experience which might be brought about in that way? (And if they occurred in the circumstances described, could you attribute them to self-assessment or to reflective learning?)

4. How critical to the type of learning and teaching situations described in this chapter is the creation of conditions in which students feel safe to take risks and to expose cherished standards and criteria, by revealing judgements and self-criticisms?

5. It is clear that the teachers and students quoted felt that self-assessment or evaluation influenced learning and the nature of the learning experience to a considerable extent. But is that process of self-assessment reflective, in the sense that the word has been used to date in this text? And, if it is reflective, where does it relate to the Kolb cycle or any of the other models set out in Chapter 4? Need it do so? Is it not more an influence on the depth and intensity of the learning, rather than an influence on the learning and development itself – which still depends on analytical reflection, occurring elsewhere or at other times?

6. Should we be going even further than choices expressed as either analytical or evaluative, and rather describe the role of reflection in learning in terms which allow both analytical (Kolbian) and evaluative (Schönian) reflection to combine, as in the Cowan model? (Perhaps this is the most important caveat of all, in this group of second thoughts?)

7. It appears that involvement in self-assessment, even when that makes no contribution to a recorded or awarded mark or grade, may have a powerful impact on learning and on the learning experience. If so – and this remains to be confirmed – how does it happen, how can we facilitate it knowingly and most effectively, and to what extent should we be passing the responsibility for monitoring the self-assessment

process, like the self-assessment itself, to the student? I have yet to find my own answers to these questions. Should that deter me, and you, from believing in the potential of self-assessment and from offering it on a pragmatic basis? Are such questions important in facilitating our professional reflections?

8. You may now wish to reconsider carefully my assertion that all the examples in Chapter 5 called for analytical reflection. You may discern some additional dependence on evaluation – in at least some of these examples. Perhaps it is best to say that the examples in Chapter 5 were predominantly analytical, while those in this chapter have been predominantly evaluative. After all, Bloom (Bloom *et al.*, 1956) would have us accept that one cannot be evaluative without being analytical first, which is why I would freely admit that the examples in this chapter (in turn) have only been predominantly evaluative.

Dear John

So far you've given me a reasonable overall description of what you are choosing to call reflection, and of activities for students which call on them to reflect. You've also, in passing, provided a set of examples of developing valuable abilities in higher education. Some of these approaches have been distinctly non-traditional. I can imagine my students looking askance at me if I ask them to do that kind of thing. And I can equally imagine my own difficulty in knowing how to introduce and facilitate this kind of activity. However, if I'm going to give it a try – and I haven't committed myself to that yet – I would need to know more about the detail of how I could persuade them to engage wholeheartedly. How can I sell this approach to students for whom it may be a new demand and a new experience, if I am to carry out my function in the process effectively?

There are some of my colleagues who have required what they call 'reflective writing' or reporting of experiences from their students – mostly in relation to the preparation of personal development plans and portfolios, which are now emerging as a component of higher education. I've had a look at some of these and was not impressed. There seems to be a lot of describing of everyday experiences, and a tendency to claim 'learning' in abstract terms, which don't persuade me that course time has been well spent, or that students see point of the activity.

So my question is not simply, 'How can I get them to do this?' It is also, and even more importantly, how to get them to engage with it deeply – and with real effect on their capabilities, as you call them.

7

What Can We Do to Encourage
Students to Reflect Effectively?

First, a digression: what is 'teaching'?

I take 'teaching' to be:

> the purposeful creation of situations from which motivated learners
> should not be able to escape without learning or developing.

I put considerable stress in that definition on the word 'purposeful'. It is the
existence of a purpose and the pursuit of it which, for me, distinguish
education as a process from the many other situations in which valuable
learning occurs. Education, for me, is a process which involves and uses
teachers, and hence is distinct from the natural (and valuable) learning or
development that will often happen incidentally or accidentally, yet is totally
tutorless and is simply learner-directed. I also link learning and development in my definition, because I believe that the highest cognitive learning
leads to the *development* of cognitive skills rather than the incidental exercise
of them in mastering particular content within individual subject contexts.

You'll notice that, according to my definition, I see (and hope for) the
real possibility of an active, and even a proactive, role for the facilitative
teacher. I subscribe wholeheartedly to the philosophy advanced by Carl
Rogers (1951, 1961, 1969, 1983), who likens the facilitative teacher to the
therapeutic counsellor. For the questions and comments of the therapeutic
counsellor are carefully chosen, and are purposefully intended to be constructive, although the counsellor may not always know in which direction
they will lead. The same could and should be said of the facilitative teacher
in open learning.

Where is all this leading me – and you? For my part, I hope I have
established that facilitation can be classed as one form of teaching, and that
teaching need not involve instruction. I further suggest, as a basis for the
grouping of my examples in this chapter, that there are facilitative learning
and teaching situations in which the influence of the teacher in achieving

their purpose is virtually restricted to the design and provision of initial structures and tasks. There are also, however, situations wherein the engagement of the teacher continues throughout the learner's pursuit of tasks or activities, and may depend upon some almost disruptive (if creative) interventions for its effectiveness.

Outline

In this chapter, I begin with four examples of 'teaching' which facilitates reflection, principally by providing a structure for the learning situation which will occasion reflective thinking. I leave the second type of proactive facilitation until later – in a further four examples – since it can be provocatively nearer to the authoritarian model of teaching which I would call instructing, and with which we are both undoubtedly familiar. In such facilitation, a tutor's interventions prompt reflection – often in action. The last of these examples is unusual, in that the facilitator had no specific intended learning outcome in mind, and the consequent learning emerged both for a student and a tutor.

Example 7.1: Needs emerge from an experience

In the first week of their studies in civil engineering, I asked entrants to think about their learning needs in respect of communication skills. I gave them a checklist with a number of suggestions, one of which was the ability to describe apparatus. Almost all of them left this and several other boxes unticked. Questioned, they would politely, or otherwise, assert that they had done that kind of thing ad nauseam at school, and had no need to dwell upon it further.

Once they had assembled in class for the first lab work, I invited them to choose a partner with whom they would work for the afternoon. Having done that, they were somewhat surprised when I immediately split each pair. For I had arranged that they were taken away in different directions by tutors (postgraduate students), who assembled groups of about ten students in rooms which contained a piece of strange apparatus. The tutor reminded them briefly that one of their tasks in laboratory and experimental project work was to describe apparatus adequately. The tutor next asked them to describe on paper the particular piece of apparatus before them, in the most effective manner possible, and for the benefit of their partners. The tutor indicated willingness to answer any questions about the apparatus, its use and mechanisms – and did so when asked. The students, split from their partners, were encouraged to consult with any of the others in the room, while they each prepared their separate descriptions.

When the descriptions were complete, a postman or postwoman collected them and carried them to another room, containing the second half of each of the split pairs. She or he returned with the descriptions which had been prepared in that room by these partners, who had been faced with a totally different piece of equipment. In both rooms, the students were now given red pens and were invited to comment constructively on the descriptions prepared by their partners.

It was at this point that most of the students discovered that they had made a truly unfortunate choice of partner. For they had opted to work with someone who was apparently incapable of producing a description which could be comprehended. It failed to convey all the information which they, the readers, felt that they needed. Happily their tutor encouraged them to annotate the description they had received, indicating where they found it lacking, what additional information they wished, and also those parts of it which they found confusing or were unable to comprehend. Shortly, the postperson went into action a second time, carrying the descriptions with requests for clarification and amplification back to their originators.

Most of the students now discovered, a second time, and with even more intensity, that they had definitely made an unwise choice of partner. For the person who had received their clear and explicit description had asked all sorts of silly questions about it, had failed to understand points which it undoubtedly conveyed with devastating clarity and generally had displayed an inability to think, as well as to understand. However, the authors were given an opportunity to revise their descriptions. So, this time, and bearing in mind the undoubted limitations of their partners, the important information about the piece of apparatus in their room would be effectively, if painstakingly, conveyed. Once again, they could consult with others in the same room, seeking advice, inspiration and (often) sympathy.

A second time the descriptions were carried back and forth, to partners. The partners now worked individually and were prohibited from consulting the other students in the room. They were immediately asked and required to answer ten fair questions about the piece of apparatus in the other room, which was described to them on the paperwork which they were now studying. A fair question was taken to be one which asked for a rough estimate of the size of the piece of apparatus, the location of the on/off switch or an indication of the function of the wheels, levers and switches by which the apparatus would be operated. An unfair question would be one which asked about colour (unless that was particularly significant) or the name of the maker. The questions were chosen so that none of the students who had described the apparatus could reasonably quibble with the question list, since it contained only requests for information which should have been provided in their description. Therefore, their partner, having received their description, should have been able to answer all correctly – or should, at least, have been able to score nine out of ten in the total test.

The sheets were quickly self-marked, according to answers provided by the tutors. Few partners scored more than half marks. It was at this stage announced that the mark awarded to the writer or artist of the description would be that scored in the test by the recipient of the description. Descriptions and marks were returned to the writers – and the pairs were reunited. But perhaps reunited is not an apt description, for a number of embryonic friendships had, by this time, been rather bruised by the experience. Indeed, on the first occasion I ran this activity, one of my colleagues urgently advocated the need to lay on coffee and chocolate biscuits, to restore the blood sugar level, and the equilibrium, of some of the more agitated students.

Most of the students had by then concluded without intervention from the tutors that they had quite a lot to learn about the simple task of describing a piece of apparatus, and even about comprehending a description of a piece of apparatus. From the unprompted reflections which rather frenetically began when the process went so badly wrong, there had emerged a particular type of generalization – namely a generalization which specified one particular learning need. What I have chosen to call reflection-for-action (Model 4.4) was revisited. Knowing that their confidence had been misplaced in at least one skill area, the students retired thoughtfully to ponder anew over their list of learning needs in the area of communication skills. More ticks were added to their checklists.

It was the structure of this activity and the experiences which it created, rather than any subsequent interventions by a tutor, which led students to reflect for action, and rethink their self-judgements about their ability to undertake the simple task of describing apparatus.

I have dwelt at length on this somewhat trivial example, because the principle on which it is based can be applied in so many other, more complex, situations – to prompt constructive reflection by otherwise unjustifiably self-confident learners. (See also Example 8.3.)

Example 7.2: Structured dialogue

In a third level Open University (OU) course (D321: *Professional Judgment*), which I studied as a student before taking a post as a tutor on its successor, D300 (Example 6.3), roughly half of the assignments were to be written in Socratic dialogue. That was also the form of presentation chosen for both the 'learning units' and the television programmes in the study plan. Few, if any, students had ever encountered this mode of presentation in a distance learning course. Few, if any, had ever written assignments, or anything else for that matter, in the form of dialogue. Yet that mode of writing was required of them, while the choice of topic was left open to the student. This all rendered more awe-inspiring the demand of the dialogue assignment, first time round.

In this context, the essence of effective dialogue is that the partner who is written into the script should be rather more active in questioning than were some of the 'yes-men' who attended on Socrates himself. I vividly recall the occasion when I sat down at my PC one Sunday afternoon, to write (for my first time ever) an assignment which was to be in dialogue form. I had notes that would have sufficed for something which I would hitherto have presented as an essay and which I must admit I had already prepared in my mind along such lines. For the first thousand words or so, as I keyed away at my word processor, I did indeed produce an essay, loosely disguised as something in dialogue form. I had John (myself), explaining points to an attentive and dutiful Ian (my alter ego), who asked helpful questions, such as 'What then?' or 'And how do they do that?' With about 1200 words drafted, Ian tired of this role and began to rebel. I found that my fingers had acquired a life of their own, and suddenly had Ian challenging, 'But you don't really believe it's as simple as that, do you?'

I was nonplussed. Almost beyond my control, my fingers keyed in the honest response that indeed, I did have some inner doubts about these explanations from the course materials which I was repeating, amplifying and trying to illustrate. My alter ego came back at me even more firmly. He demanded to know what I really thought – and, when I told him, he pressed me to justify that standpoint. He challenged me to grope for the truth amid the inadequacies which I felt I had encountered in the course materials and which he pressed me to acknowledge. By the time I had keyed in 2000 words, Ian was totally in charge. John was frantically rereading the course materials and reader, studying these in greater depth than ever before, in order to present something which Ian would have no option but to accept. Thus John was now grappling with the material and the concepts on a distinctly fundamental level. Deep learning, in the Gothenburg sense (Marton *et al.*, 1997), had been prompted by the dialogue structure.

Fortunately, a call to the family evening meal intervened. Even so, it was only after I had devoted Sunday evening and more time besides to a considerable amount of additional study and thinking that John was able to recover something of his poise, and provide at least semi-adequate explanations and conclusions for Ian. The dialogue, which was by now heavily edited, reached and exceeded the word limit, with a different message from that which John would have offered in the original (and somewhat predictable) essay-style argument he had prepared and set out to present.

Since that memorable afternoon and evening, I have heard many other students report their own versions of that experience of mine. It is an important learning experience. It represents for each of us a significant stage in our self-development, and has led each of us to use the self-questioning dialogue format subsequently, both privately and publicly, for a variety of purposes. The dialogue format strongly encourages us to reflect-in-action on the soundness of our thinking.

Had I written an essay or report, I would merely have reordered and summarized the learning which I felt I had acquired in my dealings with the course materials. However, through the imposed structure of the dialogue, and with the emergence of a partner remarkably like Karl Popper in his liking to challenge and to offer counter-examples, I was obliged to reflect. I had to reflect on the validity and coherence of my learning to date, and I discovered the need to revisit some of my conclusions. I also had to explore other areas of the subject, and generally to progress and develop my generalized understanding, in the deepest sense of that word.

No tutor had had any contact with me from the time I started to write until after I had finished, and consigned my assignment to the post. So, if there was something in that turbulent educational situation which prompted me to reflect deeply and constructively, and has since prompted others similarly, then it was the structure of the activity, and not the overt actions of a tutor. That structure occasioned my reflective encounter with my incomplete and inconsistent thinking. It led me, as it has led other learners on this course, to decide that something needed to be done about it, and it motivated me to take that remedial action in hand and seek the development I desired.

Example 7.3: A letter-writing task prompts reflection-on-and-for-action

(You may find it useful in due course to compare this variant, and its contribution to learning, with Examples 10.2 and 10.6, with their primarily evaluative purpose.)

I had encountered a useful practice for the end of the academic year. In a lightly structured activity, classes were brought together to generate a 'letter' (George and Cowan, 1999b). In each case they worked first as small groups, and after that in plenary. Finally, and after full class discussion, they were able to pass on a remit in bullet point form to two or three writers, who would compile the final letter on their behalf.

The desired epistle was to be addressed to each student in the class group in the following year, to whom it would be sent without editing by staff. This letter was to set out to be as helpful as possible to that new student. It was to be written to provide advice which would enable them to get the best that was possible from the course, to identify in advance the difficulties which would possibly or probably arise, and to apprise them of the positive outcomes and experiences which they might expect. It also indirectly provided feedback to the teachers about the learning experiences of those who had drafted the letter.

Many students volunteer that the assembling of such advice for the personal letter has been a most useful review experience for them. They find that it has pushed them to reflect, and to formulate end-of-course generalizations about the way they should have tackled their studies. It has also drawn their learning together in a way that hadn't quite happened until then, Thus a reasonably attractive, and certainly non-threatening, structure for an activity with formative intent for others can in addition generate overall reflection-on-action on an individual basis, which then proves a constructive influence on further learning for those who contributed to the compilation of the letter.

Interestingly, a number of those experienced lecturers who applied through the fast-track route for membership of the Institute for Learning and Teaching in Higher Education (ILTHE), as it then was, have reported a similar experience. It doesn't involve a draft letter, but it does prompt useful reflection through asking for something rather different. Called upon to describe how they tackle course design, teaching plans, assessment, student support and so on, some established university teachers have volunteered reactions which I would classify under two quotes. The first, on the complete process: 'This has been my most searching staff development experience in over 20 years as a university teacher, and has left me with so many issues I can see I need to address.' The second, from someone pushed to articulate how she goes about course design, and responding to the suggestion that perhaps she had never talked to anyone else about how she does that until now: 'I don't think I've ever talked to myself about how I do that until now.'

In these three examples, the activity prompted the reflection – as it did in the next one.

Example 7.4: Self-assessment

At the end of their first term of IDS studies (Example 2.4), my first year students worked with six or seven others in a carefully structured activity wherein they were asked to draft a list of the qualities against which they would judge their performance to date in that course. This was their first encounter with self-assessment. They had not gone through the preparation described in Example 2.7, which I only developed later.

They were to prepare to appraise the enhancement of their personal and professional capabilities. The activity was introduced by a task which encouraged students to identify in groups (though not necessarily to accept for their own subsequent use) qualities which might feature on individual lists. The activity was prompted by mention of one or two of the qualities which had been instanced to them, during the term, as valued behaviour. One teacher, for example, had made it clear that he valued students who 'identified and asked good questions'; another had said several times that she valued 'critical thinking', without explaining what she meant by that.

The students were now free to assemble their own personal and com-posite list, from the group list or otherwise. They should each produce a compilation which sincerely represented their beliefs and values about the importance of the educational outcomes of IDS studies, and which they would use (individually) as their own.

The students, working on their own lists, were next and individually asked to do the following:

1. Describe what you mean by each term or heading, giving an example taken either from your own behaviour, or from something which you have seen someone else doing, or from something which you wish you could do, or had done.
2. Now rate yourself against each quality you have specified.

Once the students had completed and submitted this self-appraisal, they were given a photocopy of it, and asked, in their own time, to address the next part of the task:

3. Identify in your learning journal, and in your submitted work during the past term (which has now been returned to you), the most suitable examples which you can find to endorse the claims you are making in your self-appraisal.

Most students discovered, and volunteered frankly, that their genuinely formulated self-judgement was not justified by what they could find in their own records of their performance over the previous term. They reported that they now wished to change that self-appraisal – with all the constructive implications which this reassessment, based on evaluative reflection, would have for their aspirations for focused improvement in the second term. They were asked to draft their own plans for remedial, constructive or developmental action in the second term. Thus their generalizations, arising from reflection on the events of the first term, prompted them to formulate aspirations and plans for development which were soon to be worked on, in the challenges of the second term.

From the outset, this was admittedly a rather devious design of both activity and structure. Students were nevertheless prompted by the format to make their own discoveries, through reflection, of mismatches between their aspirations and their perceptions of reality as evidenced in the records of their work, and to 'reflect-for' the action needed in the second term.

Facilitation through tutor intervention

Having dealt so far with examples in which the structure of the activity itself has been the catalyst for reflection, I will now relate four examples in which tutors have a critical role, by being proactive in nudging or coercing the student into or around the various stages of the Kolb cycle. This amounts to intervention during the activity, to accelerate movement by the learners through what Vygotsky (1978) called their zone of proximal development (ZPD), where something you can do 'today' with the prompting of somebody more experienced than you can become something which you will be able to do on your own, 'tomorrow'.

The classic example of such nudging, for me, was repeated in scores of workshops, year after year, in the OU summer school for foundation level mathematics, M101 (Open University, 1978–97). It occurred in the activity described in Example 7.5.

Example 7.5: Teachers prompt movement round the Kolb cycle

Until 1997, all students on the Open University foundation course in mathematics had to attend a one-week residential summer school (see also Example 3.1). This week occurred roughly at the mid-point in their first year of studies. One striking feature of the programme was a strand which had been elegantly designed to develop problem-solving abilities, through a range of small-group activities (Mason, 1984). In these activities, which continue nowadays in other settings, the students (often working in pairs) are led busily around the Kolb cycle on a number of occasions, prompted by what I would describe as buzz words. The methodology is never made explicit in terms of Kolb, to either students or tutors.

A problem is set. Perhaps the students are asked how many squares there are on a chessboard. Someone immediately volunteers the answer, '64'. The tutor gently points out that there must be at least 65, because there is also the larger square which surrounds the whole board of 64 smaller squares. Convoluted, and successful and unsuccessful, discussion busily commences.

The tutor intervenes with the first buzz word: 'Specialize!' 'How many squares are there, for example, on a 2 × 2 chessboard?' Readily the answer of 5 emerges. 'And on a 3 × 3?' Less quickly comes the answer of 14. And so on to 4 × 4 and even a 5 × 5. As the results emerge, the tutor surreptitiously begins to prompt reflection, by summarizing the numbers in a table (Figure 7.1), with some scribbled figures in the margin.

Board size	Number	
1 × 1	1	
2 × 2	5	4
3 × 3	14	9
4 × 4	30	16
5 × 5	55	25
6 × 6		?

Figure 7.1   Tutor's summary during chessboard problem-solving

Now it is time for the second buzz word: 'Speculate!' – followed by a sequence of prompting questions. 'Can you see a pattern in these results? Can you explain it? Can you guess now what the answers will be for a 6 × 6 and a 7 × 7? How did you get that?' Now it is time to move on to the third buzz word: 'Generalize!' And then more questions. 'What do you think the answer will be for an 8 × 8 – the normal chessboard? Or for a 20 × 20 chessboard? Test that out in practice, and confirm the answer, or otherwise.'

Now another buzz word: 'Rationalize!' 'Can you produce a sound explanation of the pattern of numbers which you think you have established?' And so the students move rapidly around the Kolb cycle, once they have grasped the process. They almost go straight back and forward from particular examples to generalization (or at least the assembly of data which leads to generalization), being rushed somewhat quickly through reflection into generalization, and then from generalization, back through the planning to test it, in a more demanding particular example.

The pattern continues, with more and more complex problems. In every case the students are encouraged to simplify the problem first of all to an easily solved form. One such problem describes the familiar case of the man searching in the dark for socks, in a drawer which contains many individual socks of several colours. The tutor suggests that the students should first reduce the number of colours in the drawer to two – and next perhaps work out what happens if there are three colours, and so on. But once the generalization has been assembled and rationalized, the tutor will urge that they should test out their conclusion on something which is even more complex than the stated problem. What happens if the socks are being obtained for a four-legged pet, and if there are five colours of socks available in the drawer? And so on to a centipede seeking to be properly dressed from a drawer containing 15, or more, colours of socks.

The tutor's role in all of this is simply to urge the students, just when they have begun to get comfortable in the pattern of dealing with particular cases, to move from particular examples of *experience* through quick and almost natural *reflection* to *generalizing*. And, similarly, the tutor nudges them from generalizing to *testing*. In so doing, the tutor conditions them to associate the approach they are following with his buzz words, which have been introduced and understood in the first encounters because they were accompanied by simple questions to be answered. Just as students have begun to be comfortable with their generalizing or specializing, and settle into these discussions, the tutor urges them on to the next part of the cycle. The tutor is an intervening facilitator, albeit someone who does that in a gentle and encouraging way, and even with humour. Nevertheless, the tutor's interventions are not always welcomed by the students. Many prefer to settle into a pattern of thinking about any one point in the cycle. This static position becomes settled and seductively comfortable; it also becomes relatively undemanding and, more importantly, less productive.

The programme traditionally commenced with a demonstration in plenary to about 100–200 students in a lecture theatre. There, a course director, working from the front, introduced both the ideas and the buzz words in one or two opening examples. This 'master tutor' gently coaxed the entire class to work with him or her, in the manner I have described, through the first of the many problems which the students were to encounter in the plenary and in the group work which followed. Thereafter, the tutors, who were charged to be facilitative, worked in individual rooms with small groups of about 10–12 students. Some of these tutors had not worked with this activity or in this way. They found that they could readily assimilate from the previous demonstration what was required of them. Hence they could perform effectively in this role on their first attempt, urging the students to move swiftly from specializing to speculating, or from speculating to generalizing.

The outcome was that, at a later stage in the week's programme, students successfully, and independently of tutor support, were able to tackle a very demanding problem in an assignment where half of the marks were for a reflective analysis of the process which they had followed, and only half for the extent to which they obtained an adequate solution.

I suggest to you that the significant features in this example – for the tutor, and for the tutoring – are that:

- the stewardship of the pedagogy is vested in the tutor;
- the tutor actively intervenes to prompt cycling according to Kolb;
- the tutor works deliberately to bring about frequent cycles, in quick succession, around the Kolb diagram;
- there is increasing awareness, on the part of the students, of the process they are following;
- there is a natural reluctance on the part of the learners to move on round the Kolb cycle, which is overcome by the proactive interventions of the tutor.

Example 7.6: Tutors intervene to occasion reflection-in-action

Not long after they began their studies, I would present my first year students of civil engineering with a problem situation, and ask them to respond to it by designing and constructing a model structure. This was sometimes to be made from balsawood and glue, or sometimes from spaghetti and adhesive tape. I might call for a tower, a bridge or a cantilever. I asked the groups to begin by summarizing, step by step, the process which they would follow while analysing the problem, and in formulating a number of distinct and competitive responses to it, until they could eventually choose which one to work through in detail as their favoured design. At the outset, the groups spent little time on this part of the activity. The descriptions of the design process which were produced, and which were set out on flipchart sheets behind the area in which each group was working, were sparse in detail, thoughtless and often inaccurate in wording.

This modelling activity was competitive and motivating. Hence the groups were understandably keen to get on to the practical work. They wanted to decide on a design, to fabricate it and to test it tentatively. They then wanted, as quickly as possible, to enter the arena in which their model might gain the maximum possible marks by sustaining a greater load before failure than any of the others. In this setting there was, however, one disruptive rule of the game. This was that any peripatetic tutor, wandering round the groups and observing their activity, might challenge any group at any time – if the description of the process which they were supposed to be following, as it was displayed on the flipchart behind them, did not conform with what the tutor observed them to be doing. If that proved to be so, the students had to stop in their designing and fabricating activity, and had to rewrite a more accurate statement of the process in which they were now engaged, in sufficient detail to satisfy the tutor. A similar challenge could be made if the process was not sufficiently detailed on the flipchart sheet; the group accordingly had to amplify, so that their description was reasonably comprehensive and informative.

There was naturally much frustration on the part of the students when they were interrupted. They found it difficult to see the point of these interventions. After all, they knew what they were setting out to do, and how they intended to achieve it, so why should they bother recording that, in pedantic detail, on a flipchart sheet?

I tried out this activity, with and without the declaration and amendment of the design process on flipchart sheets. Matched groups were pre-tested and post-tested. It was thus possible for me to compare results and to demonstrate, to my own satisfaction at least, that the next performances in designing effective model structures improved with concentration on, and awareness of, process; and that, if groups were left undisturbed by tutor interventions, their performance did not improve to the same extent as it did when reflection on process was required, in the manner I have described.

At that early stage in their studies, the students had yet to acquire the ability to describe the process which they follow when they are designing an artefact. Their descriptions tended to be vague, and too general to be useful. More importantly, they were often inaccurate – the rhetoric being distinct from the reality. Interventions which prompted reflection-in-action focused attention on this weakness.

There is a school of thought which claims to show that awareness of process goes hand in hand with the ability to execute that process and to improve it. That is why it seemed useful for tutors to intervene – to encourage students to reflect by ensuring that they articulated, in general terms, what they were doing, and that they scrutinized what they actually did do in order to decide if their general description needed to be revised, and hence rethought. In other words, it is potentially creative to construct, in a particular situation, something of a dialogue between the description of process and the reality of process – a dialogue which, in effect, implies rapid circulation around the Kolb cycle and hence reflection-in-action. That reflective interaction was occasioned in this example by the tutor's interventions during the activity, more than by the mere structure of the task.

Example 7.7: A teacher intervenes by providing an input

My first year Heriot-Watt students followed a programme which contained a wide assortment of group activities. Consequently, one of the goals of the first year IDS programme (Example 2.4) was to help the students to develop interpersonal skills which could contribute to effective group working. And so the groups which met on the Tuesday afternoons and on the Wednesday mornings were often treated as 'home' groups, having been chosen so that they did not contain any two students who would be working together in other groups during the remainder of the week.

In these IDS activities dealing with interpersonal skills, the students were often provided with an input. This might exemplify a methodology for observing, analysing or understanding the behaviour of people in groups. Such examples were garnered in the early weeks of the programme, in order to introduce the basic methods and vocabulary of transactional analysis. This was done through simple reporting of an analysis of transactions which the tutors had drawn up, having unobtrusively observed the very groups who were now receiving this analysis, while they had been engaging in a preparatory activity a few minutes previously.

Having grasped a method of enquiry or a theoretical explanation of behaviour, students proceeded to test it out on some of the group activities with which they had been engaged in the previous week or ten days. On that basis, they went on to reflect constructively on means of rendering more effective and productive the group working in which they would be engaged in the week ahead.

As the teacher, I had felt that we had needed to provide significant theoretical inputs which could be put to good use. I thought it ineffective and almost irresponsible to leave the students to analyse experience of interpersonal transactions without a basis on which to do so. Thus I started the students' progress round the Kolb cycle with a generalization to be tested out (Figure 7.2). The students reflected on the initial input in relation to their recent experience that afternoon, thus consolidating and refining their understanding of the theory or generalization. Then they applied their method of analysis to other recent experiences, taken from a variety of current group-working situations.

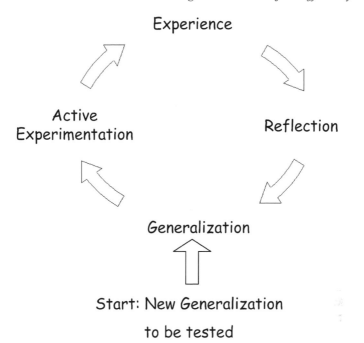

Figure 7.2 Entering Kolb's cycle from a provided generalization

The significant features of this example are that:

- the cycling began at a different point in the cycle from that of Example 7.6;
- a tutor intervened to make an influential input at the generalization part of the Kolb cycle, in order to arm the students to test this out in a forthcoming experience or set of experiences;
- the students accepted that tutors could act in that way;
- the input was a description of a conceptual framework, linked to an example of its use as a method of enquiry;
- the outcome was deep and informed reflection-on-action.

In the last three examples, the learning has depended on the activity of a tutor within the activity. My closing example, as I indicated in the opening to this chapter, is rather different. It is also unusual in several ways:

- the facilitator did not take part in the event, other than to organize that it would happen;
- the learners were a student and a tutor;
- there were no specifically intended learning outcomes in mind, although it was the facilitator's clear goal to prompt useful reflection on process.

Example 7.8: A structured activity provokes reflections-on-action

This example centres on a student of second level science, who came to a personal tutorial with three genuine enquiries in mind. The consultation, which was one to one, took place, by arrangement, in a room where there was a video camera focused on the tutor. Video recording of the event commenced just before the tutorial exchange began.

The student posed her first question or difficulty. The tutor and the student worked on this together, in the usual manner, until it appeared to the tutor that the difficulty had been resolved. At this point the tutor awaited and indeed expected the student's endorsement of that judgement. The tutor expected an indication that the student was ready to move on to the second problem or difficulty. The conversation quickly became distinctly hesitant and sticky.

(I will interrupt my description of the tutorial exchange at this point, to explain the action researching purpose for allowing the television camera to intrude. This experiment concerned an adaptation by me (Cowan and George, 1992a) of a process called Interpersonal Process Recall (IPR). This had been devised originally for an entirely different purpose by a counsellor called Norman Kagan (Kagan *et al.*, 1963). I have been employing this technique over the past ten to fifteen years, to extract recall of thoughts and feelings, as they have occurred in the minds of learners and tutors at the time of their dialogues together.)

IPR was used in this particular example as follows. A colleague of the tutor, acting as an enquirer, went with the student immediately after the event to a separate room, where there was a replay facility. Enquirer and tutor between them had selected three or four minutes of the exchange which appeared to the tutor to be likely to be of interest, and worth exploring in detail. The student, who knew in advance of the technique and how it would be employed, was reminded that the question to be asked of her would always be the same, each time the tape was paused: 'Does that remind you of how you were thinking or feeling at the time?' After her reply, there might be further questions of elucidation, seeking simply to clarify or amplify her original answer.

(In all my experience of the use of this technique, with just one exception, those who have not experienced it before have always found it an exciting revelation. For they discover to their astonishment the extent to which they can have access to what virtually amounts to a replay in their mind of their feelings and thoughts. These impressions come back from memory with sharpness of detail which they would never have imagined possible. They thus provide information which subjects could certainly not have been able to recall without the prompt of the recording.)

In this instance, the tutor naturally chose the four-minute section of the recording which covered the end of the dialogue around the first difficulty, and the hiatus which had occurred thereafter. Although it was the student's thoughts and feelings which were 'unpacked' initially, it will make my point more effectively for our present purposes if I first describe what the enquirer extracted from the tutor.

The tutor felt sure that something had gone wrong – but he did not know what. He had noticed and been perturbed by the look on the student's face, and by the student's reluctance to speak, to answer, to table the next difficulty, or – generally – to respond. The replay was stopped frequently, either at an appropriate break or because the tutor's eye movement as he watched the replay suggested to the enquirer that important recall was occurring. Each time, this tutor recalled vividly the anxiety he had been feeling, and his various frantic speculations about what he might have done wrong. Eventually he progressed to the part of the recording which prompted him to recall his clear judgement at the time, which was that he had done something quite wrong, that the student wished the exchange to end as soon as possible and that he, the tutor, should quickly find a way of allowing the student to terminate the appointment without further embarrassment on either side.

The student's recall, which the enquirer had obtained earlier but had not declared to the tutor at this point, followed rather different lines. Her facial signals had also led the enquirer to stop the tape frequently, at almost 15-second intervals. This staccato replay of the tape had prompted her to recall (first) her satisfaction that her difficulty had been resolved, and (subsequently) her consciousness that her new understanding now began to answer a lot of associated difficulties which had occurred in the studies of the previous week or ten days. She had immediately begun to think these through, as she was then recalling in detail. She remembered – also vividly – her anxiety not to lose that which she felt she had just begun to grasp, her acute need for time to think all of this through again and, above all, her fervent hope that the tutor would just stay silent for a minute or two, leaving her to tidy all of this away before moving on to her next question.

Here we have a classic example of one of these mismatches in perception between a tutor and a student (or a group of students) which are a common discovery in IPR enquiries. When this student and her tutor came together to hear the reports from the enquirer, both were adult learners, and both were learning in their different ways – and to their surprise – about transactions in learning and teaching. The student learned that her facial expressions and her silences could be misread by at least one tutor. She eventually began to discuss, and see the desirability of, feeding back information to a tutor about the immediate outcomes of tutoring, to enhance its effectiveness for her. The tutor learned to his horror how badly he had misjudged the facial expressions and behaviour of the student, and particularly the reasons for the student's reticence. He saw the need to develop for the future a tutorial style in which silences might figure rather more often, and without unease on his part. He would also devise and use more effective questions than hitherto, in order to ascertain the process of learning which was occurring in response to his teaching. He planned to introduce that suggestion in future, by a brief reference to this particular experience. Thus, from this relatively brief experience, both went off resolved to test out the tentative conclusions of their deep and fairly lengthy discussion on process, and to do so in the next tutorial exchanges in which they were engaged, and whose effectiveness they wished to enhance.

Student and tutor, as I have described, began from a particular experience of the learning and teaching relationship; they each progressed through extensive reflection which they undertook together after it had been occasioned by the prompting of the feedback from the enquirer. They next moved into tentative generalizations about their roles in learning and teaching situations, which each was immediately eager to test out or verify in practice, in the next similar, but hopefully now also dissimilar, situation.

The significant features of this interaction, in terms of what the facilitator had planned in an open-ended way, were as follows:

- The facilitator, in effect, arranged in advance for intervention immediately after the event, in order to bring about – or at least prompt – powerful reflection without, in the event, even being present.
- She did this by arranging for the use of a proven technique which – by that point in time – had become fairly standard in the institution in which it was (once again) being used.
- The enquirer's only intervention was to stop the tape replay when the subject's face suggested that significant recall was happening; to ask, if necessary, the same prompt question; to follow up that question, when appropriate, with simple questions of elucidation; and to note the information volunteered, and pass it on to the other party.
- There was no active facilitation of the reflection itself, but only the creation of frequent occasions for recall and reflection thereon, which was akin to reflection-in-action.
- The outcomes of the activity were valued – but had not been predicted or anticipated.

This example raises two important issues – the value of unintended, or at least unspecified, learning outcomes, in a day and age when the reverse is the norm; and the extent to which someone planning an event, as in Example 7.1, in effect determines the approach which will be followed by the participants, including in this case the enquirer.

Other examples

- The reflection in Example 2.3 (Study skills for OU students at Dumfries) depended on the structure of the activity.
- The reflection in Example 2.2 (Identifying and using algorithms in applied mechanics) also depended on the structure of the activity.
- The Aalborg supervisors, in Example 2.5, intervened throughout the

progress of the projects, and especially to require review and reflection of the processes being followed.

Possible non-examples

- Woods (1987), who is one of the gurus of problem-solving education, explicitly declares his specific problem-solving methods to students, and teaches them almost by instruction.
- Rogers (1983) advises against the structuring of activity or of intervention by the teacher, who is simply to be empathic and responsive (see Chapter 12).
- The journal commentators in Example 2.4 (the Interdisciplinary Studies course) did not impose structure, although they actively (if non-directively) provided comments which the journal writers might accept as facilitation of further reflection. (Is this a non-example, then?)

Generalizations

The question with which this chapter began asked for guidance on how to set up, and facilitate, activities with which students will engage to good effect. I would suggest in summary that any such activities, if they come as a change in approach for students, should be carefully planned to offer these features:

1. A challenge or activity which is intrinsically motivating.
2. A very carefully planned task which is simply, clearly and adequately explained, such that it will require no amplification, adjustment or subsequent explanation.
3. Equally well-considered facilitation, if necessary, by tutors whose role is to provide minimal or no instruction, and who will seek to support learning and development mainly by nudging learners into their ZPD.

Interestingly, these requirements are becoming apparent as very necessary features when one is planning to use the VLE or online activities to support learning and development (Cowan, 2006).

In addition, a number of noteworthy features emerge, for me at least, from my eight examples:

- The designer of each activity (other, perhaps, than the last) had a clear notion of the intended outcome, and chose an arrangement which, if successful, should have achieved that outcome.
- The demands made on the learners were fairly straightforward, at least in terms of the explanation or description of their task.
- Where the structure of the activity could be made to achieve the desired

purpose, minimal tutor engagement was incorporated, other than to describe to the students what was to be done.

- The structures chosen were such that good (or better) practice should have ensued for the learners, or were such that ineffective practice would become apparent.
- On occasions, and in some activities only, success apparently depended heavily on interventions by the tutor, to nudge learners around the Kolb cycle.
- The tutors did not attempt to instruct the students in the exercise of the ability which was the focus of the activity.
- The more learners were to have autonomy over the outcomes of learning, the more tutors appeared to take responsibility for the *structure* of the learning activity, and vice versa. Tutors also, consequently, gave more thought in advance to their roles within learning and teaching situations.
- As in all learner-directed programmes, in my experience, the teacher must get the structure of the activity right from the start. And, to promote effective reflection purposefully, they must have thought about if, when and how to make interventions that will be regarded by the learners as legitimate within the structure, and not seen as interruptions being made because things are not going well.

Before you test this, some second thoughts from me

1. Is it a valid reflective summary to conclude that it is through the design of the structure of an activity or programme that the teacher sets in place the Kolb cycle, or the potential to follow it? And is it by facilitative interventions or interactions that the teacher will most effectively encourage constructive progress around that cycle?

2. Demanding structures and powerful interventions can be threatening and, if so, will then inhibit rather than nurture worthwhile learning and development. How can teachers judge in advance how far they can go in the search for methods and approaches to develop learners' potential to the full?

3. The human race progresses because we build on the experience and learning of those who went before us. So should it not have been possible, as well as desirable for the sake of efficient use of the time of all concerned, to condense the experience of those who went before the learners in the examples described in this chapter, and thus to expedite the learners' progress? Couldn't learners have been taken directly to established generalizations, to begin from there?

4. I have been urging you to form your own generalizations from the examples I offer you. Are these generalizations genuinely 'better', according to criteria for your development which you value, than they

would have been if I had gone straight into an exposition of my approach to the development of abilities, and only then justified it by quoting examples – while still leaving you to decide if you were convinced?

5. What place is there, even in reflective learning, for the teacher who instructs and directs rather than structures and intervenes? Surely these options, like many in this book, are not mutually exclusive?

6. You will undoubtedly have recognized that, as the writer of this text, I am an example of a teacher who has opted to make substantial inputs to his readers. I have clearly had a devious intent from the outset, stemming from a clear decision about the view I wish to 'sell' to you, and to other readers. My many examples appear to be simply a way of presenting my view and my preferred approach to learning and teaching, with an intended conclusion. If you follow me through the reflections I have structured for you, and into the generalizations which I have in mind for you, are you genuinely free to generalize, and to decide how to do that, in your own ways? Should you be? Is it acceptable for a facilitative tutor to have intended outcomes in mind?

7. Notice that in Example 7.1 the students had an experience which led them to reflect on their competence, and to generalize about more than this particular learning need accordingly before formulating a judgement. That sequence appears to be almost self-contained. Sometimes (and in more examples than this one) it seems unnecessary to go round the Kolb cycle more than once, or even to go round it completely, before some learning outcomes are achieved. Is that a valid simplification of the Kolb cycle?

A final thought

Finally, I offer a long-standing reflection on the progressively diminishing role of a true teacher:

> The whole function of the teacher is epitomized in two sayings from the Fourth Gospel: 'I have come that men [*sic*] may have life, and may have it in all its fullness' (John 10:10), and 'It is for your good that I am leaving you' (John 16:7).
>
> (paraphrased from H. G. Stead, in Davies, 1971)

Dear John

Most of your examples come from engineering or the study skills area. So I'm afraid they are not of much direct use to me, because my subject is quite different, and I mostly teach at final year level or to postgraduates.

I presume I question on behalf of the majority of your readers, who will not be engineers, either. I'd like you to show me, and others who don't teach in your discipline area, examples which could be directly useful to us, please. Or do you seriously believe we can translate something from your teaching to ours? If so, how can we do that – how can we adapt your ideas to fit our disciplines and situations?

8

How Can You Adapt Ideas from My Teaching, for Yours?

Introduction

On my rough count so far, I admit to having seven examples taken from my own discipline area of civil and structural engineering; but there have been five from social sciences, four from arts and three from science – which is not a bad spread. Similarly, although I have two examples from the basic study skills area, I have four that concentrate on higher level cognitive abilities, which I would call core skills rather than study skills. And there are two examples which are utterly general, in that I challenge the reader to identify from the text the discipline area in which I last used them. More importantly, my models in Chapter 4 are non-disciplinary, and relate to the development and evaluation of higher level cognitive and sometimes interpersonal abilities.

However, the letter asks a question about adaptation which is often posed – sincerely and validly. Even though I had hoped this book would have answered it already, I anticipate that it may still be in the minds of some readers. I will try to answer it effectively, giving examples to illustrate that response. And I am glad to do so, because it allows me to make explicit a methodology for switching examples from one context to another.

If this question doesn't bother you, then please skip to the next question – and the next chapter. If you are interested in seeing what my answer will be, then first allow me to set out my answer in brief.

Outline

The whole message of the Kolb cycle, for me, is that one way to learn is to look for patterns within families of problems or tasks, which link them together because the underlying framework, structure or shape of plan is common to them all. If that is true for our students in their studies within our disciplines, then it should be true for us, too. In this chapter, then, I propose to show how some examples of teaching which we have met already in these pages in a particular disciplinary context can be set out in a different context. I will operate on them in two steps, following the Kolb cycle, of course.

First of all, I'll try to extract the underlying framework – as I've called it – which will be a Kolbian generalization. Then I'll test it out as a generalization, by checking if it can apply in two other disciplines and situations. The result will be the use of the same framework, and virtually the same words, in each example and transfer situation; but, if so, I hope it will answer this worry about transferability. Then, when we move on to the second and third examples, I'm leaving it to you, the reader, to do a bit of work to follow the parallel which I am claiming in the frameworks used before and after transfer from one setting to another.

I believe I can illustrate my methodology in an introductory and general example. I sometimes find myself asked for suggestions, by a teacher who has to deal with the design of a learning and teaching activity, for a specific situation with particular features – outwith my own discipline. When I respond with an acceptable solution, I am generally given credit for being creative. But usually I'm not being very creative at all. I'm simply applying a framework with which I am familiar in one setting, having clad it with new details appropriate to the new situation. If there are only seven original jokes, I suspect there are not many more original frameworks for learning activity. I believe firmly that these effective frameworks or structures for learning and teaching are, or should be, interdisciplinary. So there aren't too many different basic schemes, and we don't really need too many – because we have so much we can utilize again and again, taking the same framework and just giving it different cladding.

To illustrate that point, I will not work here with any of the examples which would make my task easier. The Dumfries study skills story (Example 2.3), for instance, is already interdisciplinary, since it brought together students from a variety of faculties and courses. And the Interdisciplinary Studies course (Example 2.4), although it only involved students of civil engineering, had widespread interdisciplinary aims. These present insufficient challenge in the present context, where I seek to show that ideas about how to teach can transfer readily from one disciplinary context to another.

Example 8.1: Framework A fits engineering, classics and social sciences

Let's test this assertion of mine by starting from an example which often turns off listeners or readers who claim that they don't understand anything about engineering. I'll try to identify and transfer the framework in

Example 2.2, which concerned the use of solution cards – as it happened, when studying applied mechanics, although I cheated slightly by referring to it as a numerate subject area. I hope you'll remember that this was the example in which I helped my students, when they were in difficulty, to draft in their own words an algorithmic 'recipe' to be followed when tackling common problems of a familiar type. You should compare my framework with the full description in Example 2.2, to check that I am playing fair at this stage.

The underlying framework – framework A

1. Assemble a family of examples which can all be tackled by the same method.
2. Choose one example, which exemplifies the characteristics of the method in use.
3. Take the student through that example, nudging them into their zone of proximal development (ZPD), when necessary.
4. Summarize the steps taken, in words as general as possible but using the student's words.
5. Get the student to test out this method on another example, with as little assistance as possible.
6. Modify it, if necessary, so that it applies to both first and second examples.
7. Make notes of any complications or ways of presenting the problem which can obscure the standard nature of the problem.
8. Ask the student to test out the method on examples as yet unconsidered.

Using framework A in classics

In an Open University (OU) classics course dealing with fifth-century (BC) Athens, students would have encountered the classification of Greek vases – according to a methodology which we need not detail here. Similarly, the students may have been told how to classify Greek swords and shields. Let's use the generalized framework and see what we come up with. I'll leave it to you to keep an eye on the steps in the original, and to make sure that I'm not oversimplifying.

Here was my advice to the tutor, Judith George, about what she might (and did) do:

1. Assemble a family of examples of vases which can all be classified by the same method.
2. Choose one vase, likely to exemplify the characteristics of the method in use.

3. Take the student or a small group through that example, nudging them into their ZPD, when necessary.
4. Summarize the steps taken, in words as general as possible but using the student's words.
5. Get the student or group to test out this method on another example, with as little assistance as possible.
6. Modify it, if necessary, so that it applies to both first and second examples.
7. Make notes of any complications or slight peculiarities in a vase which can obscure the standard nature of the problem.
8. Ask the student or group to test out the method on vase examples as yet unconsidered, and then to extend the approach to swords or shields.

Using framework A yet again – in social sciences

In the OU course, D300: *Professional Judgment* [sic] *and Decision Making,* students with a strong study background in the social sciences often had difficulties with the quantitative part of the syllabus. When I was tutoring this subject, I decided to borrow and slightly adapt the framework I had used with my first year civil engineering students. I planned to move on from this to a numerical topic, which created problems for many students with a social science background. This was the offputting challenge of the virtually predetermined sequence of calculations to determine the predictive value of a positive test result (PVP) in a diagnostic medical test. Many students on this course found that title, and the associated calculations, demanding or offputting – so much so that the course team openly referred to this part of the syllabus as 'the hard stuff'.

I transferred my framework. This time I planned it from the start as a group activity, given the negative reactions and apprehension which I anticipated. Here's what I did:

1. I assembled a family of examples calling for the calculation of the PVP in assorted settings.
2. I chose one example, likely to exemplify the characteristics of the method in use.
3. I took the students in my group through that example, by nudging them into their collective ZPD, when necessary.
4. I summarized the steps taken, in words as general as possible but using what students had said.
5. I got the students to test out this method on another example, with as little assistance as possible.
6. Together we modified the listed method, if necessary, so that it applied to both first and second examples.

7. We made notes of any complications or ways of presenting a problem which could obscure its standard nature.
8. I asked the students to test out the method on examples as yet unconsidered.

I had provided this activity as a revision exercise, following a diagnostic pre-test which confirmed the students' declared needs. They willingly took the post-test (also diagnostic), which confirmed that substantial progress had been made.

Active experimentation – for you

The judgement should be yours, and not mine. So please try to relate this framework, as I have done, to a familiar, common and routine task in your own discipline, with which some students have difficulty. Has this first example of transferability yielded a generalization of a teaching method which could transfer to your (different) discipline and situation?

Example 8.2: Framework B fits social sciences, engineering and biology

I choose now the example of dialogue assignment writing (Example 7.2). This is an approach which many, I suggest, would regard as typical of the soft subjects, like social science or humanities. I choose to demonstrate transfer into a demandingly hard subject area, like engineering.

This example originated in a situation in which the course team valued questioning. The dialogue form chosen for the course units, the videotapes and the assignments witnessed to that. They also demonstrated their belief that there should never be a commitment to a 'correct' answer. The course materials and presentation accordingly valued questioning more than answering. That was why even the materials, which I did not describe in the earlier account of this innovation, were presented as a dialogue. There the course team chair and a guest authority argued out almost every point made, without necessarily reaching or declaring a conclusion, or agreeing. The underlying idea was that the sharper the questioning, the deeper the learners' thinking – because there was scope and encouragement for multiple interpretations.

The course team, in designing an assignment strategy, had therefore opted for a format which made it clear to the students that they were expected to question the 'wisdom' presented in the course materials. That approach was to be applied by them to a task set as coursework. In the original version, the prompt for questioning was the dialogue format, which – as I described in Example 7.2 – quickly became and felt stilted if there was not active questioning. In the dialogue assignment, the learner came to probe their own arguments, as the model which featured in the materials had exemplified. Even when the final version of the assignment was being marked, the tutor asked questions rather than offering answers or judgements.

The underlying framework – framework B

I summarize the inherent framework of this formative assignment, for such it was, as follows:

1. The teacher declares that one important course objective is to stimulate sound questioning and critical thinking.
2. The teacher chooses a task style in which sound or sharp questioning is not only expected, but encouraged and rewarded.
3. The teacher demonstrates how that kind of questioning might appear.
4. The student now tackles a similar task which is not straightforward, which calls for thinking, which may have more than one reasonable answer, but which makes considerable use of course material.
5. The structure of the activity calls for frequent questioning by the learner of what is being said, written, thought or decided.
6. The teacher does not immediately, or even subsequently, declare a 'right' answer, although gross errors and omissions may be pointed out later.

Using framework B – in a class activity in first level fluid mechanics

In this example, I take a development which occurred before the dialogue assignment, and was not derived from it. I do not see that this reverse chronology invalidates my argument, though. I simply desire to demonstrate to you that a useful idea for a framework can apply in another type of situation, group size and discipline – but not that one need be deliberately derived from the other.

For this example, I take an activity run at Heriot-Watt University at first year level by my colleague, Derek Fordyce. This was in a numerate subject called fluid mechanics.

1. On several occasions, within two-hour time slots, Derek reminded the class of the emphasis he placed on the importance of asking pointed questions (which was not new to them), and explained how that demand would figure in assignments and examination questions, for which the activity to come was a preparation.
2. He then allocated students to groups of between four and six members. He presented a fairly demanding problem which went beyond

the simplification of reality which so often happens in engineering studies. He chose, for example, the flow of fluid in a non-standard pipe system. These systems had some familiar features to which the formulae and theories of the course had already been applied, but others which had not previously been considered. The class had studied flow and pressure loss in pipes, and pressure losses at bends, but not losses at T-junctions and V-junctions. Thus the problems were not straightforward, called for thinking and might well have had more than one reasonable answer. He allowed plenty of time for the groups which had been set up to formulate their solutions, having warned them of the format of what was to follow.

3. He chose one group and asked them to come to the front and present their solution. As they did so, they were constantly questioned – at first by Derek – and questioned searchingly, even if their thinking was sound.

4. As the class began to pick up the idea of setting up a questioning culture, the questioning moved easily and naturally to the other students, with another group's solution to probe. Foolish questions were challenged in turn, across the room, or even by Derek from the front. Sound questions could also be challenged, either as a tutorial tactic or from sincere ignorance on the part of the questioner.

5. In all of this, Derek volunteered no judgement whatsoever. Even in the case of a brilliantly perceptive solution, which was rare but not impossible, he would question and probe – as if unconvinced. It was left to the class to go on thinking and judging, and to reach their own conclusions – probably after they left the room.

6. The sharper the questioning, the deeper the thinking – because the problem allowed scope for fundamental thinking about the subtleties of fluid mechanics.

Verdict

It is a far cry from professional judgement to fluid mechanics. It is also a significant change to move from self-questioning by an individual in an assignment with a teaching purpose to self-questioning within and across a class group in a class activity. You may not feel that the principle is indeed the same in both cases. Perhaps for that reason the parallel between the two examples may seem too stretched for you to accept it as demonstrating the existence of a common underlying framework. I hope not.

Let's try a simpler case, though, which adheres more strictly to the original underlying framework. It arose in a course design meeting, when a module writer bewailed her difficulty in getting students to question and think deeply about her subject matter in biology, which happened to be scientific, but was descriptive rather than numerical or formulaic.

Using framework B in biology

I took the framework of engaging in a dialogue with self, and considered it as a basis for replacing the format of examination or assignment questions which the module writer used in her existing course. This would be prompting the type of thinking she wished to encourage. I suggested to her that she might consider the following:

1. Declare a marking schedule in which at least half the marks for responses would be for exploring the other side of the position from that which the learner favours.
2. Refrain from disturbing the establishment, and the students. Hence (almost) retain one of the standard question forms. This was the one in which a statement is presented, often within quotation marks, after which the student is merely invited to 'Discuss'. But now the demand of the question would be spelt out differently.
3. Use a rubric which asks for four distinct responses, for the traditional 20 marks:
   (a) *State* whether you agree or disagree with this statement (Yes or No). (0)
   (b) *List* the main points you would make in support of your view. (5)
   (c) *List* the main points you would expect to be made in a counter-argument by someone who had good reason to disagree with you. (7)
   (d) *Explain* how you would respond to these points, in order to convince a listener to accept the position declared in (a) – but not simply by expanding on list (b). (8)
4. Provide, in tutorials, model answers to questions of this type, together with answers of varying standards. Ask groups to consider what marks they would give to each of the answers and why; these should be justified and explored in informal group discussion.
5. First, use this same rubric as a format for one or two coursework tasks, in both formative and summative continuous assessment, to familiarize students with coping with this style of demand.
6. Emphasize the demands of items (c) and (d), when marking and commenting on submitted coursework. Encourage discussion of how to meet the demands.
7. Never declare or imply a 'right' answer – although gross errors and omissions might be pointed out, but only some time later.
8. Assess accordingly.

This approach was accepted by the module writer with some enthusiasm, and with few modifications. She continues to use it.

The parallel between these uses of this framework is less explicit than in Example 8.1. However, I submit that these key features are present in all three cases instanced here:

1. The teacher makes it clear that one important course objective is to stimulate sound questioning and critical thinking.
2. The task style is chosen to explicitly encourage and reward sound or sharp questioning.
3. The desired style and standard of questioning is exemplified.
4. The students tackle a similar task which is not straightforward, which calls for thinking, which may have more than one reasonable answer, but which makes considerable use of course material.
5. The structure of the activity calls for frequent and rigorous questioning by the learners.
6. The teacher does not immediately, or even subsequently, declare a 'right' answer.

However, the final judgement should again be yours, and not mine. *Did* these examples in this set yield a framework or generalization which could transfer to your discipline and situation?

Example 8.3: Framework C, transferred to other areas

In Example 7.1, you may recall, I set up a situation in which students who felt they had nothing more to learn about communication, at least insofar as describing apparatus was concerned, came to a contrary judgement within a short time.

Privately, I give descriptive titles to my underlying shapes and frameworks for activities. This framework, for reasons which may be apparent to aficionados of A. A. Milne (Milne, 1926), I have always called 'Heffalump Trap'. With that title in mind, and having given away my secret once again, let's look for the features of the framework underlying the activity I described earlier in some detail.

The underlying framework – framework C

I sum up the framework of the 'describing apparatus' activity in these short terms:

1. Ask the learners to declare explicitly what it is that they have mastered, if you suspect that they will tend to claim (and believe) more than is actually within their ability.
2. Set up a situation in which they should be able to demonstrate that competence.
3. Check their performance against expected outcomes – in public.

4. Celebrate success – if it emerges. Otherwise, note any striking discrepancy – if it arises – and confront the learners with that.
5. Invite the learners to decide what to do about it.

Using framework C in staff development

Let's explore this framework in the field of staff development, which I suppose is the discipline area of education.

Alan Harding and I had a somewhat wicked way of beginning a week's programme of staff and educational development. We followed the same outline with lecturers coming from any single department and degree course, or even faculty – if they brought to the workshop activity an overtly declared confidence in what they were doing in their teaching, and in their competence to do it soundly. We introduced the group to the words in Bloom's taxonomy (as below) (Bloom *et al.,* 1956). Although this has been criticized, we had found that it was nonetheless a useful framework for initial and, indeed, ongoing discussions of educational goals, because it uses words of whose meaning there is a common and shared agreement:

1. We divided our participants into four or more groups and asked them to decide what proportion of their learning and teaching *should* concentrate on:

    *   evaluation
    *   synthesis – or creative problem-solving, according to the discipline
    *   analysis
    *   application of understanding
    *   understanding
    *   knowledge.

2. We required them to produce rough percentage figures under these headings, summarizing the emphasis they placed on the goals they targeted in their teaching, for each year of their course. They usually made powerful claims for coverage of items at the top of the scale, and especially so for final year classes.
3. Once the groups had each told us that they had reached agreement, we gave them prepared acetates on which they entered their figures, which they then returned to us for display in plenary. We had arranged the columns in different positions on the various acetates, so that the results from all of the groups for, say, the final year of the course could be displayed at one time. I cannot recall an occasion when these showed an acceptable consensus. Clearly there was disagreement here on which they, and we, needed to work. We pointed out the lack of agreement, but made no comment thereon at that stage.
4. As they struggled to digest that inference, we asked them in passing if they felt that the end-of-year assessments should reflect what they

wanted the students to learn. This trivial question, which was of course answered affirmatively, diverted attention from their dilemma about their disagreement over goals. We then produced some of their past examination papers, usually for the final year, which we 'just happened to have with us'. We asked them to show us, in the examination question coverage, the amount of testing of the higher level goals for which their acetates had made bold claims. There were few such examples to be found, and certainly nothing akin to the claimed proportions – something I have also encountered, incidentally, during Teaching Quality Assessment and external examining in some of our most highly regarded British departments.

5. We asked them what (if anything) they wanted to do about it – and then left them on their own, with time to come to their own conclusion that they wished our help in redesigning their curriculum.

This Heffalump Trap, like the original one, had caught people who had dug it for themselves. They were consequently more prepared to make a new beginning – provided the reception of the embarrassing message had taken place in circumstances which did not occasion embarrassment, an angry defensive reaction or hurt.

Using framework C in connection with project work

In virtually any discipline, I have encountered the following:

1. When I contact a department for which I have recently been appointed external examiner, I often ask them to tell me about their final year project. Invariably, it sounds good – especially when I ask about the criteria against which it is judged. I ask, without making a fuss about it, if these criteria are made known to the students. And I tend to be told – with some mild surprise – that of course the criteria are tabled and explained, and naturally influence much of what the students do, during the year.
2. Later in the same conversation I suggest that, in the course of my travels and therefore at no cost to the department, I would quite like to meet with the students, after they have made a start on their projects. 'That would be grand,' they say. 'We'll arrange that.' 'Perhaps I could run a short workshop, to let them make the acquaintance of their External, and his attitudes?' I suggest. 'Oh, we've never had an External who did that, but it seems a fair enough idea.' 'Would the staff be interested to join in?' I ask. 'I'm *sure* some at least would want to come along,' they say. 'And perhaps share with me in the workshop?' I suggest gently. 'Why not?' comes the unsuspecting reply.

3. On the day, I gather the students in one room and put them in groups of about six. I ask them to summarize for me on flipchart sheets what they expect me to be looking for when I am judging the worth of the projects which will come to me at the end of the year. And what will be the qualities which I should notice in a very good piece of work? They work with a will to answer my question. In a separate room I give the staff, almost all of whom have come along out of curiosity, the same task. In their case, I let them work together, with one of their number acting as scribe.

4. I go back to the students' room, and we Blu-Tack the sheets on one wall. They are written in the students' own words, but much the same message comes from every group, although I have discouraged collaboration.

5. I then invite the staff to bring their flipchart sheet through and display it on the opposite wall. The staff immediately go to see what the students have written, while the students flock around the staff summary. The symbolism of the use of opposite walls is apt. For both walls carry starkly different messages, which differ in much more than the choice of words.

6. As tactfully as I can, I point out from the centre of the room, with crossed arms and challenging index fingers, that the staff seem to want the students to go *that* way, while the students think that they are expected to go *this* way. I suggest that it might be an idea for the two groups to talk to each other. For, if the students have got the wrong idea of what's expected of them, how can they be expected to deliver work which will be judged sound? I tell them that I had a colleague whose granny was prone to point out that, 'If you don't know where you're going, any bus will do.' Staff begin to protest loudly that, 'We *told* them.' I point out as gently as possible that the evidence on the walls suggests that, whatever message was *sent* and with whatever force and conviction it was *told*, it has not yet been heard and understood.

7. I suggest that it might be an idea for them to talk to each other. Then I depart, quietly – and await developments which seldom fail to emerge, constructively.

Verdict

Again, I leave the decision with you, asking if the underlying framework for these three diverse activities is indeed a common one. If so, is it one that you might use, whatever your discipline, should your purpose be to confront complacency?

Notice that the argument here is again that frameworks can function acceptably and usefully in various discipline settings – provided the teachers concerned share commonality of purpose.

Overall generalization

It will be clear that I firmly believe that the close marriage of underlying principles and the desired learning outcome can usefully determine a pedagogical shape or framework (e.g. Cowan, 1974a, 1974b) for a commendable learning and teaching situation. It is this basis on which we should be designing our learning and teaching activities for students who are to achieve our intended outcomes. Only thus do we arrange for one part of what Biggs has called constructive alignment (Biggs, 2003) – the alignment of outcomes and learning activity, so that learners should actively achieve what we hope for, for them. I argue that such a sound framework is independent of the discipline in which it happens to be used, since it relates only to the category of intended outcome. For that reason, I believe that such formats are usefully transferable in principle (though not in detail) by any teacher who has a similar learning goal and is prepared to exercise a little ingenuity while pillaging good ideas.

It has been, and is, for you to actively experiment with that input from me, in your own discipline and setting. If it proves valid, then the outcomes for you as a teacher will be rich ones. For you, like me, will not need to do much of your own design of class activities, but will be able to abstract discernable frameworks from a subject area wherein you spot a particularly effective learning and teaching situation. To these frameworks you will simply need to add particular cladding, to suit your particular situation.

A second thought from me

I'm afraid I didn't originally have any reservations to offer regarding the sincere beliefs which I have aired frankly. My sole comment would have been to ask if you noticed that I have not made any reference to, or use of, the Cowan diagram or Schönian reflection. You may wish to consider why that should have been so.

But then, with hindsight and on reflection, a worrying question emerged for me. Have I got it all the wrong way round in this chapter? I have been urging you to see ways of stripping a method of its disciplinary detail, and finding underneath a framework which you can transfer into your own situation. Perhaps I should instead have been urging you to start from the learning need, to think in general terms about how the achievement of that need could be supported, to spell that out as a general description of the framework for learning which you seek – and then to look around to find if anyone else has been filling out the detail of a framework like that in their own subject area, something which you could usefully borrow, or pilfer?

Dear John

It's time to get back to what I was hoping for, when you told me the title of this book. You've written a great deal about reflection – which certainly features in the subtitle. So far, though, you haven't written directly about becoming an innovative university teacher – which is what most of us readers will have been looking for. I'd like you to get back to the promise of your main title, and say something about being innovative – about why, and how.

You have given an enthusiastic account of innovations which have clearly brought great satisfaction, as far as you yourself have been concerned. Reading between the lines, though, it's clear that they also meant a lot of hard work – and that sometimes the risks involved were considerable, for you and maybe also for the learners. Why should someone today wish that workload on themselves, and take these risks?

We find ourselves today in an environment where education is treated as a business, and where lecturers are constantly expected to deliver, in quantifiable terms examined in appraisals, under such performance indicators as Research Assessment Exercises, direct and grant income, and entrepreneurship. It's an environment where staff have less and less time in which to think about changing their teaching, and where senior management are more and more involved in decisions about priorities and innovations. In that context, it seems to me that change cannot be a matter for individuals, and must be carefully and expertly planned, lest it fails to deliver. So what place is there in that process for ordinary teachers like me?

I suppose what I'm getting round to is the view that teaching is no longer an activity where we can each do our own thing, and are answerable only to our classes, if that. Development nowadays surely has to be in the hands of trained and professional specialists in institutions, in specialist units, in the subject centres in Britain, and even in the new Higher Education Academy. Why and how should teachers like me bother to get directly involved?

And what about that operation at programme level and above? If we have an idea about what we'd like to change, or how we'd like to change it, what then? How should we individually engage with this process of innovation nowadays, within the context of our institutions, their demands and their processes?

9
Why and How Should We Start Innovating Nowadays?

Outline

This will be a chapter in a different format from those which have gone before. I shall still try to respond to the introductory question, and include generalizations and second thoughts. It will also be a chapter with a somewhat shared authorship, for I asked an educational adviser who has a remit for the development of e-learning to offer me his comments on my draft, as a critical friend. I include his remarks as he made them, which should ensure that this important chapter contains genuine second thoughts, from someone other than me.

University teachers operate nowadays in a situation which is in a state of flux, where much that matters is changing radically, and where we each have to engage fully with working out the particular implications for us, and for our students, of these changes. In this context, I'd say firmly that:

- There is much need and scope for innovation.
- Each programme, module and activity presents their own individual challenges – and calls for their own individual solutions.
- Considerable support is available to innovators.
- Once innovation is in progress, it is certainly subject to sharp scrutiny, but getting the innovative show on the road often calls for a bit of tactical nous.

Accordingly, I'll aim to finish what will be a long chapter by setting out specific advice to the apprentice innovator. I shall consider first, though, the factors in our present situation which call on each of us to be engaged with change in our teaching. I will close that first part by presenting a brief generalization and the usual 'second thoughts'.

Let's begin, then, by considering an assortment of calls on us for innovation, before we go on to think about how to overcome some of the hurdles.

Much of what should be in our curricula is new

Nowadays, as I argued in Chapter 3, the computer effectively handles most of the lower level demands in the cognitive domain. For example, computers can carry out routine tasks, following well-established procedures. Most employers thus expect even recent graduates to have developed, and be able to use, the higher level cognitive abilities which they should exercise in much of their employed time. Consequently, we – the teachers – are expected to have devoted much of our curriculum goals, learning experiences and assessment to outcomes which featured almost marginally for our predecessors, and in their practices. Probably, as an additional challenge for us, these are outcomes which did not really feature explicitly in our own experiences as students.

In regard to the affective domain, we face demands generated by our multicultural society, the internationalization of the curriculum and an increasing awareness of the need to have sound ways of 'handling' values and principles in the same way as we handle subject matter and disciplinary principles (Gardner *et al.*, 2000; Cowan, 2005). All of these factors have highlighted the need, as seldom before, for the development of learners in respect of affective outcomes. Here, again, teachers lack models and exemplars – and even personal learning experiences – to build upon. Innovation, and especially effective innovation, is thus much needed if we are to deal as we should with affective outcomes.

A similar challenge has emerged in respect of interpersonal abilities. An increasing and important amount of graduate time is spent in interaction with other people. We now appreciate the need to train effective listeners, negotiators, collaborators and investigators. These are abilities which used to be developed only to a slight extent in course provision, and to be given attention incidentally rather than deliberately and purposefully. They now need to feature strongly and explicitly in our curricula, in our learning and teaching methods – and in our assessment. In most disciplines we teachers don't yet have proven ways of tackling that type of learning outcome, or of integrating it with our other programme aims. This is another need calling for evaluated innovation.

I will illustrate these points with three brief and general examples, which call out for innovation, at the time of writing:

1. In the cognitive domain, the stimulation and effective development of creativity, across disciplines, is a troublesome challenge with which many are wrestling (JISC, 2005).
2. Those dealing with the affective domain have not yet assembled a pedagogy. They need a methodology with associated practical applications to enable them to generate on the part of students belief in, rather than mere adherence to, critical professional values (Cowan, 2005).

3. In the interpersonal domain, the new technologies have had an impact on how people may and should assemble written work, such as reports. That they call for radically new manners of so doing is appreciated, but how best to teach effectively for the development of those new abilities has still to be demonstrated (Hartley, 1998).

In this context, let us not forget that some keen and able graduates can only find themselves employment in undemanding and low status posts, because the job market is difficult. For them, an awareness of the market situation and keenly developed higher level abilities, which enable them to display their competence and potential at the slightest opportunity, are vital. This is yet another reason for us to concentrate on higher level, transferable capabilities.

Nevertheless, these changes in the desired learning outcomes are far from the only factor calling for change and innovation in higher education. There are, for example, economic pressures. These factors raise questions whose answers should be carefully considered, and should not emerge merely as knee-jerk reactions.

To sum up, for a variety of reasons, teachers in higher education should now be dealing predominantly with learning outcomes at higher levels, and in areas which have not traditionally featured strongly in curricula. In addition, governments and industry expect teachers to prepare students as a global workforce (Winner, 1998: 9), and to be managers of information rather than employees who just make great use of higher level skills. The extent to which that challenge has been taken up is questionable. Consequently, we should plan our teaching in ways and forms for which there are few models, few successful exemplars and few well-established principles to be found in the literature. Making a response that should prove as effective as possible inevitably calls for innovation, followed by evaluation of that, and then by dissemination of effective practice, in respect of greatly changed curriculum goals.

Resources are being reduced, again and again

Each year university teachers are expected to cope with ever-increasing student/staff ratios and ever-decreasing class contact hours. Both are an inevitable consequence of nationally determined attritions in funding levels and increases in intake targets. Higher education thus cries out for innovations which will deal effectively with these increasingly demanding resource levels. Senior management may well declare unhelpful dictates as their response to these pressures. Contact hours can be cut unilaterally across the board; pass rates may have to remain at previous levels, whatever that implies; options which do not attract large numbers may be dropped.

Admittedly there is already some pedagogical endorsement for reducing the number of lectures. It has been known for some time (Bligh, 1998), though not perhaps appreciated or accepted, that heavy timetables and large numbers of lectures are not the ideal recipe for educational effectiveness – even with lower level objectives. But there is no similar justification, other than economic limitations, for increasing the size of seminar and other groups (Benson, 1987). Formerly, remedial interactions between individual students and their teachers were possible, with relatively small class sizes such that informal contact could happen before and after formal events in the programme. But as Quality Assurance Agency (QAA) audit reports repeatedly state, individual tuition is now very much a thing of the past, other than in Oxbridge. Consequently, the cracks in the system have begun to show, sometimes alarmingly. In particular, personal tutor systems, which are increasingly necessary for the learners in difficulties, are so under-resourced and overloaded that in most universities they fail to serve their vital purpose.

In the face of these pressures, the innovator who can generate arrangements which lessen the problem, let alone make it disappear, is welcome indeed. If the virtual learning environment (VLE) can be harnessed to store, and effectively answer, easily pinpointed and frequently asked questions, the innovation would be taken up immediately – and valued.

Similarly, the innovative structuring of tasks and expectations for group work, which resurrect in the VLE the old-fashioned 'self-help' group or the newer co-operative learning group, will rightly be highly rated as an innovation, both by students and by their overworked tutors. Equally, our induction courses (and more besides) now need to go, innovatively, far beyond basic study skills, and to nurture innovatively in learners the core ability to self-manage their own learning, with and without peer interaction, as never before.

Keith Smyth (2005), whose professional role is to advise innovators, comments:

> This can't be over-emphasized in relation to the VLE. Most students entering or returning to HE don't have the mindset to study effectively online. This is partly because their expectations about studying at university revolve around ideas about lectures, seminars, and of the lecturer as an 'instructor' rather than tutor or guide. It's also due to the diverse range of ways in which online support and resources can be used from one course to another, and also because despite being more IT-literate, many of the student population have not previously studied in heavily blended or fully online contexts and are not used to the self-dependence this involves. These challenges are often still there even for those who self-select to study on an online course.

The implication of under-resourcing and lower contact hours is thus that there is a strong encouragement from all quarters for innovators to find cost-effective practices which will provide individual support and direction for learners with whom there is less and less contact time. This need is accentuated by the range of abilities which nowadays characterizes the average class cohort. That point leads in turn to the next factor calling for innovatory responses.

The range of abilities within student groups is ever widening

Most programmes nowadays recruit student groups within which there is a wide range of abilities and prior experience. The exceptions are a relatively few elitist universities and some highly popular programmes with selective intakes. Most university teachers are thus confronted by the challenge to deal with learning needs at the tail-end of the student group, which seldom featured to any great extent in the past, and so did not feature even covertly in the teaching methods of the past. In all forms of programme delivery, innovations to enable teachers to provide effectively for the range of needs, and to support and stimulate the wide range of abilities within one group, are consequently sought after.

Furthermore, we much need practices which will provide cost-effective remedial tuition for those whose grasp of prerequisites is weak or non-existent, while at the same time avoiding the danger of boring or frustrating our more able learners. And we have to do so within a lightly staffed structure of group work, rather than in intensive personal tutorials. One way of dealing with this may be to develop innovative group styles which build upon, without exploiting, peer support.

We also need approaches which cater for a much greater range than hitherto of learning rates, learning styles, prior learning, learning preferences – and learning misconceptions. In all of this, here again the implication is that those who can pilot and consolidate innovative approaches which deal effectively and cost effectively with such challenges will be much appreciated – within their hard-pressed departments or schools, and in their universities.

In our present situation there is great belief, at government, management and policy-setting levels, for the contribution which can be made by IT. This expectation has been taken up with enthusiasm despite there not being over-much evidence to justify it. That limitation applies in particular to the VLE and/or the managed learning environment (MLE). These are widely regarded as the most powerful way to enhance higher education cost effectively, although there are few fully developed and rigorously evaluated working examples to justify either aspect of that assertion. There is, nevertheless, much expectation of innovations in this area, and so a need for evaluated innovations. How this is to be achieved is yet to be worked out across the board, and points us to our next major factor.

We are expected (if not almost obliged) to harness IT in meeting our challenges

It is difficult for anyone to conceive how the political decision to increase the number of students in higher education in the UK can be realised without considerable increases in off-campus and online learning. For the possibility of enlarging campus accommodation appreciably is as unlikely as the possibility that even nominally full-time students will not be engaged in appreciable part-time employment. Fortunately, IT and the VLE offer us possibilities for learning in higher education which we are only beginning to appreciate and exploit. IT will not solve all our problems, but it can certainly make a noteworthy impact on many of them – provided it is used thoughtfully, innovatively and cost effectively. However, if it is simply used as a replacement or reinforcement for face to face delivery, then it will surely flounder. We do well to remember that earlier attempts to use technologies to directly replace live teachers were not particularly successful (e.g. MacLean, 1970; Cowan, 1975).

Furthermore, under pressure and in responding to approaches favoured by government, management can become worryingly simplistic in its decision-making, and seriously myopic in not seeing problems, whether potential or subsequently realized. Even for the innovator and enthusiast, the VLE and MLE are complex environments, with much potential – even in capable hands – to create as many problems as they solve. A blended or transitional approach is difficult to administer, and depends in its conception on technical and specialist staff whose decisions must be trusted and supported, which it is difficult for management to accept. So truly mixed mode and even thorough piloting are eschewed – and the consequences can be discouraging for innovation as well as progress.

Regrettably, much of the initial effort put into the use of (expensive) VLEs has been to encourage, or even coerce, lecturers to put their lecture notes and PowerPoint sequences on intranet pages, to which students have ready access. This has had two main effects, neither of which I would regard as either innovatory or desirable. It transfers the cost of printing out hard copy from the lecturer's department or school to the student, and there is a fear that it may encourage students' absence from the classes which are based upon these notes and the PowerPoint presentations. However, Keith Smyth (2005) comments usefully on the known facts:

> A couple of recent studies have suggested the online provision of slides/notes does not encourage this absenteeism to the extent previously thought. From personal experience, all I was able to observe when I provided notes online was that those students who did not turn up were those who tended not to turn up consistently, anyway. Then there were the students who used the notes provided in advance to come better prepared for the lectures, including a couple of international students who commented that it allowed them to interpret subject-related words and phrases from English into their own language in advance, and not during the lecture itself. Not a huge point, but maybe enough to suggest the issue isn't clear cut?

Today's true innovator, I suggest, will want to build upon a rather deeper vision of what education might be, rather than simply to consider how this powerful tool can be used to replace teachers and reduce teachers' workloads. To such an innovator, IT and the VLE do indeed offer great possibilities for learning, whose depths few have yet attempted to plumb fully:

- First and foremost, students and teachers have access through the Web to a wealth of resources, including complete courses, which were never before accessible to student learners. This is a rich basis for wide-ranging learning – but one which can lead to much inefficient or even shallow learning, if improperly used. Or to mental indigestion!
- The online medium is ideal for presenting subject matter in realistic forms through the use of multimedia, therefore allowing more opportunities to see relevant examples and to practise knowledge application (e.g. viewing medical procedures, virtual field trips that would prove difficult or hazardous to do for real, models and simulations).
- The online environment is well suited to particular types of activities that can be conducive to higher order learning (e.g. problem- and case-based learning, which tend to require a rich range of resources 'upfront' and to hand).
- VLEs offer great advantage to those who, through geographic location or a disability, simply could not access a traditional campus environment to undertake a course of study.
- Asynchronous interactions in discussion boards allow the reader to ponder over a remark or a question before responding, and to consider that response before sending it off. This potentially time-consuming individual interaction is undoubtedly an inducement to deeper thinking, but it is also an opportunity for students in a class or group to progress so differently that meaningful contact between them is then almost impossible. Nevertheless, in provision which is increasingly internationalized, the advantage to students writing and reading in a second language of a situation where they can communicate slightly less speedily than native speakers, and where a strong accent is not an embarrassment, should not be overlooked.
- An *almost* synchronous communication can take place in the chatroom. Therein succinct statements are almost essential, and there is a brief opportunity for reflection before responding. Chatroom exchanges, in a well-structured task, can expedite decision-making, encourage clear expression and bring together widely separated learners at a time convenient to all of them, to transact group business. However, chatrooms whose use has not been thoughtfully considered and planned for can degenerate to trivial exchanges akin to the social use of text messages on mobile phones.
- Email, with or without attachments, permits one to one interactions and supports the distribution and discussion/revision of group drafts. It can be especially constructive if some of the software facilities for reviewing and highlighting changes in documents are imaginatively used.

The telephone, fax and texting by mobile phone further enlarge the options, and should not be overlooked. For example, in relation to the last of these possibilities, I recently encountered a simple but clever use of mobile phones, in what the innovators called 'm-learning'. This featured students of nursing and paramedical professions, who were on placements and unable to access a PC from which to contact their academic tutor or supervisor. When they felt out of their depth, particularly in regard to an ethical or highly specialized matter, they could seek advice urgently by mobile phone and text messages. The medium called upon them to sum up their dilemma or enquiry succinctly – which was no bad thing. It permitted the tutor to respond speedily, but not immediately, if that should be inconvenient. And it gave the tutor enough time to assemble a pointed and sound response.

In another situation based on IT, I noted that the students, who were engaged in group work centred upon a discussion board, had drifted rapidly out of the group convoy during an interactive activity. They had also used the thread facility very ineffectively, and thus found it, as one student put it, 'difficult to get back in when I have been out of things for a while'. For the next activity, the tutor carefully and helpfully specified occasions and uses for the chatroom meetings. These reader-friendly explanations were linked to a requirement for scheduled circulation of minutes – circulated as attachments to emails – with reports to be made upon agreed action points (according to their ascriptions). Almost miraculously, the discussion boards in the next activity articulated to the overall structure, and groups began to contribute what was expected of them. Definition of structure, without change of task, changed learning performance to good effect. Note a later comment from Keith Smyth (page 143), which reinforces this point.

Another example involving what was at first ineffective use of IT emerged in an open-ended enquiry skills project. The tutor was concerned to note energetic but ineffective use of the internet and search engines, in considering the choice of a research question in a given field. Next time round, she introduced the simple innovation of offering as a starting point half a dozen extremely diverse, but sound, papers of recent date. She required these to be read, and to be summarized by one or other of the group, in the opening stages of the project. The subsequent process of arriving at a research question and of searching relevant, but not irrelevant, literature was speeded up, and strikingly transformed. The group enquiries were as diverse, sound and often as unpredicted as hitherto.

I hope these examples have illustrated that, provided we use it and structure it thoughtfully and creatively, IT offers us wonderful possibilities – which we have only just begun to explore and to consider thoroughly. That is a powerful incentive to innovation – including innovation in on-campus learning supported by IT in remedial or in blended form.

There are also great challenges for the teachers, especially arising from the hazards associated with the not always ideal flexibility of the situation – such as the possibility that groups who depend upon each other in their learning, in one way or another, may diverge. The 'convoy' may split. This may not simply be because some race on ahead and others lag, which is something with which a system can be designed to cope. It may also be because, like a convoy in the Second World War breaking up on the prospect of a U-boat attack, members may surge off in a variety of directions, and lose their common purpose and the possibility of effective interaction.

Smyth (2005) expands on the problems arising from flexibility, which are to some extent covered in what I have already written:

> The idea of 'flexibility' in online learning can definitely be taken, and implemented, in too literal a way. There needs to be a structure (including clearly communicated responsibilities and deadlines) within which the considerable benefits of self-paced studying and increased opportunities for reflection can be effectively harnessed. In addition to helping students plan and manage their learning in a medium that naturally offers considerable scope for procrastination, it helps ensure that online exchanges occur within a period of time that is likely to be useful to the majority of the students, rather than a student being ready to engage with their colleagues to find that either they've moved on, or are just not ready to converse yet. This message cannot be stressed too strongly for the reader who is new to thinking about online teaching and learning.

Finally, I switch the subject somewhat, to avoid falling into the common trap of talking only about innovations in 'learning and teaching'. It is a significant and dangerous omission to neglect assessment in any context where we are thinking about learning and teaching. For assessment has long been recognized as the hidden curriculum (Snyder, 1971) which powerfully influences student learning. It has also been appreciated that much assessment, when badly designed, encourages learning in pursuit of outcomes which, though worthwhile and in accordance with the course objectives, were neither desired nor intended. Assessment has long needed to be brought into line, or aligned, with learning aims and outcomes (Biggs, 2003; Cowan, 2004b). Hence my next heading, in this sequence of points which provide the backcloth against which to plan innovation today.

We need to ensure valid assessment, in the face of changes

Assessment features here for two reasons. The first is that if we change outcomes and learning and teaching methods in our innovations, then, to ensure alignment, we need to make corresponding changes in assessment. The second is that much review of assessment is long overdue, in any case. Consequently, many factors currently compound the need to develop our approach to assessment, and hence to innovate with forms of assessment.

Such factors, emerging from one or other of the causes I have mentioned, are as follows:

- The important need to devise aligned modes of assessment which will validly and reliably test the development of abilities, and which are appropriate to predominantly or fully online contexts, so using a range of online resources effectively. These methods must take forms very different from traditional assessment of the acquisition of understood knowledge, and its application in routine situations (Heywood, 1989). They must also avoid the dangers of mismatches between task and the specific nature of the online environment (such as avoiding discussion board interactions where rapid decision-making is a desired outcome – Smyth, 2005).
- The increased use of continuous assessment, in various forms and for various reasons. This is usually summative, in that it contributes to part of the overall mark or grade. But there is also an expectation on both sides that it will or should be formative, assisting students to progress their learning and development through the associated feedback and feed-forward (Sadler, 1983). Combining these two contrasting functions is not readily contrived, remains in my judgement an outstanding need, and so calls for especially ingenious innovation.
- There is an obvious need, in a semesterized system, to assess speedily, and to be able to declare and use marks and grades before the beginning of the next semester. At the same time, double marking and moderation (in this case meaning monitoring and checking for consistency) must feature strongly, lest the integrity of the assessment process is challenged. Innovations in assessment which will enable early and valid judgements to be declared are needed.
- The proliferation of various forms of plagiarism, directly using material drawn from web-based sources, or entailing the submission of 'sub-contracted' work, is now recognized as a major problem. Innovations in assessment which validly and reliably preclude the use of copied material, or the delegation of assignment writing to a friend or employee, will be one way of dealing with this problem.
- Greater use of self- and peer assessment has brought many benefits, including deeper and better directed learning (Boud, 1995; Heywood, 2000) and socio-constructivist influences on learning and development (Cowan, 2004b). In most cases we have yet to deal innovatively with the need to train students to judge the work of others objectively and comment constructively in such situations.
- There is greater use of portfolio-based assessment, in disciplines where this is something of a novelty for assessors as well as for students. Especially in relation to personal and professional development, this has increased the time required for assessing, and has raised doubts about reliability and validity. Innovations which could ease these problems would be useful (Heywood, 2000).

- The rapidly growing potential of computer-aided assessment, to test more than recall and understanding, and even to mark essays against model answers, is still in the developmental stage, wherein further innovations will be useful (Brown *et al.*, 1999).

There is thus great scope and need for innovation to explore and consolidate the potential of what is available to us in our assessing, and so to improve alignment in all respects.

Intermediate second thoughts from me – at this point

1. There's no mention of the effect of QAA and other UK quality units on innovations and educational development. Am I seriously implying that my summary has covered these demands? Funnily enough, I think I will indeed be so doing in the next part of this chapter – but I appreciate that the logic of that claim will be rejected if you are one of the many who are critical of the whole QAA operation.
2. I have dwelt here mainly on responses to the pressures and demands which I have identified. Yet, in contrast, many of the innovations I have instanced in earlier chapters were occasioned by a personal desire to change goals, methods and values for the better – without societal or institutional pressures occasioning this. There is clearly a difference in these two types of innovation nowadays. For demand-driven innovation does not need to justify itself, but innovations conceived by the innovator will be challenged from the outset to establish merit and need, which may call upon innovators to be somewhat devious in their tactics in the early stages. Does that difference matter?
3. I have given a great list of challenges with regard to assessment – yet the chapter, and the book, offers few examples of innovation in assessment. Perhaps there is room at some point for a second book?
4. I haven't answered the point in the opening letter concerning the need to involve trained professionals in what is becoming an increasingly demanding business. That leads us on to the next part of this chapter, where I hope that point may be at least partly answered.

First, some general advice to innovators

So far in this chapter, I have tried to explain why we must engage with the need to make changes in our teaching. Now I must settle to the task of offering practical advice about how we can and should tackle this challenge. Before that, however, another noteworthy comment from Smyth (2005):

I realize you give personal advice to the reader, but my immediate reaction after reading the three points with which you open was to think 'Hang on . . . ' there's something that comes before any of this, at least for me. That's to do with being open-minded to innovation.' By that I really just mean deliberately trying to keep abreast of current developments and the claims made for new practices and innovations. This isn't with a view to being driven by 'the latest thing' (jumping on bandwagons without reason is always to be avoided I think), but just so that we're in a better position to be aware of and open to the possibilities.

I'd see this as a pre-cursor to your '1. Pinpoint an aspect of your teaching . . . '. In working with staff I'd say there are definitely some individuals who arrive at point 1 by having been open-minded to innovation in the first place. Although open-mindedness is required beyond the point of an idea being conceived, it does often kick-start an initiative.

From that starting point, then, I offer my three very general, but heartfelt, pieces of advice for the experienced or the inexperienced innovator:

1. Pinpoint an aspect of your teaching where you can see use for an improvement in the standard of learning or the quality of the learning experience. Work towards a goal where you are clear in your mind about what you want to improve, and how you will know if you have been successful. Once you are clear about what such a goal might be, consider the options open to you, weigh up their potential and make a considered judgement about the possibility that your effort will bring adequate return. If what you set out to improve is already seen as a need, institutionally or nationally, you should be able to access support – and suggestions. If not, be prepared to go it alone, for a while at least.

2. Don't make a start unless you have reason to be fairly confident that your intended innovation can be successful for you, and for your students. There are various ways to inform your judgement of feasibility. You may be building on an idea which has already been used to good effect in a different setting or discipline. You may be applying a principle which seems to be well established. Or, if neither of these apply, you may have carried out a tentative pilot, on a small scale and perhaps outwith your own programme, to inform your judgement. It's worthwhile doing your homework on feasibility, and, perhaps even more important, to be seen to have done so. Something which appears risky to your immediate colleagues could well have a rough passage in its early stages. If it looks promising, and is presented in that light, local support or at least lack of opposition is much more likely – and will be something that you will value. Beware the support available from private companies. It can often be a mixed blessing, and one to be taken up only after careful scrutiny.

3. Don't run the risk of rediscovering the wheel. Too many innovators, for one creditable reason or another, work away in relative isolation. Yet we have ready access nowadays to many people, disciplines and sources which can be of great assistance to us. We should not overlook the advantage of discovering and building upon what they can offer us – beginning with our immediate colleagues. It makes sense to discover what they are doing, what works for them, what they can show or how they can guide you. Colleagues are a less formal source of support or advice than most of those listed below. But many of us often end up innovating, or getting ideas for innovations, in response to what we see our peers doing, and as informal networks of like-minded folk begin to form and gather pace in what they are doing.

The more formal possibilities of support for innovation, certainly in the UK and with similar facilities in many other countries, include the following:

- The requirement for institutions to produce learning and teaching strategies – and to report and review progress in achieving targets therein. Any innovation which is in accord with an institutional or faculty strategy can expect and will deserve support and endorsement.
- The creation in most institutions of effective and well-staffed Educational Development Units, of whatever name. Most universities nowadays have units which embody a range of specialists, usually well versed in practice as well as theory. It is increasingly becoming part of the approach to educational development that such units provide non-directive consultancy and partnership, rather than simply running staff development workshops. It is likely that an innovator can obtain assistance of great value from such a unit, without losing autonomy in what has been planned and is later decided.
- The establishment in Britain of subject centres in a support network for learning and teaching. The main role of these centres is to promote development and enhancement. They are already a wonderful source of contacts, ideas, reports of successful innovation and advice.
- The move towards obligatory training and accreditation for newly appointed university teachers, which is gathering momentum. Where such training is not mandatory, it is usually strongly encouraged. In consequence, there is a growing population of 'Young Turks' in our course teams – teachers with a sound knowledge of the basics of learning, teaching and assessment. These are colleagues who can support, advise and prompt us, as we plan an innovation – provided we tell them what we are trying to do! They also, increasingly, ensure a sound hearing for our plans at course team level and above, where what has been called 'the changing of the guard' is seeing the retirement of the old guard, who often resist any change and are sometimes sadly deaf to pedagogical argument.
- The growing engagement in creative curriculum development of specialist staff from libraries and computer centres. Increasingly, the core

concept on which innovations are based comes from some of the striking developments in information science or computing science. Specialists in these and other areas can see needs – and especially possibilities – of which academics may be completely unaware, even if they have identified a need or an inadequacy in the status quo. Often such developments call for the specialist to take a leading role, and even to take up responsibilities for learning and teaching.

- The establishment of Teaching Fellowship schemes, with an increasing emphasis on plans for further work rather than recognition of past achievement. These offer resourcing for innovatory plans and generate constructive comments on proposals.
- The creation in Britain of the Higher Education Academy, with expectations that this will play a leading part in bringing about, and supporting, a professionalism in teaching in higher education. This professionalism will be especially relevant to innovatory efforts.
- An ever-growing institutional engagement with deliberate quality enhancement, through various mechanisms. This must entail encouraging and supporting innovations which promise enhancement.
- The progression in the field of quality assurance towards systems which encourage the evidencing of standards and quality against self-set criteria, thus calling merely for auditing of claims rather than for external evaluations. This strengthens the position of those who innovate, evaluate, and hence have data to table against agreed needs and goals.
- The change in the role of senior staff, to become managers of businesses which work to targets defined by agreed performance indicators. They may arrange backing for innovations which they see as offering them returns related to their plans and targets. (On the other hand, they may lack the background and perception to engage with change in imaginative and farsighted ways!)

Now, some rather more specific and personal advice, to individuals

When I was making preliminary notes for this section, I pushed myself to be utterly realistic. What advice would I truly give a young friend, minded to launch out into educational innovation, and presumably with at least a vague intention in mind? As a result, what follows is worded somewhat colloquially and peremptorily. Here, then, are my detailed suggestions, expanded in each case with a few words of explanation.

1. Attune what you are proposing as closely as possible to learning and teaching strategies

If your university or your faculty or school has a learning and teaching strategy, then find out how well your goal fits in with the plan, and (with integrity) reword what you have in mind accordingly. Find out what is being done at institutional and local level, and make yourself and your intentions known there. Seek whatever support may be available for your effort, if it is in accordance with the plan. This support could be in the form of resource, secondment or assistance from specialist units or personnel. Try to be cautious if your plan appears likely to be hijacked, or seriously amended; but be prepared to modify, in order to enlist support.

2. Find an expert to look up to

Find a person in the field of your intended innovation whose ideals, thinking and track record inspire you. Study all that you can ingather of their written work and their conference and other contributions. If you have the chance to hear them speak, take it. Keep referring back, reading and re-reading, looking for ideas, prompts and above all inspiration.

I have described earlier how, when I first signed up to the concept of learner-directed learning, I soon found myself looking up to Carl Rogers (1969, then 1961). I later read all of his work that I could lay my hands on, and went back to him again and again. For 20 years I pushed myself further and further towards student autonomy, responding all the while to Rogers' writings and arguments. When that led me into exploring self-assessment, I similarly looked to the writings and thinking of David Boud and those whose contributions he ingathered and edited (1981, 1985, 1988). Then, after Tristine Rainier (1980) led me to consider the potential of reflective journaling, I eventually found myself treating Jenny Moon's writings (1999a, 1999b, 2004) as my guiding texts. In terms of computer-based learning, I began from Bonk (Bonk and King, 1998) and moved on to find Garrison and Anderson (2003) as the writers to whom I currently wish to return. These all have been, and still are, great influences on me, although I never feel inclined or obliged to follow them slavishly. You can benefit by finding your expert to look up to – and I hope you may do that from your perusal of Chapter 11.

3. Find kindred spirits to work with

In the spirit of socio-constructivist learning and development, it makes great sense to find and work with a kindred spirit – someone with similar priorities and similar ability, though probably in a different situation or even a different discipline; and with usefully complementary ideas. My first such partner was a chemist, with whom I felt almost confident enough to experiment in the teaching of materials science (Cowan and McConnell, 1967). I had useful partnerships with several engineers, as my publications show (Cowan, Morton and Bolton, 1973; Cowan and Morton, 1973; Brohn and Cowan, 1977; Cowan, Fordyce and Asfari, 1987). In staff development, and more besides, I gained enormously from working with a metallurgist (Cowan and Harding, 1986). However, my most productive partnership, as far as innovations were concerned, was with a classicist (Cowan and George, 1989, 1992a, 1992b, 1993, 1997; George and Cowan, 1999a, 1999b).

In such partnerships, both members have a colleague with whom to discuss and refine plans; a partner with whom to review the first tentative experiments; a person whose interest leads them to unearth what the other may have missed in the literature or elsewhere, or whose background enables them to teach or to explain. If they are in a different department or institution from our own, then in assisting them on their own patch with something new we can sometimes take risks to good effect in respect of our own development – without the possibility of losing face with our own students or colleagues.

Such partners need to be of roughly our own fighting weight or calibre, so that the collaboration is genuinely one of two peers, working in harness together. While each will look up to the other, neither should justifiably feel inferior or indebted when taking something from the other. There should be traffic of that sort in both directions – although we all tend to be more aware of what we take than of what we give.

4. Go into partnership with your students

Even once you have progressed beyond pilots, you cannot responsibly take the great risk of adversely affecting a part of your students' education. So tell them what you have in mind and what you hope they will take from it as a benefit for their studies. Take their advice if possible when shaping up your plan. Reassure them that you have a safety net in place, should the innovation prove ineffective – so that they will not lose out. Make provision for them to provide immediate feedback on their experiences, and to suggest immediate and long-term improvements. Involve them in the first evaluations, and even later in conference presentations (Agnew and Cowan, 1986; Cowan *et al.*, 1999), perhaps presenting papers in which you have had no hand (Boyd *et al.*, 1984).

If your innovation involves something unusual, then you will be aware that you cannot inform yourself about the nature of the learning experience you have created, or the immediate learning, without the help of those for whom this is happening. Beyond these somewhat negative motivations, I would stress as more important to me the firm belief that learning and teaching should be a partnership. That is a belief which has underlain my own innovating for 40 years, and of which I will write in the final chapter.

5. Negotiate appropriate endorsement (and engagement) from your line manager

Some line managers will wish to know no more than what you intend to do, what you hope to achieve and what support you wish from them. Others will look for regular and moderately detailed reports of progress. A few may wish to be directly involved, even if only to 'get the feel' of what you are doing.

At every stage in the process, you could be thwarted if your line manager has doubts, feels bypassed or does not support you when colleagues raise criticisms in the mid-development phase. Your line manager may be either enthusiastic, initially convinced and willing to give you licence – or dubious and downright unsupportive. It is essential to be aware of their position, whatever it is, in order to operate accordingly, to keep them as informed as they would wish, to optimize their endorsement and support – and to have negotiated and confirmed your goals with them. (See Further second thoughts, point 7, page 156.)

6. Build up a small circle of 'critical friends' – and use them

Find people who share your interests and priorities, are working in similar areas and are so far away (geographically or otherwise) that they can hardly work with you directly as kindred spirits. You may already know them. You may meet them at conferences or workshops after you start innovating. They may read one of your papers and email you. You may only meet them in the VLE. Tentatively at first, invite them to offer constructive comment – on a plan, an evaluation or an incident. If and as they may make the same sort of request of you, check that they are willing to extend the relationship, and to make use of it for mutual benefit.

I have perhaps eight or ten such critical friends within my email address list. One is someone I haven't met in the flesh for over 20 years; one was a student on an innovative course of mine and opted to keep in touch; one is someone who is so unlike me, in style and educational position, that his views are as useful to me as are mine, he tells me, to him. One is a Greek PhD student in another university who sends me exciting papers which he has found about the VLE and e-moderation. He invites my thoughts on them, and we discuss deeply and at length electronically – a process from which I learn a lot, but which he professes is of use to him, too. One I save for important advice about things which matter most to me – and he never fails me. One is a former close colleague and kindred spirit, now retired and with whom I no longer work. I shall seek her views on the draft of this chapter before closing my 'second thoughts' – because I'm conscious that the writing style and direction has changed from what has gone before.

7. Evaluate ahead of external expectations

You will, I hope, wish to evaluate formatively, seeking scope and ideas for improvement, before you evaluate summatively and judge the effectiveness of your consolidated innovation. But the world is impatient about innovations. Your development will come up for scrutiny before you have had time to refine it in successive iterations, or to carry out a thorough summative evaluation of a reasonably finished effort. Make sure that you are ahead of time. Despite the imperfections of rushed summative evaluations in these circumstances, ensure that you can provide as comprehensive an objective judgement as possible *before* you are asked for it.

Require of yourself that any evaluation is objective and rigorous. Identify from an early stage in your planning what will constitute success, and what parameters that will be judged by. Specify then, not later, the sources of data for the evaluation. Arrange for data to be ingathered, independently if possible, and analysed against your criteria.

Throughout all of this, ensure that you have at hand relevant analysed data which you can offer management and colleagues – at every stage. Link this explicitly to the goals you have negotiated with your line manager and to the university's learning and teaching strategies, especially if you anticipate problems higher up the institutional structure. When what emerges is positive, and supports the value of what you are doing, ensure that it is available and can be offered proactively, without your coming across as a fussy obsessive. Probably that means tabling brief summaries, with further details readily available, if and when you are asked for them.

8. Ask more of yourself than is asked of the status quo

Critics will do just that. They make demands of an innovation which they do not make of the status quo. You won't change them, I'm afraid. I recall the time when I was embarking upon resource-based learning. I was often asked to speak about my Learning Unit (Cowan *et al.*, 1973). I could almost guarantee there would be a small man in the front row, poised belligerently to ask, 'What proportion of your students don't like this way of learning?' I would reply that I knew the answer, and would happily share it with him – provided *he* told *me* what proportion of *his* students didn't like *his* way of teaching. He usually just became angry, because he saw no occasion to challenge or even check the status quo.

You should prepare and table evaluations which are more rigorous in approach than the methods used elsewhere, and which preferably compare the outcomes you have enhanced with those in the status quo. Then let that comparison speak for you.

9. Publicize

Go canny with making bold claims about what you are setting out to do. Wait until you've done something, before you say much – other than to close colleagues and critical friends. But as soon as you have some evaluated results, find a way to publicize – even if you don't yet have enough for a paper. Mention what you've achieved, when that is appropriate, in an institutional or national workshop. Take an opportunity to refer to your results when contributing to discussions, written or oral, of papers by others. Keep it brief; let those who are interested make contact and ask to be told more.

Expect this kind of publicity to bring you contacts, perhaps potential critical friends, useful suggestions, questions which make you think, awareness of some aspects of what you are doing which will trouble others and so on.

10. Publish

Offer to run a workshop or seminar in your university, with a short support paper. Contribute papers, or better still workshops, at relevant conferences. Publish 'pot-boilers' in lightweight but widely read publications. If what you've done makes good news, consider the local press. Join a relevant mailbase, and look for the opportunity to make a brief and apt contribution which will prompt anyone who is interested to get in touch with you. Aim, in time, to get sound papers in refereed journals.

Publishing gives your work status, exposes it to scrutiny, brings you contacts and establishes reputation for you in your own university and department. It also pushes you to analyse and evaluate, and to see both scope for enhancement and gaps in your reasoning and planning so far.

11. Accept your limitations when at variance with out-of-date senior staff

Many of the old guard who remain are now in senior positions, occupying influential posts. They are sometimes difficult or impossible to shift. Worse still, they may deem themselves able to conceive major proposals, which emerge without pedagogical foundation. Then, at a late stage, they may invite you to apply an educational gloss. If the central gatekeepers in an institution don't even know what is missing in their planning, someone coming in with an idea for innovation is going to meet with blank faces. And someone who declares it impossible to apply the desired gloss, as an afterthought, will simply be regarded as incompetent or obstructive. In these circumstances, it's wise to advise or suggest, but to make it gently clear in your wording that the decision to which you defer is theirs, and by implication that the consequences of any failure (in due course) will be theirs, also.

When I asked Keith Smyth for his thoughts and experience about dealing with the barriers to innovation which you will meet, he responded:

> What about stressing the need for the practitioners to ask themselves 'What could stand in the way of a successful innovation?' and 'What would I need to do to reduce this risk?' I was thinking here about institutional and personal barriers of all kinds, with types of advice to include:
>
> * 'anticipate and be prepared to address needs of those senior to you';
> * 'attend relevant training events to develop the skills you will need but don't have';
> * 'identify and enlist help of relevant support staff from the outset';
> * 'can you do anything to free up time to work on larger scale innovations?';
> * 'can you make a case for your innovation being of wider benefit to the school/faculty/professional community?'.
>
> I realise that some of these issues are addressed or implied within the points you've given, but it felt to me that they could perhaps be more explicitly stated as it seems quite a critical concern.

Point made, and taken. Of course, all that I've written here so far assumes successful progress towards the development and establishment of a successful innovation. But what if it goes wrong? What if something already well established elsewhere doesn't transfer; or if local politics amongst students or staff lead to rejection of your scheme; or if you haven't really anticipated problems for which, when they emerge, you cannot find solutions? What then? How should you cope with failure?

I'm assuming that you've taken reasonable precautions, along the lines I've suggested at several points in this text – piloting, building in safety nets and taking the students with you, for a start. But it can still go wrong. And you will find that those who are willing to share experience and advice tend to clam up if the topic of failure arises in conversation, or if it is something on which you seek advice. I recall that a refereed journal intimated editions in which writers would contribute on lessons they had learnt from failures. They weren't overwhelmed with responses – and I cannot recall any feedback on my own contributions, which were frank and dealt with real mistakes and failures (Cowan, 1984c, 1989). I responded recently to a call for papers on the problems teachers have been having with online learning. My paper was slight, coming from restricted experience of innovations in that area. Quickly it was promoted from a tentative contribution to an opening chapter (Cowan, 2006). Failure, I suggest, is not far from being a taboo subject. But it behoves me to close with some advice regarding that possibility.

Keith Smyth (2005) comments supportively that:

> However well prepared a practitioner might be, in doing anything innovative or new for the first time, some things will go better than anticipated, and just as surely some things will go less well or perhaps not work at all. In instances where this happens, personally I believe it's important to view these as positive opportunities to reflect, understand why, and refine for next time. It's a message I stress in working with staff who are trying to innovate online, and it seems to not only make them feel more at ease in what they are trying to do, but maybe also be a wee bit more philosophical in their approach and attitude. This isn't to say they stop fearing failure, mind you! Just that they are a little more constructive if they find themselves needing to accept 'little failures'.

Perhaps this is the one point on which Keith and I differ slightly. I have suffered from the backlash from one or two modest innovations which didn't work out as I had expected. My advice on the prospect of failure is therefore perhaps unduly blunt and cynical. I'd say:

- Avoid failure! Don't do anything in the formal course provision until you have good reason to know that it will work with these students, with your teaching and in this situation.
- Cover yourself when piloting, to ensure student support for a pilot which they see as being in their interest, and from which they can opt out without damage to their progress.
- Retain your confidence by differentiating between public and private judgements. Let the public, summative ones be in comparisons to the status quo – did you improve on learning or the learning experience? Keep your more important formative judgements to yourself and close colleagues, privately – did we achieve what we set out to do?

Generalization

The success or failure of an innovation will owe as much to the tactics followed and the practicalities of the chosen interactions within the institution as it will to its merits.

Further second thoughts (third thoughts?)

1. Much of the innovative work for which I was responsible at the Open University in Scotland arose when I floated an idea, recruited a team of four to six willing tutors and handed the idea over for fleshing out and subsequent action. The model advanced in this chapter doesn't seem to cover that approach, in which a team was recruited, prompted and briefed. Is that not a noteworthy omission?

2. When Lewis Elton heard that Alan Harding and I were to collaborate on staff development in Iraq (many years ago), he remarked that, 'The two great individualists of British staff development plan to work together. I'd love to be a fly on the wall when they try to make that work.' Nowadays, much educational development is centred upon teams. To what extent have my views in this chapter reflected the approach and experience of someone who works better on his own, or in a pair? A great deal, I suspect – though I doubt if the principles are any different.

3. There's no mention of active experimentation in this chapter, from start to finish; and no mention of which of the models in Chapter 4 the apprentice innovator will be learning from. What does that imply? Perhaps that innovation is inherently active experimentation, and that the planning of it leads into an experience on which reflective evaluation takes place? Or is that wishful thinking?

4. I've said nothing about the MLE. Some writers expect this to be as significant for development as the VLE. I confess that the omission here is simply due to my lack of working experience of an MLE. I dislike offering second-hand advice. What effects from the development of the MLE could affect the thoughts in this chapter?

5. I've written quite a lot on evaluation and comparisons, and have included more on this topic in Chapter 10. But many existing arrangements, especially for student support, have not been evaluated in a way which lends itself to objective comparisons. And any attempt to evaluate what has been done up until now is likely to be resented by those responsible, who will suspect that we collect data about their efforts because we propose to criticize. It's difficult to see how to avoid that hazard. Changing for the better is, after all, a form of criticism. We can't deny that we intend to compare – but we needn't parade it. How can we make these comparisons which we need, without being regarded as critical of our colleagues?

6. I haven't mentioned dealing with the problems which arise when validation, review and internal institutional processes are subjective in forming their judgements of innovatory provision. Other than my suggestions about anticipating the need for objective evaluations, I am afraid I should admit that I have sometimes found it helpful to follow the principle that 'what the eye doesn't see the heart needn't grieve

over'. But what complications can arise if we beaver away quietly, making changes which will eventually have to become public knowledge?

7. I have long and often taken much comfort from Machiavelli's advice:

> There is nothing more difficult to take in hand, more perilous to conduct, than to take a lead in the introduction of a new order of things. Because the innovation has for enemies all those who have done well under the old conditions, and lukewarm defenders in those who may do well under the new.

(Niccolò Machiavelli, *The Prince*, Book VI)

Maybe you and I can find it possible to take comfort and encouragement from that. But comfort alone will not enable us to prevail when our moves for worthwhile development are opposed by senior staff with engrained prejudices and little acquaintance with what is happening, respected and expected in the processes of higher education today. I'm afraid I've offered no magic recipe for the situations that arise, even today, in which progress is blocked, unreasonably, by those who are senior to us and who consider that they know best. How can we reason to good effect with those in power who are unreasonable and upon whose endorsement we depend?

8. I recall one newly appointed head of department who told me, firmly, 'I don't know anything about what you are doing, but I know that I disapprove of it.' In the face of such lack of sound and uninformed reasoning, the unattractive options include accepting defeat, changing jobs or finding a way to carry on, privately. One other, more attractive, option is to work towards contriving external scrutiny of the practices of the Luddite. The head of department I mentioned lasted three years in post.

Dear John

Well, we seem to have moved on now, from innovative activities involving reflection to educational innovations in general. In a way, that's fine by me, yet thinking back over the many examples you have given, I find myself apprehensive, even when I restrict myself to those which I could see myself adapting and trying out.

There must be many times in innovating when we don't anticipate everything as we should, and require to make adjustments and even changes. How do we make sure that we pick up such points early in the process? There must be occasions when we will be subject to detailed questioning, by colleagues, reviewers and external examiners, all seeking confirmation that what we have done is effective for the students, and not overly demanding.

You put great stress in the previous chapter on the need to evaluate, to do so objectively, and to have data ready to table. I could see the importance of that. I can see that we need to evaluate formatively if we are to refine and progress our innovations through successive iterations of a systematic process. And I can see that we need summative evaluations to inform the self-evaluations which are demanded of us in annual and periodic reviews, and audit. But I cannot yet work out what I would have to do, in order to live up to the expectations you outlined.

How would you advise me to go about evaluation?

10

How Can Such Innovations Be Evaluated?

Introduction

I should warn you that I'm not really going to answer this question as it is posed. For I feel strongly that innovations should be evaluated in just the same way as any other, established, learning and teaching activities. So I shall write here about how learning and teaching activities in general should be evaluated. Some of my examples, then, will be based upon innovations in respect of reflective learning and development; others, upon what are well-established methods of teaching.

In all of this, please remember the distinction between formative and summative. Personally, I would much rather have the opportunity to benefit from formative evaluation before I am judged summatively. That is because I have naturally always desired to receive feedback which will suggest to me the need and scope for enhancement, with opportunity for me to do something about that – *before* I or anyone else reaches any summative judgement on the efficacy of what I have been doing. Thus the examples which I have set out here usually begin as an enquiry seeking data to inform formative evaluations. Nevertheless, most of them will often also generate data which can be used in summative evaluations.

Hence this chapter centres upon ten examples for predominantly – but not exclusively – formative evaluation. I suppose that, collectively, there are as many examples of innovation in evaluation as of evaluation of innovation. Roughly speaking, in the first five of these, my evaluative interest is with the nature of the learning experience; and in the remainder, with the immediate learning in the activity concerned. A few other brief examples follow, after which I offer a generalization, and then some second thoughts.

First, though, I wish to comment on what, as far as my personal practice is concerned, is the (almost) *non*-example of questionnaires. For these have created many problems for me over the years, and have generated grave reservations on my part, whose origins I shall illustrate.

Example 10.1: Questionnaires

In my early days as a university lecturer, I encountered what seemed an excellent Australian questionnaire, which enabled students to provide feedback on the lectures they had been given, by ticking boxes and grading qualities on five-point (Likert) scales. I had copies made, explained my purpose to my students and issued the sheets one morning to one of my third year classes. The forms were to be completed anonymously and returned before the students left the lecture theatre. I collected the piles of forms from the ends of the rows, and took them home – to read them privately.

The feedback was reasonably encouraging – until I came to one form which puzzled me. Like the majority of the returns I had read up to that point, this one informed me that I had mannerisms, and that they were sometimes slightly amusing. But happily, like the others, it reassured me that my mannerisms were not really distracting. Then it volunteered an additional comment, in handwriting which fortunately I did not recognize, to the effect that 'He eats chalk'. This struck me as a facetious and unhelpful comment – until I came to another in similar form, and yet another which offered much the same feedback. It was clear that these students had not been sitting near to each other, so I was apparently reading independent comments, with the same remarkable message. It was remarkable in substance because I knew that I hate even the feeling of chalk on my fingers, which at that time I frequently encountered as I lectured, since chalkboards were still in use. I would definitely abhor the contact of chalk with my lips or my tongue. Clearly, however, I had a mannerism which made me *appear* as if I was eating chalk – a mannerism of which I had no sooner learned than I immediately desired to eradicate. And so in its place I quickly developed a curious and evasive mannerism. Whenever I was conscious of my hand moving from my side, and up towards my face, I whipped it smartly down to the vertical position again. That noteworthy and idiosyncratic flailing action was not, I submit, a valuable outcome from this questionnaire enquiry.

Nevertheless, I went on using questionnaires – even after I was well into resource-based learning and seldom in the position of speaking to a complete class. However, in Scotland it has long been the custom that the professor lectures to the first year. Consequently, despite my commitment to individualized learning, I was called on to take six lectures at the beginning of the first year, with a class who naturally did not know me, and for whom I had to introduce one of the main curriculum topics. At the end of my six lectures, I took some time to issue (as in the previous example) a simple questionnaire on lecturing, which was again completed by ticking boxes or by circling one number on a five-point scale. Unfortunately, I didn't allow quite enough time for this operation. As a result, only a third of the class managed to complete the last section – which dealt with my use of the overhead projector. However, from this part-sample I was delighted to learn that my acetates had been clear, that I had not obscured the image with my body, that I had left the acetates on the projector for long enough to allow the class to assimilate them and that these acetates contained neither too much nor too little information. It will not surprise you that I was pleased with this feedback – although it will perhaps surprise you to know *why* I was pleased. I was pleased because, as the sceptic I have explicitly declared myself to be about the reliability of questionnaire returns, I now had good reason to endorse in public my private scepticism. For I had not used the overhead projector once during these six lectures.

Please bear with me a little longer as I relate one further example in justification of my distrust of questionnaires. It concerns a situation way back in 1971, when the Cement and Concrete Association first put on sale sets of slides and lecture notes, for use in universities and colleges. I decided to assemble tape-slide sequences using these slides, and based my commentary heavily on the published notes. I arranged for my tape-slide sequences to be viewed by small groups of students, and prompted them to engage in informal group discussion once the programmes had finished.

As the students emerged from their group rooms, I asked them for their feedback. It was strongly positive. They stressed with enthusiasm that this was a good way to learn, and that I should do more on the same lines. They were happy to complete a brief questionnaire which I gave them, and in so doing warmly affirmed their informal verdict. Thereafter, I gave them a simple little test – to be completed anonymously. I explained that this was a 90/90 test – one in whose ten questions I would expect 90 per cent of the class to score nine correct answers from ten questions. With obvious confidence and optimism, my students sat down to tackle the test, returning the papers five minutes later with long faces. 'John, I know I should be able to answer these questions – they're quite fair, and the sequence *did* cover them. But I can't remember many of the answers.' The evidence of the test paper did not coincide with the evidence of the questionnaire, nor with the 'gut reaction' of the students. Since then I've never trusted someone who tells me about their judgements based on gut reactions, unless they can tell me how they distinguish between gut reactions and indigestion.

I caution you to find a moral in these three anecdotes. In my experience, questionnaires can be a useful instrument of enquiry, provided we are aware of their limitations. Questionnaires will often suggest questions which should be asked and pursued, or issues which should be explored. But, on their own and without corroboration, they can yield misleading or incorrect, although sincere, advice – because they tend to be reports of opinions, which require to be substantiated, rather than of facts on which we can rely.

It is also important that we analyse, and do not merely summarize, questionnaire returns. I recall a recent visit overseas, when as an auditor for the Quality Assurance Agency (QAA) I was auditing the quality assurance of courses offered overseas by UK universities. Our team visited one centre, where the UK university claimed (rightly, as we found) to offer an experience equivalent to that which the students would have enjoyed had they studied in the UK. I had noted the very positive endorsement of the experience in the module questionnaire returns. I asked if I might have sight of the forms. The person responsible, understandably, told me indignantly that these had been summarized accurately. I assured her that I did not doubt that fact, but that comments on such forms often told an interesting story. Grudgingly, she drew out the forms and passed them to me. Quickly I settled in on two modules with commendably high scores of around 4.1 on a five-point scale, for almost every feature queried. One, under each heading, had scored mainly 4s, some 5s and some 3s. The other had scored mainly 4s, a fair number of 5s and 3s, and a notable though small clutch of 1s. I enquired what had led that minority of students to be so disgruntled with this module. She hadn't noticed this aspect of the returns – and so no one had asked the students to expand. It's important that we not only summarize but analyse questionnaire returns, and act accordingly.

The great strength of professionally designed questionnaire studies as a research method comes when they are used after sound qualitative research has been undertaken, so that we know enough about individual experience and can encapsulate that in the wording and choice of the questions whose answers we require and will use. The quantitative coverage of whole populations or large samples of students then allows us to judge what weight to give to each of the diverse reactions to our teaching, and provides guidance for change. Questionnaires can be a helpful tool in formative evaluations under these conditions.

Example 10.2: A 'letter' to the tutor or course team

I have found it helpful to use less than an hour of class time towards the end of a semester to arrange for the class, in private, to draft the bullet points for a 'letter' to me, or to the course team. I suggest a couple of introductory sentences for such a letter and recruit a student to act as clerk, writing on the whiteboard in full view. Next, I invite students, first in buzz groups and then in plenary, to assemble a list of bullet points of 'advice' (with perhaps accompanying comments) to those who may be revising the module for delivery in the following year. I then consider the list, with my colleagues, and provide feedback to the class group on decisions for change which we have taken, or not taken – and why or why not. That has worked well for me, in generating an agenda of points for consideration – leading with aspects of the course which have clearly created problems for students in the year of delivery.

Working in the Virtual Learning Environment (VLE), I have adjusted this approach somewhat. After the module results have been declared, I approach perhaps three students with whom I seem to have developed a fairly resonant virtual relationship. I ask them for their advice and then summarize it – in their colloquial words, but anonymously. I take that summary electronically to the full class group, asking them for their endorsement or rejection of the various points – and for anything else relevant which they wish to tell me.

The items in such letters of advice tend to originate from weaknesses, and hence mainly suggest needs or possibilities for enhancement. They can generate many specific suggestions for improvement which I welcome and act upon. It was from this source that I confirmed the effectiveness of talking about 'headings' instead of 'criteria' in introducing the practice of self-assessment. Similarly, it was from one such letter that I learnt that a minority of my students were strongly irritated when I used the form '(s)he' in documents on screen.

Example 10.3: 'Taking in each other's washing'

I devised this method when I was undertaking an evaluative study of 'good practice' in telephone conference call tutorials at the Open University in Scotland (George, 2001). It has since been used more extensively in evaluating tutorial practice in the OU's HELD project (George, 2001; Cowan *et al.*, 2004). The arrangement is quite simple:

1. Recruit perhaps eight tutors, from various disciplines.
2. Arrange them in pairs, across disciplines if possible.
3. Recruit perhaps two students per tutorial (or seminar) group, to be contacted immediately after a tutorial. Advise them of the main questions they will be asked. These might be, 'What was the most important learning or advance in learning for you, in this tutorial?' and 'What was the most effective thing the tutor did to help your learning?'
4. Tutors should prepare to give thought, probably post hoc, to what they hope would be the students' answers to these questions.
5. After the tutorial, the enquiring partner telephones first one student, then the other, to pose the intimated questions and tease out the answers with relevant follow-up questions. The enquirer summarizes, confirming with the student that they have no objection to these responses being reported.
6. The enquirer telephones the tutor, asks for the answers to the tutor's version of the questions, and then reports what came from the two students. There need be no discussion at this stage, unless the tutor so wishes.
7. The tutor may, subsequently, decide to check out the feedback with other students in the group.
8. After perhaps two paired enquiries, in which each tutor is once a tutor and once an enquirer, pairs are rearranged.
9. The full group meets to report and discuss outcomes.

In my experience (Cowan and George, 1997), this approach generates no endurable findings of a general nature – for it feeds data into situations which are constantly in a state of flux. Its main impact is in personal development of the teachers' abilities. Tutors identify ideas for their own development from the feedback from their students, and in the practice of those of whose teaching they enquire. The plenary discussion in stage 9 above is not so much a summary of findings as an enthusiastic report of particular developments in progress.

I was not going to quote examples here, because the changes are essentially individual rather than generalizable. But perhaps I should instance that, in respect of my own known practice in chat room discussions, it was from this feedback source that I learnt to try to restrict myself to one-line messages – and to accommodate positively two or three threads of discussion occurring in the one multi-tasking chatroom conversation.

Example 10.4: Talk-aloud protocols

One of my colleagues, in a Department of Mathematics, developed some computer-assisted learning materials which set out to consolidate meaningful conceptual understanding on the part of first year learners. That understanding was then to be applied in problem-solving situations, with the aim of further developing the appropriate abilities. He was anxious to find out the impact his materials and their presentation were having on the students' learning.

I arranged to meet with trios of students, over and after an informal buffet lunch, in his small staff room which contained a PC. When the students were ready to work, we booted up the computer and set the program in action. One student sat at the keyboard, and began to work with the learning materials in the normal way – but at my request she talked out her thoughts aloud, in a running commentary, as she did so. I had briefly modelled the type of commentary I hoped to hear. The other two students, standing one at each of her shoulders, were told firmly that they were not to initiate discussion. They were charged by me to ask her questions if they needed to do so, so that they should be able to carry on, just as she was doing, if she were called away to the telephone. They were not to discuss her actions, nor to compare what she was doing with the ways in which they themselves would have tackled the tasks had they been on their own. They were simply to ask questions so that they could empathize with her approach. I explained that, in so doing, they would incidentally extract further information from her about *why* she did things, as well as about *how* she did them.

After a little while, they changed positions. One of the men sat in the chair, and worked on the keyboard on new material, while the woman and the other man questioned from the other positions, and operated in the same way as hitherto. And so too, and in due course, with the third student problem-solver. Thereafter, we engaged in a four-way discussion. This brought me into the picture for the first time, as I had so far been standing somewhat detached from all of this, unobtrusively making my notes of what they had been doing and describing to each other.

I summed up what I had heard of the processes followed by each of the three students, checked these summaries for accuracy and completeness, and with the students' help compared and contrasted their three approaches. I tried at the same time to transfer what I was extracting into a generalized form, which I eventually reported back to the author of the computer software. He responded to the feedback accordingly, and in his own way – by finding out how many students in the class would identify with the points I had reported to him.

Much of the illuminative data I obtained confirmed my colleague's previous design decisions or influenced future ones. Some findings, however, revealed striking mismatches between his assumptions and expectations on the one hand, and the reality of student preference or performance on the other. This was particularly so in respect of the range of individual responses and differences, and of the sometimes astonishing manipulation of the resource by the more able students – to good effect.

I have used this method on several occasions when evaluating computer-assisted learning, in subject areas from economics to languages. It has informatively revealed ways of learning which have at times astounded the creators of the resource materials. It reported in one setting the widespread and intense loathing by students for carefully chosen screen colour schemes, which had not until then been criticized. And on another, it identified the common evasion of sequences which called for mouse/keyboard/mouse operations. In my own case, it led me to appreciate the needs of the minority of my learners who chose to begin their learning from the end, and not at the 'beginning'. In my experience, the talk-aloud protocol often generates information which leads the teacher to remark, 'I'd never have imagined that. I'm glad I know. I know what I'm going to do about it.'

My most extensive use of something akin to this approach (and nearer to the purists' view of talk-aloud protocols) came during a period when I was perturbed about the shallow nature of my students' learning, and the inappropriate demands of traditional assessment, in a well-established part of the civil engineering curriculum (Cowan, 1975, 1977, 1980a, 1983). It had long worried me that students of engineering might learn little more in some of their numerate subjects than to carry out calculations, of whose meaning and significance they are really unaware. One simple example of this is apparent in exercises which involve the calculation of what are called second moments of area (Figure 10.1). It is possible, and indeed convenient, to set out these calculations in a tabular form, which virtually eliminates the need for thought. Hence, given a cross-sectional area which can be divided into geometrical shapes having positive or negative area, the position of the centroid and the magnitude of the second moment of area can be calculated methodically, and with no use of, or dependence on, understanding of what is being done.

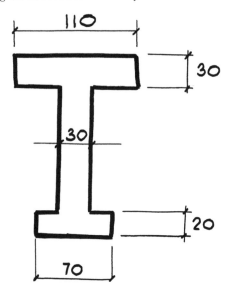

Determine for this section:
   a. the position of the centroid
   b. the value of I_{xx}

Fig 10.1   A problem calling for an algorithmic approach

Some time ago, almost by chance, I invented a style of test question which set out to assess the acquisition of the qualitative and conceptual understanding that I valued, in this context as indeed in others (Cowan, 1982). This understanding had not hitherto featured explicitly in the traditional hidden curriculum, as conveyed to students by assessment in the form of the numerical type of question and task I have just described. I now presented students with a number of familiar shapes, with certain dimensions in common. None of the shapes had dimensions given for them, though sometimes I used algebraic symbols to indicate relative values. My questions called for students to place sections in ascending order of second moment of area, where that was possible, without doing so by carrying out calculations (Figure 10.2). It would have been an appallingly complex process to calculate and compare positions of centroids and second moments of area using these algebraic symbols – and any others which the student might choose to add to my diagrams.

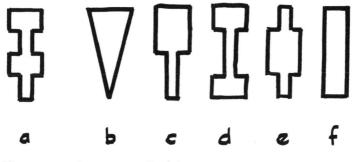

These sections are all of the same area.

Where possible, arrange them in *ascending order* of second moment of area about their xx axis.

Give reasons for the order chosen, or for your inability to place any section within it.

Fig 10.2 A problem calling for understanding of a concept

In the early stages of my enquiries, I paid a nominal fee to student volunteers to provide recorded talk-aloud accounts of their wrestling with the problems. These confirmed powerfully that the task had to be attempted by reasoning, and by using grasp of concepts which had not been called for in the traditional 'number-crunching' questions. The protocols astounded, and in this case pleased, me in revealing and confirming the extent to which the innovatory form of assessment aligned with deep and valued curriculum goals. However, talk-aloud protocols, in my experience, have more often revealed to teachers a serious mismatch between their expectations of the learning experience and the reality of what happens there for learners.

Example 10.5: Interpersonal Process Recall (IPR)

I have already reported (Example 5.6) the reaction of the student in the experiment where I tried to use audio rather than video recordings to prompt recall of thoughts and feelings during a telephone conference call. It was hard work to extract in such enquiries much that was of formative use to the tutors, and I would not encourage anyone to emulate my efforts. Working as I did by telephone, I missed out on the information given by the changing facial impressions of the subject; and sound quality, first recorded and then replayed over the telephone, suffered as well. However, there were still several striking and useful findings. The most general of these were (again) the mismatches between commonly accepted 'folk wisdom' (what was widely accepted as 'good practice') in telephone tuition (George, 1983) and the (sometimes positive) reactions of students when model practice was not followed.

One example of that concerned the 'principle' which was declared and explained at that time to all who were training to offer telephone conference calls – 'Don't deliver long monologues!' (George, 1983). Yet in two of my enquiries, tutor monologues had contributed greatly to student learning and reassurance. In one case, the longish contributions were valued as organizers, then to be dissected by the students in the next parts of the call where the tutor did little but ask short, facilitative questions, and the discussions deepened understanding. The other noteworthy finding was the predominance (see again Example 5.6) of affective learning needs, whereas the same students, when attending face to face tutorials in the same courses with the same tutors, wished the greater focus to be on cognitive learning needs, which they had identified, in advance, without prompting. Once again, IPR revealed surprising and thought-provoking mismatches between the reactions of students and the tutors' assumptions and expectations, which could be confirmed in more general enquiries with a wider sample group.

Example 10.6: Drafting a letter to next year's students

(See also Example 7.3.)

On the face of it, this example is very much like Example 10.2. Certainly it is set up in much the same way, with just one important difference. In this case, the buzz groups and class plenary are asked to assemble bullet points for a letter of advice to the next group of students to take this class. And the writers have the teacher's assurance that their letter, once they have edited it, will go unaltered to the next class group. It may, however, be accompanied by a note from the teacher or course team, indicating any changes they are making as a result of this and other feedback.

The letter serves two purposes. First, it establishes that the teacher genuinely wishes incoming students to be advised by those who have gone before. Second, it provides valuable information about the difficulties, misunderstandings and pressures which the current cohort have encountered. These letters, then, tend to concentrate on difficulties and problems, which are usually accepted by students as almost immutable; whereas the letter to the course team or tutor focuses on matters where the class feel change and improvement are possible.

As an example of the type of data generated by a letter to incoming students, I instance use of this method of evaluation after the first run of a module on Personal Development Planning, based upon workshop activity which was new both to the students and to my colleague. We learnt of the difficulties encountered by students during the introduction to collaborative group working (as in Example 5.1), which had had the purpose of fostering immediate learning and development.

Example 10.7: Observing and noting facts

I made a major change in the way I presented a design task to a first year class. For years I had used an activity where groups were called upon to plan, fabricate and test a balsawood or spaghetti model, according to a different brief each year (Example 7.6). I had worried that, in the past, groups had not tackled this task according to what I saw as 'good design practice'. Despite the advice and best endeavours of myself and my colleagues, our students had spent little time in conceiving a range of options, or in critically comparing their strengths and weaknesses. They had not even devoted much effort to an analysis of the brief, out of which should have emerged their ideas for successful designs. Analysis – in my judgement – is a neglected skill in engineering education, and in practice (Cowan, 1981a, 1986b). In this instance, rather than analysing, my students had immediately rushed, like Gadarene swine who believe themselves at the forefront of progress, into an ill-conceived plan and the construction of an ineffective structure.

So I changed the task. Previously, the students had been given a brief, and asked to design and fabricate a structure which would be tested to destruction – with marks awarded for the ratio of failure load to weight of structure. This was in direct competition with the models produced by groups of fellow students. But my new task, in truly Machiavellian style, required them to produce *two* models which satisfied the brief, but which were to be distinct and so had to embody features which were significantly different. They were told that they would be awarded their group mark according to the performance of the *poorer* of their two models. Thus, I hoped, they would be encouraged to analyse the brief, and to think about how to generate two competitive and distinct responses to it. They should then act in a manner more akin to the process which is followed by a thoughtful designer, for whom analysis and creative consideration of competitive options precede any decision for action.

I evaluated the effects of this change pragmatically – but validly, I believe – from observations of behaviour. I carefully, but I hope unobtrusively, observed and recorded certain aspects of my students' behaviour, in comparison with that of students in previous years. Two stark discrepancies were immediately apparent. The first was that teams now spent a much greater amount of time than hitherto in preparatory thinking and discussion –

before they reached their decision about the models they would build. The second was the greater amount of time which they spent in comparing options, before they decided on their final choices. (This was a subset of the first time measured, of course.) It was then my subjective view that the teams produced better models in consequence.

This impression prompted me to enter teams of first year students to compete in a prestigious annual structural modelling competition, for students from the universities throughout Scotland. In the national competition (which on this occasion was for a model retaining wall – something quite new to my students), I observed that the able students from the third and fourth years of the other universities had decided on their model form, and had commenced fabrication, within 10–15 minutes. After 40 minutes, my first year students were still discussing and deliberating. At that point a colleague from a neighbouring university came across to point out to me, tactfully, how lost and out of their depth my unfortunate young students obviously were, and how embarrassed they would be as the evening progressed. He suggested we should find an easy way out for them. His worries had been compounded when he noted the time which they spent 'ponderously' deliberating over the options which they had identified as being open to them, once these had eventually emerged from their creative brainstorming. As a result, he commented again and with real concern, they were spending at least three times as long on group discussion as were the other teams. I gently reassured him that the blame, if there was to be a blame, would be mine, and that I would conscientiously shoulder it when the time came to do so. I pointed out that, in any case, there was little that we could now do at this late stage, without causing more embarrassment than he sought to avoid.

Two hours or so later his fears were proved groundless, and his reflections on process were jolted, when one of my first year teams won the competition – and the other came third. My factual observations (of both the competition and of that entire class group, in comparison with their predecessors) had described behaviour. This was in terms which had already provided some data for my ongoing formative evaluation. The competition result provided some reassurance about learning outcomes – although there could, of course, have been other explanations for the students' success. However, I felt that it was primarily a convincing summative evaluation of the changed teaching strategy I had followed, although I recognized that the sample was small.

Counting and noting observations in factual form, as in comparing discussion times devoted to problem analysis, can provide helpful evaluative data about learning and the teaching activity which occasions it, without requiring much effort or subtlety on the part of the evaluator. It can be helpful for summative evaluations, if a comparison with the behaviour of groups before a change has already been recorded.

Example 10.8: Immediate rehearsal and review of learning

George (2001) has described how, just before the end of OU tutorials in classics, she stops ahead of time and asks students to take a sheet of A4, landscape-wise. She suggests an appropriate word or phrase to summarize the focus of the tutorial, to be put in a box in the middle of the page. She then asks them (individually) to draw a mind map, summarizing the new learning which has been acquired by them during the course of this tutorial. She now invites them to swap and compare, while at the same time she displays on the overhead projector what she had hoped, at the outset, would have been the main points to be learnt. Brisk discussion breaks out. Students wish to clarify discrepancies between their various mind maps and that of the tutor. Some remedial learning follows the consolidation of learning, which had already occurred when the maps were being drawn. It is pedagogically a sound activity (Bligh, 1998); it also informs the tutor what was learnt, not learnt and mis-learnt. She may even ask permission to borrow the maps, and photocopy them, before returning them.

In an activity with a similar purpose and rationale, I have given students the opportunity to complete 'crib cards' in a period borrowed from the end of the class. They can sum up, on a small card (or, for an activity which has been carried out on a PC, in a file of limited length), the main points that they have taken from this activity, and to which access will be welcome when the exam comes along. Ingathering the crib cards, I promise to correct (and report) wrong learning, and I analyse them to compare my teaching intentions and the reality as recorded.

Just as lecturers who have ingathered lecture notes have often been surprised by noteworthy omissions and appalled by serious errors, so too can this review activity be a reality check on the impact of teaching. It is also sound pedagogical practice, to consolidate learning.

Example 10.9: Dynamic lists of questions

Two facilitative lecturers planned a series of half-day events in which students should develop, through reflection on experience, certain cognitive abilities which the tutors considered important in their subject area. The lecturers made the assumption that they would be able to judge the overall impact of this programme from the students' subsequent performances in tests or examinations. They also felt that they could themselves judge the general competence of the students and compare it with the work of similar students in previous years, when there had been no special programme devoted to the development of their abilities. However, the lecturers were aware that factors other than tuition can influence learning and development, and they were alive to risks presented by confounding factors. So they also wished to know what immediate impact the various components of each new half-day programme would have on the learning and development of the students. They asked me to evaluate each half-day thoroughly.

I devised a plan which I was later to refine for a different setting (Cowan and George, 1992b). Before the three-part event began, each student completed a simple proforma, on which as learners they had listed the questions with which they hoped to make progress in their learning during the course of the event. These lists of questions were credited against a pseudonym, and taken in for photocopying. The lecturers also arranged that the students took a pre-test, just as they would later take a post-test (see page 111), which concentrated on the declared learning outcomes.

At the end of the first discrete component of the programme, the students retrieved their own question sheet, and amended it – so that it would now represent their outstanding personal agenda for the remainder of the event. Where the student deemed learning to have occurred, the corresponding questions were deleted; sometimes questions were added, when new needs had become apparent. For example, a student deleted a 'How do you ... ?' question, and added a new one, 'Now I know *how* to ... , but I don't know *when* to ... ?'

The sheets were taken in again, and photocopied a second time. After the next component in the programme, the sheets were once more returned to the students for amendment, and again collected by the lecturers for photocopying. Quickly in so doing, the teaching staff were made aware of the progress of learning, and could to some extent plan their activity in the third section of the event accordingly. There was thus a strong incentive to persuade learners to identify and anonymously declare outstanding needs. At the end of the programme, the procedure was repeated yet again.

Three sources of illuminative information were thus available to the lecturers:

1. They had a clear listing of the aspirations and expectations which were in the students' minds, at the beginning of the event.
2. From the questions which had been scored out at the various stages in the programme, they had an account from the students of the outcomes which the students *perceived* that part of the event to have achieved for them. The lecturers could check that perception, to some extent, against the students' subsequent performance in the pre-test/ post-test comparison. However, that could only be done on a group basis, as the anonymity of the reporting had rendered individual correlations impossible.
3. In some ways the most thought-provoking information of all was that the lecturers were able to obtain the learners' impression of the element in the programme which had written off declared questions, or had provoked new questions.

Programme revision was informed by this data, which the lecturers judged in the light of their expectations and considered criteria. The method, above all, provided a summative account of the learning outcomes achieved during the programme, and of the learning expectations for the class group.

Example 10.10: Reflective learning journals

Following a week of IDS activity (Example 2.4) which had concentrated on problem-solving, I extracted and analysed the accounts which students gave in their learning journals of their reflections and progress.

One student wrote of a wonderful problem-solving method which he claimed he had devised. He wrote in a complex style and gave a condensed description of his methodology. By the last few lines of the first page of his description, he had left me without any understanding of what it was that he, the learner, was describing, and without a single positive idea on my part for a supportive or facilitative comment. In my role as commentator, I worried over this for some time. Never, in my previous experience with learning journals, had I left as significant a page as this without a single comment. Yet, in all honesty, and with my commitment to an approach according to Carl Rogers (Rogers, 1961), I could not think of any non-judgemental or non-directive comment to add to that script. For my reaction – starkly – was one of total incomprehension regarding what the student was writing, and hence of complete lack of empathy with the message which may have been contained therein.

After agonizing, I decided to maintain my integrity and refrain from commenting. With a feeling of acute embarrassment at this implicit inadequacy on my part, I turned over, only to encounter the top lines on the next page in which he had written, 'I don't expect the first page meant anything to you – but it means a lot to me.' I confess that, at this point, I found myself fervently wishing that this helpful comment had been written at the foot of the first page, and not at the beginning of the second one. I read on, to follow the student journal-writer's description of how this obscure (and to me still totally incomprehensible) problem-solving method had been applied by him to various activities in the second half of the study week – with what he deemed remarkable success.

This journal-writer next recounted how it had occurred to him that, if his method was valid for the situations which he encountered in his studies, perhaps it might also be valid for the rather different difficulties which he encountered in his part-time engagement as a Scout leader, with two inept assistants. There followed another page or so of journal entry, in which the student narrated his account of how the same method, still incomprehensible to me as the journal-reader, had been applied by him to the difficult situation in his Scout troop. And there, as in the writer's undergraduate studies, it had apparently led to a successful outcome which the journal-writer reported in some (convincing) detail.

All of this spread out into an entry of nine or ten pages. At the end of these, in a cryptic and business-like conclusion, the journal-writer said that he didn't really expect that any of this would be terribly meaningful to the reader. 'But it's meaningful to me. It has worked for me in a variety of situations, and I'm sure it's going to work for me next week as well. I know I've written far more in this journal entry than you wanted from me – but it's been a very exciting and successful week, and I wanted to tell somebody about it.'

This, like other journal entries in that particular week, provided subjective and possibly distorted first-hand evidence of positive outcomes which the journal-writers judged to have been 'successes' as far as they were concerned, in response to the ideas encountered in the IDS activity of that week. They confirmed, in credible terms, that the activities had had impact. Being someone who taught this student and his fellows in class and group work, I tried with little success to make some indirect checks of the authenticity of the claims which he made in his journal. For triangulation is certainly important, as I hope I established in Example 10.1. Equally, we must sometimes face up to the fact that the ease of obtaining and verifying evaluative data is often inversely proportional to its usefulness and meaningfulness. The evaluative innovator must strive for an optimum balance. Roughly two years after graduating, this by then ex-student wrote to remind me of his method, and to tell me that he was still using it, successfully.

Notice that the 'byproduct' information from learning journals, about the learning experience, provides much more than can be obtained from questionnaires or focus groups.

Other examples

Evaluative data is often generated, but not so often assembled, analysed or used, I regret to say. There was provision, for example, for the almost direct generation of evaluative data in Examples 2.6, 5.3 and others; this sourcing of data could be virtually embedded in the structure of the learning and teaching activity. However, one of the most powerful resources for the evaluation of teaching is to be found in examinations scripts and assignments, which – sadly – are usually only analysed student by student, and not outcome by outcome. For a detailed treatment of the ways to obtain useful evaluative data from this source, see George and Cowan (1999b).

Although I have already instanced many different ways of formatively evaluating the learning experiences we arrange for our students, the long list above could readily be doubled. For example, I will simply mention briefly the following:

- Observing informally, while tutoring: Wandering round a computer lab, in the early stages, and while few students have yet discovered that they want to talk to me about anything, I tend to make mental notes (unobtrusively) of what is on their screens when neighbours break off to talk to each other. At the end of the session, it is natural and easy to ask them what prompted these exchanges – and hence, often, to discover instructions or content which puzzled the enquirer, and so which might be worth improving, or which stimulated deep thought and so are worth retaining.

- Tracking use of hyperlinks: On one current course, with carefully designed hyperlinks, my colleagues and I have been troubled by growing evidence that students have not only forgotten some of the vital information or requirements which were presented and explained in the links they visited. They have also forgotten that they visited this page, and so are unaware that the information exists and existed. Tracking student use of links, and the time spent on them, assists in the evaluation and redesign of what should be on offer and when – in order to minimize this problem.

- Post-mortem files: In large classes, where there are many tutors and tutorial groups, it can be useful to have a readily available file, physical or electronic, in which tutors lodge each week a rough note of frequently asked questions, or frequently encountered misunderstandings. This file can be sorted by topic when the time comes for the annual review of the materials and activities, and decisions made in one businesslike meeting about whether or not changes are needed.

- Focus group follow-up: I have long found that representative focus groups (Krueger and Casey, 2000) can be somewhat taciturn, and that articulate focus groups are usually, almost by definition, unrepresentative. I try to overcome this by assembling an articulate and helpful group, telling them the aspects of the provision on which I wish feedback and advice, and summarizing that in the usual way as terse statements. These then form the basis for a Likert-scale questionnaire, nowadays online, offered to the entire class.

- Pre-tests and post-tests: Where part of our programme calls for relatively immediate learning, and especially when this is to be used in a subsequent activity, I find it useful to devise two matched test papers, and pre-test students in matched groups with one paper or the other. Thus I make myself aware of the range of prior learning. After the event, I administer matched post-tests, by using for each group the paper they have not seen. Thus I make myself aware of the learning gain, and the students and myself aware of deficiencies which might usefully receive remedial attention, on an individual or class basis.

- Unintended learning outcomes: Careful scrutiny of the nature and frequency of some of these may suggest items I would wish to add to the list of intended learning outcomes, and to my plans for learning and assessment.

- Long-term feedback and contacts: Two of my former students, now senior academics in Scottish universities, have confided to me (and generously declared to their current colleagues) that, though they didn't appreciate at the time what I was getting them to do, they had come to appreciate it – and now followed much the same practices with their own students. It has been my experience that students who have struggled with Personal Development Planning often make contact some six months or more after completing a module, to report enthusiastically the progress which they are making, and to explain why. Long-term feedback which is not simply polite stroking of a former teacher can provide reassuring reinforcement of practices about which we may have had doubts at the time, occasioned by immediate student reaction.

Generalizations

I have inferred that a suitable way to find out about the effectiveness of teaching is to discover both the nature of the learning experience and what the learning outcomes actually are. It has been implicit in at least three examples in this chapter (Examples 10.4, 10.7 and 10.9) that, with new or even subtly different learning outcomes in mind, new or different methods of assessment and evaluation are necessary in order to identify or measure them validly. Suitable methods for assessment – and for evaluation – must always be sought and used, if reliable outcomes and judgements are desired.

In Examples 10.1 and 7.8 in particular, but also from other points in this text where I have written of mismatches, I have suggested that we should be wary of relying merely on the opinions of students (or of teachers) about the nature and effectiveness of a given situation or method in achieving the desired outcomes. I thus offer three fairly simple but directly useful thoughts on the subject of evaluation:

- If we pinpoint what it is that matters to us as teachers in a learning and teaching situation, it is then not too difficult to find direct ways of observing or extracting data which will inform us about that outcome, or its absence.
- Structures for formative evaluation can soon usefully become part of the weft and weave of the design of the learning and teaching activity (as was carried out with Examples 5.4 and 10.9). They will then continue to inform the teacher constructively, even as the very process of learning and teaching is progressing.
- Questionnaires can be a shallow, suspect and naive way of seeking the evaluative information we require, but – when they are well designed and the evidence they yield is corroborated – they can be a source of useful data, or at least of suggestions for further enquiry.

Comments

Many of the examples described in this chapter have concentrated formatively and usefully, I hope, on the scrutiny of events during a learning experience or a closely linked sequence of learning experiences. They have had the following features:

- All of the enquiries sought to extract information which would be of use to a particular teacher, taking a particular course with particular students; no attempt was made to extract generalizable findings.
- All the examples concentrated on the immediate learning or learning experience, or on the learners' behaviour while learning or doing.
- The enquiries entailed evaluative activity which took place as near in time as possible to the event. In two of the examples, it was not delayed after the event by more than 20-45 minutes.
- Enquiry was, in some cases, in two steps – with the second stage of enquiry digging deeper and more meaningfully into the detail of the learners' experiences. (Example 10.6 and Other examples: Focus group follow-up.)
- There was often a careful emphasis on obtaining and considering the learners' accounts of a particular piece of action or an outcome, rather than invite them to generalize, philosophize, describe rhetorical daydreams or give a global view of their thinking. (Examples 10.3, 10.4, 10.7, 10.8 and 10.9.)
- There was often an attempt to triangulate the information given by the learners, with their observed behaviour, and other data.

Before you test this, some second thoughts from me

1. Most of the data collection which has been described took place where there had been a radical change in teaching methods, and where (perhaps regrettably) there was no attempt to distinguish between differences which arose due to novelty and differences which might be a feature of learning under the new arrangement, once it was well established. How can these be separated?
2. One factor which often militates against the introduction of new teaching methods with new goals is that the educational system may still retain old methods of assessment. In trying to measure or identify the results of new teaching methods in pursuit of *changed* objectives, one of the most acute challenges we have to face is that we are obliged to devise and obtain acceptance for appropriate methods of assessment. Or we may even be obliged by the status quo to continue to use inappropriate but established methods, which consequently generate meaningless or misleading data – or, worse still, encourage shallow learning within an innovation which sets out to promote deep learning. Thus development will only be in the directions we desire if the methods of assessment are appropriate and aligned with our intended learning outcomes. If we eventually succeed in devising

suitable instruments of enquiry, our tests can then serve both for formative enquiry and in summative assessments. In the latter, they figure as an additional encouragement to learners for development in the directions indicated to them by the hidden curriculum of our novel assessment scheme. How can we ensure that? *Can* we ensure that?

3. And can we ensure objectivity in our evaluative observations, and in what they record? In the circumstances described in some of my examples, the learners had a subtle appreciation of what their teachers were expecting. So it is quite possible that the learners' descriptions of what they were doing were a reflection of the teachers' expectations – rather than of the reality of their learning behaviour. (This is an issue which would be a relevant worry in Examples 10.3, 10.6 and 10.9.)

4. In addition, you may wish to consider how much we are entitled to assume, from what is possibly wishful thinking, about how much learners' thinking is actually influenced by teaching; and how safely we can extrapolate from that, to the conclusions inferred in some of my evaluative summaries. There are sound reasons, in other words, for questioning the objectivity or even the potential for objectivity in much of the methodology I have described in my examples.

5. Several of the examples I have given also raise an interesting fundamental question with regard to the ownership or leadership in the search for the type of information which a teacher requires or desires. This applies both to assembling summative assessments and, formatively, to informing and shaping the process of curriculum development. Given all that I have written earlier (Chapter 6) about the influence of self-assessment on learning, why have I not relied more on the learner, as a self-assessing and self-aware person? It is arguable that evaluation based solely on enquiry by teachers or researchers cannot ever be sufficiently well informed about the thoughts and feelings of learners to provide or inform authoritative conclusions. Should we not be moving even more to schemes in which it is the learners who provide us with those sound self-evaluations we require of the learning, which is deeply personal to the individual – evaluations which we, the teachers, will then only have to audit (and not assess or re-assess) before we endorse them?

6. When the Quality Assurance Agency refined its process for academic audit in 2002, auditors were required to undertake extensive training. One point which was made firmly in that programme was that we should be as ready to identify and celebrate joys as well as weaknesses. That is not a bad principle for self-critical, or even Calvinistic, academics to remember. For we are often slow to identify our strengths; there is sometimes even a danger that we may overlook and neglect them. In the self-criticism which features in self-evaluation, we do well to remember that a theatrical critic, for instance, may be as likely to enthuse as to condemn. So too should we; but do we?

7. I have argued recently that we are on the threshold of progressing from alignment to integration of teaching, learning outcomes and assessment (Cowan, 2004b). Perhaps this integration should be extended to include programme evaluation. For example, the dynamic list method for evaluation, when used in the context of Open University induction meetings, soon became the format for the event, and hence a structure for learning and teaching, within which evaluative feedback was obtained and immediately put to good use (Cowan and George, 1992b). Similarly, early problems for qualitative problem-solving (Cowan, 1982), which were devised to facilitate action research, quickly became tutorial questions, then examination questions, and then the basis for a programme specification. This interweaving of mechanisms for formative evaluation, as I have called it, with learning and teaching activity, is typical of many formats devised for formative evaluation, as witnessed in the useful texts by Cross and colleagues (Angelo and Cross, 1993; Cross and Steadman, 1996). Note that when they write of 'classroom assessment', they dwell at times upon what I have been calling formative evaluation, and at other times on the assessment of students' learning in class.

Dear John

There's an awful lot of you in this book, and almost all the examples are yours, too.

There must be others who have thoughts and theories on the subjects you have touched on, just as there surely must be other practitioners who are engaging in innovations as you have done.

Where can I read about the ideas and practices of others, both in line with the thinking you have advanced and, I hope, perhaps taking a different stance?

11

Where Should You Read about Other Work in This Field?

Introduction

Please don't expect this chapter to be a delayed and overdue literature survey on the topic of supporting the reflective learner. Rather, it will simply offer you a list of my suggestions for some further reading, which I hope and believe may enrich the coverage of the previous chapters. I couple these suggestions with comments about why I recommend such readings to you, for I have tried to identify writings, particularly in books, which I believe to have something worthwhile to offer. References to published papers can be time consuming and sometimes frustrating to chase up. But the texts which I cite provide references to articles which may be of interest and use, if you wish to read in more detail.

Coverage

I have amplified the question which heads this chapter, drafting the following questions which I hope will concern you – and which on this occasion I do not attribute to an imaginary letter writer:

1. Where can you access a wider coverage of the current thinking about reflection in learning and development, and of the ways in which writers have described this, in theories and models which you may find helpful?
2. What should you read to set and extend your thinking in the broader context of current developments and thinking in the field of higher education?
3. What does the recent literature have to offer with regard to metacognition and deep understanding?
4. What about self-assessment? There seems a considerable amount of

writing and thinking on this practice. Where can you best read to obtain a current view of this approach and its potential?

5. If you are minded to engage in action research, to inform you about the nature of learning and the learning experience which you occasion for your students, what writers offer you sound and practicable advice about how to proceed?

6. Finally, the commitment to promote student-centred learning has been around for some time now. Where did it come from – and what is current thinking on this topic?

That is a formidable list. So let's begin without further ado, with the first item.

Going deeper into reflection in learning – the literature

Jenny Moon is a psychologist with a keen interest in the processes of reflection and metacognition. Recently she has published three texts (Moon 1999a, 1999b and 2004) which are rich in their content and coverage, noteworthy for their rigour and valuable for their ability to communicate to good effect with readers like me who seek to progress our practice on a sound basis. My copies are well worn and contain many post-it notes which await my attention. I have returned to each of these books again and again, and have always found therein yet more food for thought and yet more ideas which I can take up. I wholeheartedly recommend Moon's texts as the next reading for anyone minded to move on from what I have been able to offer here. If you search for theories, then Moon is your best and certainly most rigorous source of information and advice. For, to be frank, theories are thin on the ground and are often unsubstantiated by hard data, and yet are held and followed by some – perhaps including myself – with passionate conviction. You will judge them more soundly having benefited from Moon's scholarship. Those who seek models of the process will do well to start from her 'map' of the process (Moon, 1999a), and from the reasoning she advances for its development.

The most commonly cited model of reflective learning, in my current experience, is that which is based on the picture of 'ripples in a pond'. (Race, 2005). This one has been assembled, iteratively, and widely promoted by the energetic and effective educational communicator, Phil Race. It clearly says much to many people in the world of education. My reservation is that it barely features active experimentation, which is also missing from Moon's map. However, the same reservation could be expressed about a thoughtfully developed and earlier model by Boud, Keogh and Walker (1985), which they explained at length in their opening chapter to the collection of writings which examine the nature of reflection and its role in the learning process. This model expands, and portrays in a different and linear way, the three steps of Experience/Reflection/Generalization in the Kolb cycle. But, again, it does so without explicit mention of the possibility of the active experimentation which should, in my view, follow. You will no doubt wish to consider, if you have not already done so, the emphasis which I have been placing on that component of the process of learning and development, which seems less important to other writers than it is to me.

Boud and Walker have edited, with Cohen (Boud *et al.*, 1993), a much reprinted volume about using experience for learning. In their introduction, they describe their book as 'a struggle to make sense of learning from experience'. They assist their readers' learning from their contributors' struggles, with an introduction which is a useful advance organizer for those who go on to read the remainder of their book. It is also a very useful re-organizer for those who have been following my thoughts and experiences, and may wish a succinct summary which offers and substantiates several propositions about learning reflectively from experience. You can then go on to test out your own thoughts on this topic by referring to Boud and Walker (1991). These writers have assembled, as part of a course on adult learning in the workplace, a fine set of readings to provide a foundation for subsequent thinking and development about reflection.

Another way to encourage your thinking to reflect from a different perspective is to take time to absorb the approach set out in the book by Brockbank and McGill (1998). This was published around the same time as the first edition of my own book. It has always seemed to me a useful, objective and well-referenced companion reading for the highly personal approach of my own writing.

If you would go back to the beginnings, which is often no bad thing to do, then you can of course refer to Kolb's much quoted (but less often read) seminal text (1984). This somewhat weighty treatment of the theory is helpfully summarized in everyday language in the handbook by Gibbs (1988). He translates the theory of experiential learning into an attractive reality for teachers and students. This slim volume illustrates the theory with persuasive examples, and in turn justifies the examples by providing a theoretical basis for them. You will find it especially helpful that the first examples are categorized according to the phase of the Kolb cycle with which they are primarily concerned. All are transferable and none are complex. There then follows a set of clearly explained case studies, which are taken from particular disciplines and situations, but which offer many transferable suggestions. I hope you will appreciate, as I do, Gibbs' frank closing discussion of the problems which a teacher can face in moving to experiential learning. I find this book refreshingly relevant to my needs.

Next amongst the basic readings which you may wish to consult are those by Schön. I suggest that it is important to remember that Schön set out initially to address the need to educate reflective professionals in situations where theory and practice should be properly integrated. He saw learning and development as ensuing, in that context, when reflection led the practitioner to extract understanding from the problems which had arisen or were arising in professional practice. That is not quite the type of situation with which most teachers in higher education work, and so his writings and advice should be interpreted accordingly. Schön's work is summarized in the two key texts which I have already mentioned (Schön, 1983, 1987). These have been carried forward by him (Schön, 1991), in a volume which provides a helpful range of illustrative case studies which depend upon reflection. The central notion in this text is of a reverse educational approach suited to facilitate reflection. It begins by asking what practitioners need to know; it then presumes that the answer begins from reflection on the understanding which they have already acquired from everyday practice. Nevertheless, it troubles me somewhat that the practitioners in the case studies are often seen as subjects for research, rather than as thoughtful and developing researchers of their own practice.

For an alternative and yet acceptably profound account of the development of reflective judgement, you will find it helpful to read King and Kitchener (1994). They detail the stages which lay the foundation for encouraging reflective thinking by adults, and which lead to the development of reflective judgement. Another alternative perspective comes from Handal and Lauvas (1987), who treat reflection as being at the heart of teacher education. Their writing should stimulate your thoughts, if you are prepared to consider the transfer of their philosophy to your own discipline and situation.

Reflection is implicit in many of the case studies included by Boud (1988), in his book primarily devoted to developing student autonomy. For that reason it will make useful reading for you, especially from the point of view of promoting constructive second thoughts. For the discussion therein of the issues surrounding autonomy is relevant to reflection, as to many other aspects of teaching and learning. That discussion leads on to the presentation of a number of case studies in which reflection is not specifically addressed, but where it features strongly and in interesting ways. The same is true of the examples offered by Ramsden (1988), which you should expect to prompt you to the same analytical and reflective style of reading – again pushing you (like me) to extend your thinking to teaching in general, and not merely to supporting the reflective learner.

If you seek to continue to relate reflection to your teaching and your students' learning in general, you should read Boud and Griffin (1987). This is an interesting and original text which approaches, through the contributions of a range of writers, the question of what learning is like for those who are learning. It contains teachers' reflections on learning, prompted by their practical experiences of learning and of teaching, which are reported almost incidentally. There are chapters here which deal with aspects of learning that are usually neglected, such as intuition and how interdependence is conceived and learned. There are also chapters which concentrate on personal learning and growth; and there are chapters which deal with the experience of those who return to study. Finally, the editors themselves return to their two main and linked topics – learning and the facilitation of learning. The theme of reflection runs through this book; I often take it down from my shelf, to be prompted into new lines of thought.

If you find it helpful as a teacher to concentrate more on learning than on teaching, I would encourage you to read a subsequent and highly original publication (Boud *et al.,* 1993). This emphasizes the role of personal experience in learning, through contributions in which the various contributors have tellingly written themselves into the experiences they describe and analyse.

You may find it helpful to relate learning based on facilitated reflection to other approaches in current use by exploring the literature on problem-based learning, especially when it includes examples of learning in which reflection figures as a response to facilitation by a tutor or supervisor. You could make a start on this topic with Boud (1985). This again contains a mixture of case studies which provoke reflection through the contrasts they provide, as does the searching overview of problem-based learning as at 2004 assembled and edited by Savin-Baden and Wilkie (2004).

As an 'examples man' with concern to see active experimentation encouraged, I would also urge you to consider spending time on Gould and Taylor (1996). They write from the innovative background of social work education, in which many creative ideas have been developed in the past two decades. They offer a varied and useful account of cases in which the concept of reflective learning has been applied to education in their discipline area. Their book presents material from academic and practice settings, both of which feature reflective learning. I benefited greatly from the reflective and theoretical discussions which are part of most of the papers, and the examples have had much to offer me; I hope they have the same impact for you. I warmed similarly to the examples given by Tresman and Edwards (1993), in this case specifically for science education.

And so I offer you my last suggestion, in the hope that you will be prepared to grapple with mathematics – though not necessarily to contemplate teaching that subject. Mason has devoted much effort to the creation of situations (Example 7.5) in which learners have to move rapidly from generalizations to speculations and specialized conclusions, which are tested out by them in new particular situations – and hence back again into generalizations. He set this up for his Open University colleagues, as I have already mentioned, in a special course unit for the foundation course in mathematics of that time (Mason, 1984). The approach is expanded in a companion volume (Mason *et al.,* 1982), from which I have never failed to draw encouragement and inspiration. I hope it can do that for you, too.

Principles and current educational emphases in higher education

Three texts stand out for me under this heading. The first is the second edition of Biggs' very practical approach to how academics can and should improve their teaching in today's circumstances (Biggs, 2003). It offers a conceptual framework to inform that decision-making. It is full of tested practical advice, shrewd wisdom and relevant comment. It went quickly to a second edition because the first was so valued, and the writer is, as ever in his influential career, keen to remain relevant.

My second essential reading is Knight's book about 'doing teaching and being a teacher' (Knight, 2002). This offers detailed advice about the core business of teaching in higher education, and enjoying it; and it does so in an attractively collegial style. My third essential reading is Ramsden (1992), which covers a rather different fundamental approach to that of Biggs, and is therefore a useful and practical complement to that first text.

In contrast to that trio, Ketteridge *et al.*, (2002) have written a more comprehensive, businesslike and authoritative book, with a rather different purpose and intended readership from those I have just mentioned. They write for academics beyond probation, who are extending their levels of responsibility in academia. Their insights into many of the pressures and priorities in higher education at the present time are worth exploring, even for those who simply aspire to be innovative and effective teachers in this environment.

In quite a different category I would place the perceptive writings of Barnett (1997). Make your acquaintance with him, I suggest, in his review of what academics mean when they talk about critical thought – which has been described as a bold statement about higher education in the modern age. Barnett displaces the idea of critical thinking with the much broader idea of critical being. This is a text for those who are interested in how universities can be transformed for the modern world.

The pedagogical context – current thinking on promoting metacognition and deep learning

Metacognition, in simple terms, means thinking about thinking. My colleague Helen Wood shares with her students the idea of the monkey on her shoulder – which offers comments to her, on her thinking and doing, just as Pask's observer (Example 5.2) does; it is a feature of her own thinking about her thinking. That metaphorical monkey, like Pask's observer, is exercising metacognition. Similarly, when learners reflect (with or without prompting) on a recent experience, and if they are following the Kolb cycle and try to identify what they were doing in that experience, they are engaging in metacognition (Example 2.1). And when learners reflect-in-action and notice, for example, illogicalities or errors in their thinking, they are then also devoting time, however briefly, to metacognition.

If you want to go back in time to Pask's complex work on metacognition, it has been helpfully summarized by Entwistle (1978). This perhaps provides better access to Pask's thinking for the uninitiated than the researcher's own writings. Again for non-specialist readers, Entwistle (1992) sets out a clear summary of the relationships between metacognition, styles of learning and theories of learning. You should find this useful as an advance organizer for your reading around this topic. He has also written more recently on this topic in a paper for the ESRC Teaching and Learning Research Programme (Entwistle, 2000). You can find an alternative introduction, in everyday terms, in the Open University Resource Pack for courses E530/730 (Thompson, 1992).

Facilitating metacognition can be treated as a focus for teaching and learning activity. It can be integrated into an undergraduate teaching programme, as Woods (1994) and Biggs (1985) have done. This school of educational practice maintains that deep learning develops when adults devote time to analysing and talking about their learning and their learning strategies, and are prompted to do so in interventionist programmes which establish the existence of alternative or supplementary strategies which it might be worth considering or testing out. An example of that would be my own surprise reward, when students who had studied and analysed their problem-solving in one subject area moved on inexorably to explore the nature and potential of strategies for other subject areas (Cowan, 1986a).

If you are interested in taking the topic of metacognition further, and in doing so from a theoretical basis, a good and meaty starting point would be Marton *et al.* (1997). I would also persuade you to sample the more integrated combination of theory and practice to be found in Richardson *et al.* (1987). Alternatively, Biggs and Moore (1993) present the whole concept as a central component and possibility in effective teaching for deep learning and the development of abilities.

A booklet which may be of direct assistance to you has been written, for staff development purposes, by Baume and Baume (1992). They set out to help university teachers to design programmes and courses which depend on active, and reflective, learning. The basis for that approach to metacognition is detailed in lucid and practical terms. Practising lecturers from a range of disciplines then describe how they themselves have used active learning in their courses.

Next on my list, I would suggest you devote some time to reading Weil and McGill (1989) for the wealth of examples which they include, all within a framework which is helpful for teachers like you and me. Kolb and reflection figure heavily in this text. The writers begin by trying to make sense, as they put it, of the diversity of theory and practice to be found in the field called experiential learning. They then present a stimulating and oft-quoted analytical argument which differentiates between four 'villages' of experiential learning, and summarize some of the practices, challenges and influences associated with each. I encourage you to find time to read about these villages and to think through their implications for you and the location of your work, in relation to their examples which I am sure can be of use to you.

I should mention two publications in the series 'New Directions for Teaching and Learning'. Hutchings and Wutzdorff (1988) of Alverno College have assembled some good examples of learning through experience, together with a helpful review of assumptions and principles. This makes easy but authoritative reading. A companion volume by Stice (1987) adds further complementary examples.

To close this list of suggestions, however, I encourage you to become acquainted with the writings of Brookfield. He is a teacher, and a writer, concerned with helping students to learn to think critically, as one of the most significant activities of adult life (Brookfield, 1987). He includes this aim in his comprehensive, and also much reprinted, treatise on understanding and facilitating adult learning (Brookfield, 1986). And you can move on from what he calls this comprehensive 'analysis of principles and effective practice' to a book, with Preskill, full of practical ideas about how to engage students, and yourself, in effective discussion in the classroom (Brookfield and Preskill, 1999). These are the thoughts and methods of a man eager to engage his students in deep thinking and metacognition.

A closely associated topic – current practices and thinking about self-assessment

I reluctantly digress into semantics. Boud (1995), who is the leading authority in this field, often writes of self-assessment; yet most of the practice he describes, or includes in the accounts he has commissioned from other teachers, is of what I have preferred to call self-evaluation. That conceptual distinction is important to me here, whatever words we use. Boud's self-assessment, which I would myself describe as evaluation, does not contribute to the overall grading or mark for the student concerned. Indeed, he declares that self-assessment 'has the self as agent and audience' and 'is essentially formative and not absolute, although it can be used for summative purposes'. I hope you will be prepared to continue, for at least the remainder of this book, to accept a usage in which I employ 'evaluation' to describe a *process* in which judgements are made by comparing performance with criteria or standards; and if I restrict the term 'assessment' to evaluation which concentrates on an *outcome,* in the form of a grade, mark or judgement, whether formative or summative. Whatever the titles we use, I submit that the distinction between an emphasis on process and an emphasis on outcome is significant. However, given the usage by Boud and others, it would be unhelpful to diverge from their title – 'self-assessment'.

Evaluative reflection often inexorably encourages the learner to follow a process which leads to a self-assessment of learning – which is a new and for some teachers a worrying possibility. For the teacher and the examination board have long had absolute authority to judge, grade and mark learners and learning. So there are natural grounds for concern whenever anyone suggests engaging learners in what they call *self-assessment* – and this apprehension does not disappear if the innovators strive to make it clear that they will not be abdicating from the responsibility to provide the marks or grades which will contribute ultimately to certification.

I expect you will already have discerned my personal enthusiasm for self-assessment, wherein at least some of my students did award themselves, or claim, grades (Cowan, 1984b, 1988). I hope you will want to formulate your own more detached and informed judgement of this possibility. You may wish to learn to what extent self-evaluation and self-assessment are currently encouraged by teachers; with what outcomes; and how, beyond the range of examples in this book, teachers can go about persuading students to be frank with themselves and others about their worth, and to engage in an activity which some students will see as a responsibility for their teachers.

I have difficulty offering you sources on self-assessment other than those edited by Boud, in which, fortunately, you will find a great variety of views and experiences. I can only mention that Rowntree (1977), writing at the beginning of the period in which this approach began to find favour, had some far-sighted comments; and that Heywood (2000), writing on assessment over 20 years later, includes tellingly frequent references to self-assessment, and particularly to the variant favoured by Alverno College (Loacker, 2000), when he stresses the impact of self-assessment on reflection.

The issues of practice and outcomes are thoroughly addressed by Boud (1995). I strongly recommend this book to you, partly for his keen interest in this aspect of higher education, and partly for the varied contributions by other teachers and researchers who have first-hand experience of self-assessment and its outcomes. The text begins with a personal statement by Boud himself, which I find frank and persuasive. It then moves on to a clinical review of the state of the art, which is well illustrated by examples from the wide range of different disciplines, cultures and teaching styles in which it has figured. It concludes with another testimony by Boud, which is again written very much in the first person, and is a fine example of 'transparency'.

Boud's opening description (1995: 1) seems to me to endorse much that the rationale behind the Cowan diagram, as I have described it in these pages, seeks to attain:

> Whenever we learn, we question ourselves. 'How am I doing?', 'Is this enough?', 'Is this right?', 'How can I tell?', 'Should I go further?' In the act of questioning is the act of judging ourselves and making decisions about the next step. This is self-assessment.

He goes on to declare the assumptions about self-assessment on which his thinking is founded. These are that self-assessment is a necessary skill for lifelong learning, that it needs to be developed in university courses, and that it is necessary for effective learning. He then makes the significant point that the conditions which promote reflection are very much those which promote self-assessment (and vice versa?). He lists these conditions as:

- active engagement with a task which is accepted as having learning as its primary purpose;
- a task which includes significant elements of choice by the learner, which matter for learning;
- an experience which is not predictable by the learner, who is encouraged to notice surprises within it;
- a challenge of some sort to the learner's experiences;
- the learner having to make choices and follow them through;
- the new learning having to be linked, by the learner, to the old learning.

Interesting case studies in this comprehensive text include self- and peer marking in a large electronics class; self-assessment against declared criteria in engineering design; self- and peer assessment of class participation in law; and an example of self-assessment in negotiated learning in science education. In addition, there is a helpful review of several self-assessment initiatives which stemmed from the UK Enterprise in Higher Education funding, and which relate to several different domains. But there is one surprising omission from the coverage – namely the extensive use of self-assessment in the established course structure at Alverno College, and the comparably extensive evaluative research which demonstrates the impact of self-assessment on the learning there (e.g. Loacker *et al.,* 1986; Mentkowski and Strait, 1983; Loacker *et al.,* 2000).

Consequently, I have some reservations about the chapter in this book on research into self-assessment, which appears to me to dwell rather more than I would have expected on reliability and associated factors, given Boud's earlier statements about the self-relevance of the process. I would not quibble with his judgement that much of the research is 'both conceptually and methodologically unsound'. But if an effort is to be made to rectify that weakness, I would make a plea for it to focus more than hitherto on the effects of self-assessment on learning outcomes and potential – ahead of reliability, whose importance I nevertheless do not dispute.

To close this section on a practical note, I urge you to explore some recent examples of good and effective practice in self- and peer assessment, which have been assembled by Hinett and Thomas (1999).

Beyond feedback and evaluation, to a methodology for action research

There is, for me, no distinct line dividing the formative evaluation of teaching from action research; there is more in the way of a grey area where one type of activity shades into the other. With that caveat, let me never-theless try to distinguish the two concepts, and establish my use of the terms, as usual by examples.

I am engaged in formative evaluation:

- when I get my students to draw concept maps of their learning, and compare what that tells me with my objectives for the tutorial in which we have just taken part, and take immediate action accordingly;
- when I collect feedback questionnaires which ask about the strengths and weaknesses of the comments I have made on their submitted work, and adjust next time how this is tackled by me;
- when I pre-test and post-test my students after I have presented an explanation in a new way, and wish to find out how well it has been understood, so that I can plan and provide remedial tuition if necessary.

I am engaged in action research:

- when I get a colleague to interview my students, to learn which aspects of facilitative style in commenting on reflective learning journals have an impact on the students' subsequent thinking;
- when I use recorded protocols to discover how my students use and react to the resources I provide in the VLE;
- when I join with a colleague to analyse the way student discussions are influenced by the content and style of our moderation.

I take formative evaluation to be an investigation of learning and of the learning experience, which is undertaken, perhaps with the help of a col-league or my students, with the express purpose of obtaining data which will tell me where there is need or scope for improvement in what I do. I take action research to include formative evaluation, but to cover also those investigations in which I merely set out to learn more about the nature of the immediate learning and of the learning experiences for which I am responsible – findings which I expect to be of use to me, but in ways of which I am not necessarily aware at the outset.

The concept of teachers as researchers of their own practice has a well-established pedigree. Around 1970, a number of educational leaders advanced the argument for the teacher to be truly professional in responding to the need to research the outcomes of their practice. A pro-minent writer on this theme was Stenhouse (1975, 1984). In (school) tea-cher training and education, the approach has gained considerable acceptance (e.g. Heywood, 1992). But university teaching, for which until recently there has been no rigorous training or preparation, has been predictably reluctant to move onwards from intuitive development and so-called evaluation – which often amounts to little more than the adminis-tering of questionnaires designed by untrained amateurs and summarized without being analysed.

Until recently there was perhaps but one text to which any university teacher interested in evaluating beyond the self-devised questionnaire approach might be referred. That was the handbook by Cross and Angelo (1988), dealing with what in the United States is called classroom assess-ment techniques. This publication followed a provocative paper by Cross (1986), in which she had quoted Schön (1983), who had asserted that the questions driving research into teaching and learning did not seem to be the questions for which answers were truly needed to improve professional practice. In attempting to connect practice and research, Cross proposed that research on teaching and learning should be carried out in literally thousands of classrooms, by the teachers themselves. *Classroom Assessment Techniques* (Angelo and Cross, 1993), in a second and expanded edition, gained in its revision a much enlarged introduction to the process of classroom assessment. It offers a definition, a rationale, a teaching goals inventory, five steps to a successful start and advice on planning and implementation. It then lays out 12 case studies, before suggesting methods of enquiry which you, the average university teacher and reader, might use in your own classroom enquiries.

A companion volume (Cross and Steadman, 1996) is designed to be used by university teachers in groups and in workshops. In a case method approach, it illustrates how teachers can think about a variety of common learning issues, focusing on how students are learning, and on such issues as motivation, deep and surface learning, metacognition and critical thinking.

My initial advice to you is that you should begin from this small collec-tion. You will find much that you can use, and much cause to widen your horizons about what we as university teachers should and can be doing in the way of action research. If you then decide to limit your activity by concentrating simply on formative evaluation, you could focus your list of possible strategies or 'tools of enquiry' by consulting one of three pub-lications produced principally for teaching staff of the Open University (Cowan and George, 1997; George and Cowan, 1999a; Hewitt *et al.*, 1997), or else by consulting the popular booklet from Gibbs *et al.* (1988).

If full action research is a line that you wish to pursue further, then I can warmly recommend three texts. Hopkins (1993) has written a sound guide for those who wish to undertake research in their classrooms. The fact that he writes for a readership who are mainly engaged in school teaching seems to me to be unimportant. Certainly I find his advice directly relevant to me, whether I seek to enhance my teaching, to test the assumptions of educa-tional theory or to evaluate new developments. Winter (1989) has written a similar style of text, free from jargon and rooted in practicalities. It sets out to encourage and advise practitioners who want to understand and improve their work, and in rather more detail than Hopkins offers. I would suggest that you sample both, and choose to begin from the one which appeals most to you, on a first skim reading, and once you have defined the questions for which you seek answers. Last, but for me the most important, there is a handbook of methods and resources for the reflective practitioner which I rate highly as a storehouse of ideas, theories and principles (McKernan, 1996). If you make any sort of commitment at all to action research or to rigorous formative evaluation, I would advise you to buy this one, keep it handy and use it often. It is strong on the philosophy, methodology and analysis of action research.

Returning to the starting point – the rationale for student-centred learning

I have frankly declared throughout this text the influence Carl Rogers had, and continues to have, on my own thinking and practice with regard to meaningful learning – and the teaching which can nurture it. However, I am aware that there are relatively few references to Rogers in current educational writing, and that many (amongst whom are those who reviewed the outline of this text) perhaps regard him as a voice from the past. So I recommend as your starting point under this heading the second edition of a much respected collection of papers on the experience of learning, in a volume of that title (Marton *et al.*, 1997). This addresses the fundamental questions about what students learn and how that learning takes place. It also establishes a sound base for studying the work which has been carried out in recent years on the important difference between deep and surface learning – two terms whose meaning is, I hope, almost self-evident.

In this connection, the pioneer researchers Entwistle and Ramsden (1983) provided a subsequent account of research into different approaches to learning, and pointed out the implications for those university teachers who wish to improve the effectiveness of their teaching. Ramsden (1988) offered a further volume of contributions, which opened by covering research taken into practice, and went on to action and reflection – all based on the view that teaching should be directed towards helping students to understand. (You will note that helping is the everyday word for facilitating.) Ramsden (1992) again firmly promotes the view that effective teaching in higher education involves listening to students and changing how we think about teaching. I suggest that you will find this particular book helpful if you want to pursue the notion of learner-centred learning in today's context.

Amongst the early contributions to the literature in the field of higher education, Boud (1981) assembled papers around the theme that the role of teachers is not simply to transmit knowledge, but is also to assist their students to take increasing responsibility for their learning. That is a slightly different, but complementary, justification for learner-directed learning. In a text which confirmed the relevance of this perspective, Morgan presents his reflections on learners' experiences of study (Morgan, 1993). He takes his readers into a position where they view learning from the student perspective. However, for a more up to date and comprehensive treatment of the factors which affect and can enhance student learning, I would refer you to Prosser and Trigwell (1999). They argue, most persuasively, that the way to more effective teaching and education is to understand how students perceive their unique learning situations – which this book assists the reader to do.

Perhaps you can then move on to Rowland (2000). He has written an engaging account of an approach to one's teaching which is full of insights and productive enquiry. He encourages his readers to set their personal and professional values at the centre of their decision-making about what their students should learn, and what teachers should teach.

I confess, though, that Gibbs is my preferred source amongst today's writers in respect of these matters. He presents with characteristic directness the arguments for a new approach to improving the quality of student learning (Gibbs, 1992), and goes on to describe the work of people who have applied in their teaching these arguments, and the principles emerging from research into learning. The evaluations which he presents with these case studies are, to me, distinctly persuasive. Gibbs has been a powerful influence on teachers in higher education, in the UK and elsewhere, over the past three decades. He consistently offers clear justification for change to student-centred approaches, and helps teachers who are so persuaded to see how they can achieve that radical step, in their own situations. I would advise you to extend your reading of him beyond this one publication – to perhaps Gibbs (1997, 1999a, 1999b, 2004) and other references already cited.

In contrast, you may find it valuable in a somewhat different way to become acquainted with the texts of Paulo Freire (Taylor, 1993). Taylor has written a stimulating account of Freire's 'Metodo' – that method which depends on the practice of freedom in learning, facilitated by teachers who ask questions and who prompt further action in response to the learners' answers. This has messages to prompt your reflection if you aspire to facilitate worthwhile learning.

Please forgive me, though, if I squeeze in a new reference to Rogers before I close. Rogers contended that when teachers display their understanding of the meaning of the learning experience for their students in three interrelated ways (see pages 200–201), then learning improves (Rogers, 1980). That was a stark contrast to the behaviourist theories of learning which were being advanced and widely followed at the time he wrote. In 1962, Rogers met with Skinner for a dialogue before 500 people (Kirschenbaum and Henderson, 1990). This lengthy debate brought together the respective leaders, at that time, of the schools of humanist and behaviourist psychology. Skinner, the behaviourist, had committed himself to the purposeful reinforcement of observable behaviour as the way to bring about learning, and thus to enhance teaching effectiveness. Rogers, in contrast, had concentrated his approach to teaching and learning on the person-to-person relationship.

If you are wrestling with the by no means dead need for distinction between instruction and teacher-led education on the one hand, and facilitation and learner-centred learning on the other, I recommend that you dip into the Skinner versus Rogers debate in the Kirschenbaum and Henderson book. You will find much on which to ponder, especially concerning the role of freedom in learning, the difference between control and influence, and the value of genuineness. The other debates in the same text are also a useful way of testing out the Rogerian approach, if you are so minded.

Some second thoughts from me

I hope I can persuade you to try to find time to read the work of Perry (1970). He assembles from his research a nine-step scale of intellectual and ethical development, which has been much used in educational research. Perhaps the most significant outcome of his reported findings and their effect on others is that many teachers have been shocked, like Perry, to discover the intellectual immaturity of their own students. They remain puzzled about how to find ways to enable these students to make progress upwards, in the direction of qualitatively sounder conceptions of learning and of the process of learning. You can make speedy acquaintance with Perry's work in a chapter of Ramsden's book (1988), which I have already mentioned in another connection.

You should also, however, find time for the intensely thought-provoking book by Belenky and colleagues (1986), which has its origins in the fact that almost all of Perry's reported work was with male students. These women writers describe how they set out with the same aim as Perry, but with a different method and outcomes. They wanted to focus on themes which might be more prominent among women learners, and on what women learners have to say about the development of their minds. This led the writers to a classification of knowledge as received, subjective, procedural or constructed – to which I cannot do justice in a brief summary. It remains in my thinking as something which surely does not only relate to female adult students; I hope you may find it useful in prompting similar second thoughts on your part.

These two sources are where I would suggest you start in looking once again, I hope, for the facilitation of your second thoughts. Equally fruitful will be the ample and easily accessible literature on learning styles (e.g. Schmeck, 1988), which is something this book has barely touched on, and which lies at the heart of that individuality in learning which is one of the main justifications for providing learner-centred learning which copes with individual needs and styles.

An opportunity for self-evaluation

Rogers (1969) listed his ten principles for good learning, followed by ten guidelines for the teacher who would facilitate that kind of active learning. Over the years, I have often paraphrased Rogers' principles, putting them into the first person and asking teachers, as I now ask you, to consider which of his assertions *you* would say are true of *your* learning. Please take a minute or two now, just to check through your answers to these questions about how *you* learn:

- Have you a natural potential for learning?
- Do you learn more significantly when what you are learning is relevant?
- Do you find it threatening to be expected to change your view of yourself?
- When such threats are minimized, is it easier for you to learn?
- Do you find it easier to be perceptive when you are not under pressure?
- Do you learn significantly by doing?
- Do you learn better when you take responsibility for your own learning?
- Do you learn most lastingly when your feelings are involved, as well as your intellect?
- Are you more independent, creative and self-reliant when evaluation by others is secondary?
- Is 'learning to learn' the most socially useful learning for you in the modern world?

I suggest that, if you have answered 'Yes' more often than 'No', you have just confirmed that you believe in learner-centred learning, for yourself at least, and hence that you should be committed to facilitative teaching. My next question or task for you, of course, is to ask you to think about how many of the principles implicit in Rogers' questions as I have phrased them currently feature in *your* teaching – and what that says to you.

Just one, but very important, additional second thought – or question

These books are clearly ones which I have read and found helpful over the years, and mainly kept for my bookshelf. How will you gain access to the writings by those whose thoughts, ideas and practices have not 'rung bells' for me, yet may for that reason be very important?

12

Postscript

To close, first I offer some overall second thoughts, and then a rambling sequence of relevant questions and answers, upon which I feel I owe it to you to dwell.

Second thoughts on the structure of this text

You will have noticed from what I have written (and indeed from the subtitle of this book), that I regard reflection as a key issue for teachers who want to help students to develop (relevant) capabilities – and abilities. I believe that it is through the process of Kolbian reflection that particular experiences travel, to be transformed into the generalizations which are of use well beyond the limitations of whatever is the current learning and teaching context. I also believe that it is detached Schönian reflection which inspires us all, formatively and summatively, to move forward and to achieve new goals with a purposeful and meticulous self-management of our learning and development.

So in these pages I have followed the Kolb cycle on behalf of my readers. I have told stories about the *experiences* of myself and others in educational innovations, offering examples and sometimes non-examples to illustrate my points. Through the comments I have made after telling my stories, I have tried to encourage you to engage in your own *reflection*, rather than to follow my process of reflection, which led me – years ago – to my own conclusions. For I have hoped with all my heart that you would reach your own *generalizations*, from your own thinking and in your own words. I was confident that, if you just went on to test out some of your generalizations, or even if you were stimulated by mine, then a plan for the *active experimentation* would become yours. And thus the *next experiences*, as you moved on from this text, would certainly be yours, in joint ownership with your students.

What of your own reflection, then? I wonder if you have been prompted by the structure of my text to reflect. I wonder if the questions I have asked, and left for you to answer, have been provocatively facilitative – or merely frustratingly provocative. In either case, please feel welcome to get in touch with me at J.Cowan@napier.ac.uk.

Second thoughts regarding the questions which I have chosen to answer

A troublesome point for me in this text (and perhaps for you, too) has been the choice, and the introduction, of the questions which have headed the various chapters. Although there has been a pretence of dialogue in my presentation, it has been distinctly Socratic – in the sense that I myself have set up the questions. Thus the questions raised are, I am afraid, in the sad tradition of Socratic stooges, who seldom challenged what the great philosopher said to them.

But I am no philosopher. So what I have written should be sharply scrutinized, and its weaknesses, assumptions and omissions should be identified and challenged. That is something which I am aware has (understandably) been done inadequately by my alter ego – he who pops up in the second thinking at the end of each chapter. He knows me too well and has lived with me so long that he thinks in my way, asks second-thought questions or offers comments which matter to me, and tends to agree with my conclusions. But you shouldn't do that. I hope you didn't – and won't.

Second thoughts on what I've missed out

Postman and Weingartner (1971) argued that the ability to identify and ask good questions is the best measure of the quality of someone's education. I hope you've been identifying and asking good questions during your reading here – and especially that you have been asking yourself questions which go beyond those that I have chosen to address. Helen Wood, who has often been a source of both strength and inspiration for me in the past 20 years, reflected very deeply when I asked her to come up with an example of an ability which really mattered in her discipline of chemistry (Geddes and Wood, 1995). She offered me that description which I have often quoted subsequently – namely the ability to notice what is not there. This is an ability which is at once important and demanding, as Sherlock Holmes explained when he had to point out to Dr Watson the curious incident of the dog in the night-time. For the dog did nothing in the night-time – which was the curious incident, of course.

You will have found it relatively easy in your reflections on this text to notice, in what was there, the points with which you didn't agree, or the assumptions with whose justification you were dissatisfied. But I hope you also looked for what wasn't there. And, in this, my last prompting of your reflection, I earnestly encourage you again to give that search your earnest attention – as you emerge from the experience which I hope this text has created for you.

That leads us, of course, to the biggest omission of them all – the vital question which I neither asked nor answered in my Preface: Why do I 'teach' in this way? I feel we should know each other well enough by now, that I can be frank and expand on this topic as I close.

Why do I 'teach' in this way?

I was taught at school and university by people who, in effect, instructed me. Some did that well. I learnt a lot from them and I respected them. Some were less effective for me. When I became an academic, I was minded simply to emulate the best of the practice I had experienced. Five years into that career change, and far from satisfied with my performance, I seized the opportunity to attend a two-week course at UMIST on university teaching. This was to be run by a Professor Bill Morton, of whom I knew nothing. I suppose I hoped and expected to enhance and refine my lecturing approach, but not to change it radically. In the interim, I attended an event in Basle (of which I will write later in this chapter), which gave me cause to ponder on my directions and methods as a teacher, even before I arrived in Manchester.

I soon discovered that Bill Morton believed firmly that supporting worthwhile student learning was what a teacher in higher education should be concentrating upon. I had been puzzled when the pre-course documentation asked me to accept the condition that, while we were resident for a fortnight at UMIST, we were to have no engagements outwith the course. Bill set this condition because, in a sense, he was an educational evangelist. He wanted to convert people like me from our emphasis on trying to teach well. He hoped he could persuade us to concentrate instead on what, and especially how, our students should and could best learn. He never preached to us, or at us. Instead, in our two weeks together, he judged it important to establish a little community of peers – of which he was one. We worked together, we listened to capable visiting teachers who provided a range of inputs and we received some very assorted visitors who came to speak to us after dinner and to discuss their experiences with us. All of this we were encouraged to assimilate on our own terms and according to our own reactions. Bill lived in with us. He spent a great deal of time with us. He even, on one never to be forgotten occasion, lectured to us in his subject area – superbly. He prompted us to digest the experiences of each day, and then of each week, in our informal discussions, often late into the night. It was through my relationship in these two weeks with Bill Morton that I found myself valuing learning rather than teaching.

Like other members of that group, with some of whom I have kept in contact over the years, I returned home determined to tear up my lecture notes, to stop concentrating on teaching as we practised it and to concentrate on supporting student learning. That shift in my values has endured over the ensuing 40 years. It was crystallized in the context of this very special relationship with someone whom I had quickly come to value for himself as well as for his achievements. He never attempted to indoctrinate us. He was certainly someone who was willing to table his values and principles, and to answer our questions about them. Yet first of all he painstakingly and with sincere interest listened to *our* values and views, and engaged in ever deepening discussions of them. He explored with us the value which most of us initially put on trying to instruct as effectively as was within our power, and he enabled us in turn to explore his own values.

Although I did not know it at the time, Bill Morton, and his style with us, exemplified the perceptive analysis by Carl Rogers of 'Realness in the facilitation of learning' (1980: 271). Reading Rogers on my return home, I met and 'signed up to' his three basic principles, drawn from counselling psychology (Rogers, 1969, 1983). These are empathy, unconditional positive regard and congruence. I have constantly found them a sound starting basis when I am working out, 'How can I, as a teacher, help learners to develop and then pursue their own considered and reasoned values?' In addition, I was soon to confirm from experiences that learners' acceptance and trust in the teacher are vital.

The three important qualities for effective teaching

Empathy, the first quality in which Rogers placed confidence, is described as 'the ability "to put onself into another's shoes", or experiencing for oneself the outlook or emotions of another being within oneself' (Wikipedia, 2005). We display empathy when we understand (or show that we wish to understand) the position, values, circumstances or emotional state of others. A militant who is willing to understand what matters to a pacifist acquaintance, and why, displays empathy; as does an experienced teacher who takes time to explore the standpoint of a young teacher who thinks in terms of teaching rather than learning. Rogers talked of entering the private perceptual world of the other and becoming thoroughly at home in it.

His second quality is unconditional positive regard. This goes beyond empathy, for it entails wholehearted acceptance that a learner's questions and aspirations, however obscure to the listener, are genuinely of importance to that learner and hence should be so to the listener. According to McGill and Beaty (2001), it is ' ... a non-possessive caring for the learner, an attitude which believes fundamentally that the other person is trustworthy and worth caring for. It accepts the feelings of the other person as relevant to their learning.' Bill Morton constantly displayed unconditional positive regard in taking, as his starting point in his discussions with us, the views and practices to which we then held dear.

Rogers explained his third quality, congruence, as a close matching between what is being experienced at the gut level, what is present in awareness and what is expressed. Bill Morton displayed congruence when, in his discussions with us, he was prompted by us to recall the time when he himself had held and been guided by the views we were expressing.

An inclusive example

Many years later I ran a module in which students of civil engineering in their third (penultimate) year were required to choose their own objectives, study plans and standards. The only requirement was that they had to address some learning or development which they felt would enrich the civil engineering education they would otherwise experience. For instance, two students, who had already volunteered to undertake Voluntary Service Overseas when they graduated, opted to learn what they called 'Second Aid'. They explained to me that, in the UK, those who take first aid certificates (as they had done) are sternly precluded from learning to do anything beyond providing immediate care for the ill or injured, for they might do damage while acting with the best intentions. However, when they went out to Africa, perhaps a hundred miles from the nearest town, they might be faced, while working on a construction site 'in the sticks', with an accident which had led to serious injury. They wanted to be able to deal competently with that type of circumstance, to the best of their ability. Hence their concept of second aid, which would take them beyond the first aid qualifications they already held. They achieved their goal, and were to make good use of their second aid training a year or so later in cases involving fracture of limbs and serious wounds.

However, I digress. For the example which really concerns me, and is taken from this same open-ended context, concerns three students of Chinese descent, who had joined us from Singapore on direct entry. They approached me formally, with one of their number as their spokesman. He opened the subject delicately: 'We have come from a culture in which the teacher is the authority; and we have been brought up to look to the teacher to be responsible for our learning. Now we find ourselves in a situation where we understand that you value learner-directed learning. Is that correct?' I indicated cautious assent. 'We can see that it will be necessary for us to develop the ability to manage our own learning. We want to make it our objective for our personal development in this module to develop that ability, to direct our own learning.' I enthused at their choice of objective, and asked, as I would have done with any other students, how they intended to achieve it. 'We would like you to teach us,' explained the spokesman. Therein lay a powerful challenge for me – to display unconditional positive regard. I had to identify fully with this intention, despite the fact that it was about as far removed from my own standpoint as it could have been.

I found little difficulty empathizing with their intentions. That began from my assembling through enquiry an understanding, on my part, of the situation and personal history, as these students saw it. I could then summarize to their satisfaction why they set a high priority on adjusting to studying in a department with a powerfully learner-directed ethos. I similarly checked out my grasp of their prior experience in Singapore, and what they valued within it. Thus we were able to begin from a shared standpoint. So it was with genuine unconditional positive regard that I identified with these students' wish to commence their development through what some of my colleagues might perceive as the nonsense of being taught to be self-directed learners. We began from a shared standpoint, and continued with a purpose to which we all four subscribed.

In order to display congruence, I had to be the true me in all of this, while tackling a remit which I would certainly not have chosen for myself. My memory of Bill Morton's approach at UMIST, which had furthered the massive value shift in my own case, helped me greatly. I aired my dichotomy with the trio, and with them considered ways of resolving it. Eventually, we negotiated that I would 'teach', as they called it, for half of the time; this on condition that they would take charge, as best they could, for the other half, and try to work out how to direct their own learning. I have never known, nor asked, what they did in their own time.

For my own part, I went beyond a facilitative style borrowed from counselling, into the somewhat collegial relationship which I had learnt from Bill Morton, and of which I did not find Rogers writing until much later in his publications (Rogers, 1980). In our meetings together, we spent a fair amount of time explaining to each other what we valued in education and about learning, and why. I did all that I could to identify with their established position. They would talk with me about the problems which their objective created for them. I sometimes told them about the problems which I myself had had, some years before, when I felt obliged to change my philosophy for teaching, yet hadn't worked out all the implications. These exchanges of common or similar experiences established congruence, I felt. By so doing, I suspect I led them to explore, with empathy on their part, the position which I represented.

About half way through the year-long programme, I was approached by the spokesman, with the others in attendance as usual. 'Professor Cowan,' he said, 'it was our objective when we began, to learn how to become learner-directed learners'. I nodded, awaiting the expected intimation that they wished to change to a simpler objective. 'We do not think we need your assistance any longer, Professor Cowan. We feel we are now ready to take charge of our own further development as self-directed learners.'

Is this approach to teaching worth it?

This ambiguous follow-up question pinpoints and condenses two enquiries. First, does the approach which I have suggested in this book really work for students' learning? And second, is it rewarding and satisfying for the teacher?

The answer to the first question is given far more eloquently, and is more comprehensively evidenced than I could ever manage, in Rogers' rewrite of *Freedom to Learn* (Rogers, 1983). Having declared two decades earlier that he was offering 'a provocative signpost of what education might become', he was able 20 years later to quote again and again from a multitude of first-hand reports which confirmed the effectiveness of his model. So I shall not address that first question here; it has already been answered for us.

The second question is more difficult for me. While drafting this chapter, I had occasion to revisit the appendix which I prepared in 1984, at the request of the editors of occasional papers for the Education for Capability Committee (Cowan, 1984b). As I have already explained, they proposed to publish the paper (Boyd *et al.*, 1984) which had been prepared and delivered unassisted by three of the students who were involved in the year-long experiment described in Example 6.2. The editors wished a companion contribution from the facilitative teacher.

In responding to that invitation, I quoted the splendid remark by the late Ernest Bevin, who once warned a questioning audience that, 'If you will just open that Pandora's box, there's no telling how many Trojan 'orses will come out of it.' I note 20 years later that my frank account at that time could equally have been written of my reactions to many of the innovations in which I have subsequently been engaged.

I stressed then, and would stress equally now:

- the need for learning to be self-assessed if it to be genuinely self-directed;
- the significant changes in the nature of the students' learning when that occurs;
- the demands involved in being an effective facilitator;
- the importance of interactions between students, and between students and tutor;
- the role of the facilitator in creating activities and task structures, rather than in telling;
- the emotional ebb and flow, affecting more than motivation, in the demanding situation which radical innovation can create;
- the subsequent experiences of the graduated learners, in work contexts where questioning and 'rocking the boat' may not always be appreciated;
- the closeness of the working relationships linking tutor and individual students.

I expanded upon that last point, mentioning that the revelations which occur within close working relationships may be uncomfortable memories when students progress. For those who have exposed deep weaknesses in such a relationship can often find that they can only acquire subsequent independence by finding a way to reject the person to whom they have made their disclosures. Those who have been dependent on a facilitative tutor have often only achieved independence by proving aggressively that they no longer needed the person on whom they had once been so dependent. And those who have been uplifted by the almost charismatic influence which I occasionally managed to exert, at a time when they would otherwise have wallowed in a trough, only felt self-sufficient once they had rejected the stimulus which was inspirational for them in their time of need.

And so at that time I wrote, and still believe, that:

> The good teacher, like a mother eagle, must encourage the fledgling learners to fly the nest in their own strength, and must never remind them of any debt which they owe to those whom they leave behind.

And that, of course, highlights the ultimate irony. For, in our eyes as well as theirs, while failure must be the teacher's responsibility, success must belong purely and genuinely with the learners. If we set out to facilitate learner-directed learning with a strong reflective component, then if the situation, the learning or the learner fails, the major part of the blame is ours – for we got something wrong. Yet, paradoxically, when the student is successful, they must feel that 'I did it by myself'; and the teacher must believe that, too. For if I, as a teacher, really believe that my aim is to help my students to stand on their own feet, then I must acknowledge that they deserve the full credit when they do so successfully. When the great day arrives, if I do not have that conviction, I cannot claim to have achieved my educational aims of their independence and capability.

And so, as I reach (almost) the end of my book, I have come eventually to probably the most important part of it. For I now know that, when I write about a teacher's role in independent learning, I am concerned ultimately with my own self-evaluation of the extent to which I have managed to act in accordance with my values and my goals as a teacher, and of these values and goals themselves. And as a self-evaluation should begin from goals, aspirations and values, against which we judge our performance, it behoves me to close here by explaining where the goals and values for my work as a university teacher originated.

A confession

Honesty obliges me to admit, at this late stage in my text, that the rationalizings which I have set out, chapter by chapter, and even in the above paragraphs, have their true origin in what I must describe as an emotional experience.

As a young and inexperienced lecturer, enrolled for Bill Morton's course, I travelled to Basle, Switzerland, for an International Christian Conference on Higher Education. For some reason, I arrived at one plenary session after it had begun. I picked up the remarks of an eloquent Asian lecturer, who was powerfully condemning the intellectual imperialization by Europeans of higher education in the Indian subcontinent. I struggled to understand this concept. How could we have imperialized higher education in India? I found myself perturbed by the fact that this man was a mathematician, that mathematics, as I understood it, had emerged from the Indian subcontinent and that many of the leading teachers of mathematics in my country and in my time as a student were Asians. Fortunately I went on listening.

'In Europe,' he declared, 'when you say that John is teaching Paddikar mathematics, then you picture John, up here' (and he gestured to his position on the platform). 'And Paddikar down there' (pointing to the front row of the audience below him). 'And mathematics is like a parcel which John passes down to Paddikar.' He mimed the passing down of the parcel. I reflected that this was indeed a fair description of the way most university teachers in my country at that time would picture their role, and the process of learning and teaching. It has also, I'm afraid, been my subsequent experience of Asian students' expectations of learning and teaching, in Sri Lanka, Hong Kong and with my three Singaporeans. Is this, perhaps, the consequence of the intellectual imperialization which the speaker had been deploring (Biggs, 2003)?

'In my country,' declared the speaker firmly and sincerely, 'when we say that Paddikar is teaching John to learn Sanskrit, then we are describing a relationship. It is a relationship which brings together two people, one of whom is rather more of a teacher than a learner, and one of whom is rather more of a learner than a teacher.' And here he raised his hands, and clasped his fingers together, in an arch. 'It is a relationship within which the learning and teaching of Sanskrit takes place.'

For 40 years that picture and the commentary which accompanied it have haunted me. The lecturer, whose name I do not know, left me with a vision of a relationship between learner and teacher to which I wished to aspire – and which ever presents me with a challenge from which I cannot escape. I cannot rationalize or justify this position; I can only declare that this is the kind of learning with which I would wish to be associated as a teacher – and as a learner. I hope that explains, even at this late stage, the origin of some of the views and practices which I have set out, at times passionately, in the pages of this book.

References

Agnew, M.S. and Cowan, J. (1986) Exchanging experiences, *Proceedings of The Freshman Year Experience*. Columbia, SC: University of South Carolina.

Angelo T.A. and Cross, K.P. (1993) *Classroom Assessment Techniques*. San Francisco: Jossey-Bass.

Anon. (1980) *Education for Capability Manifesto*. London: Royal Society of Arts.

Barnett, R. (1997) *Higher Education: A Critical Business*. Buckingham: SRHE and Open University Press.

Baume, C. and Baume, D. (1992) *Course Design for Active Learning*. Sheffield: CVCP Universities' Staff Development and Training Unit.

Belenky, M.F., Clinchy, B.M., Goldberger, N.R. and Tarule, J.M. (1986) *Women's Ways of Knowing*. New York: Basic Books.

Benson, J.F. (1987) *Working More Creatively with Groups*. London and New York: Tavistock.

Bhattacharya, B., Cowan, J. and Weedon, E.M. (2000) Action research: A means to more effective teaching and learning, *Innovations in Education and Training International*, 37(4).

Biggs, J.B. (1985) The role of metacognition in enhancing learning skills, *Proceedings of the Annual Conference of the Australian Association for Research in Higher Education*. Hobart: AARHE.

Biggs, J.B. (2003) *Teaching for Quality Learning at University* (2nd edition). Buckingham: SRHE and Open University Press.

Biggs, J.B. and Moore, J.P. (1993) *The Process of Learning* (3rd edition). Sydney: Prentice-Hall of Australia.

Bligh, D. (1998) *What's the Use of Lectures?* (5th edition). Exeter: Intellect, School of Art and Design, Exeter.

Bloom, B.S., Engelhart, M.D., Furst, E.J., Hill, W.H. and Krathwohl, D.R. (1956) *Taxonomy of Educational Objectives, Handbook I: Cognitive Domain*. New York: David Mackay.

Bonk, C.J. and King, K.S. (eds) (1998) *Electronic Collaborators*. Mahwah, NJ, and London: Lawrence Erlbaum Associates.

Boud, D.J. (ed.) (1981) *Developing Student Autonomy in Learning*. London: Kogan Page.

Boud, D.J. (ed.) (1985) *Problem-Based Learning in Education for the Professions*. Sydney: HERDSA.

Boud, D.J. (ed.) (1988) *Developing Student Autonomy in Learning* (2nd edition). London: Kogan Page.

Boud, D.J. (ed.) (1995) *Enhancing Learning through Self Assessment*. London: Kogan Page.

Boud, D.J., Cohen, R. and Walker, D. (eds) (1993) *Using Experience for Learning*. Buckingham: SRHE and Open University Press.

Boud, D.J. and Griffin, V. (1987) *Appreciating Adults Learning: From the Learners Perspective*. London: Kogan Page.

Boud, D.J., Keogh, R. and Walker, D. (1985) *Reflection: Turning Experience into Learning*. London: Kogan Page.

Boud, D.J. and Walker, D. (1991) *Experience and Learning: Reflection at Work*. Victoria: Deakin University.

Boud, D.J. and Walker, D. (1993) Barriers to reflection on experience, in D.J. Boud, R. Cohen and D. Walker (eds) *Using Experience for Learning*. Buckingham: SRHE and Open University Press.

Boyd, H.R., Adeyemi-Bero, A. and Blackhall, R.F. (1984) *Acquiring Professional Competence through Learner-directed Learning*, Occasional Paper No.7. London: Royal Society of Arts.

Boyd, H.R. and Cowan, J. (1986) A case for self-assessment based on recent studies of student learning, *Assessment and Evaluation in Higher Education*, 10(3): 225–35.

Brockbank, A. and McGill, I. (1998) *Facilitating Reflective Learning in Higher Education*. Milton Keynes: SRHE and Open University Press.

Brohn, D.M. (1973) A test of structural understanding, Conference on 'Concrete Objectives for Education'. Slough: Cement and Concrete Association.

Brohn, D.M. and Cowan, J. (1977) Teaching towards an understanding of structural behaviour, *The Structural Engineer*, 55(1): 9–18.

Brookfield, S.D. (1986) *Understanding and Facilitating Adult Learning*. Buckingham: SRHE and Open University Press.

Brookfield, S.D. (1987) *Developing Critical Thinkers*. Buckingham: SRHE and Open University Press.

Brookfield, S.D. and Preskill, S. (1999) *Discussion as a Way of Teaching*. Buckingham: SRHE and Open University Press.

Brown, G.A. (1996) Referee's comment on an early draft of this text.

Brown, S. and Glasner, A. (eds) (1999) *Assessment Matters in Higher Education*. Buckingham: SRHE and Open University Press.

Brown, S., Race, P. and Bull, J. (eds) (1999) *Computer-assisted Assessment in Higher Education*. London: Kogan Page.

Carroll, Lewis (1935 edition) *Through The Looking Glass – And What Alice Found There*. London: Macmillan.

Cole, R. A. (ed.) (2000) *Issues in Web-Based Pedagogy*. Westport, CT, and London: Greenwood Press.

Cowan, J. (1974a) The essential features for a successful academic game, *SAGSET Journal*, 4(2): 17–22.

Cowan, J. (1974b) Identification of standard game forms with definable objectives, *Programmed Learning and Educational Technology*, 11(4): 192–6.

Cowan, J. (1975) The feasibility of resource-based learning in civil engineering, PhD thesis, Heriot-Watt University, Edinburgh.

Cowan, J. (1977) Individual approaches to problem-solving, in *Aspects of Educational Technology, Vol. X*. London: Kogan Page.

Cowan, J. (1980a) Improving the recorded protocol, *Programmed Learning and Educational Technology*, 17(3): 160–3.

Cowan, J. (1980b) Freedom in the selection of course content – a case study of a course without a syllabus, *Studies in Higher Education,* 3(2): 139–48.

Cowan, J. (1980c) Quantitative and qualitative understanding of engineering phenomena, *Proceedings of Ingenieur Padagogic '80,* 113–19. Vienna and Klagenfurt.

Cowan, J. (1981a) Design education based on an expressed statement of the design process, *Proceedings of the Institution of Civil Engineers,* Part 1, 70: 743–53.

Cowan, J. (1981b) The Truss game, *Simulation/Games for Learning,* 11(2): 92–5.

Cowan, J. (1982) Ascending order questions, *Civil Engineering Education (ASEE),* 4(2): 7–10.

Cowan, J. (1983) How engineers understand, *Engineering Education,* 13(4): 301–4.

Cowan, J. (1984a) Beyond instruction, *Proceedings of the 6th International Conference on Higher Education.* Lancaster: University of Lancaster.

Cowan, J. (1984b) *Acquiring Professional Competence through Learner-Directed Learning,* Occasional Paper No.7. London: Royal Society of Arts.

Cowan, J. (1984c) Learning from mistakes – a pragmatic approach to Education for Capability, *Programmed Learning and Educational Technology,* 21(4): 256–61.

Cowan, J. (1986a) Education for Capability in engineering education, DEng thesis, Heriot-Watt University.

Cowan, J. (1986b) Are we neglecting real analytical skills in engineering education? *European Journal of Engineering Education,* 11(1): 67–74.

Cowan, J. (1988) Struggling with self-assessment, in D.J. Boud (ed.) *Student Autonomy in Learning.* London: Kogan Page.

Cowan, J. (1989) Four fatal errors equals two lessons learnt, *Education and Training Technology International,* 26(2): 145–8.

Cowan, J. (1994) Sauce for the goose? A multi-level pedagogical pilot, *Education and Training Technology International,* 31(4): 325–9.

Cowan, J. (1995) Research into student learning – Yes, but by whom?, in S. Tornkvist (ed.) *Teaching Science for Technology at Tertiary Level.* Stockholm: Royal Swedish Academy of Engineering Sciences.

Cowan, J. (2004a) Beyond Reflection – where next for curricula which concentrate on abilities? In C. Baillie and I. Moore (eds) *Effective Learning & Teaching in Engineering.* London and New York: RoutledgeFalmer.

Cowan, J. (2004b) Education for higher level abilities; beyond alignment, to integration?, in V.M.S. Gil, I. Alarcão and H. Hooghoff (eds) *Challenges in Teaching & Learning in Higher Education.* Aveiro: Portugal, pp 53—76. University of Aveiro.

Cowan, J. (2005) The atrophy of the affect, in S. Robinson, and C. Katulushi (eds) *Values in Higher Education.* Vale of Glamorgan: Aureus Publishing.

Cowan, J. (to be published in 2006) An Introductory Refelction (Formerly New wines in an old bottle), in J.R. O'Donoghue (ed.) *Technology Supported Learning and Teaching: A Staff Perspective.* Hershey, PA: Idea Group Inc.

Cowan, J., Fordyce, D.S.E., and Asfari, A.F. (1987) Cultural influences on student learning – a preliminary study involving students of engineering, *International Journal of Innovative Higher Education,* A(1/2).

Cowan, J. and George, J.W. (1989) Non-numerate study skills: a mathematical approach, *Open Learning,* 4(1): 41–3.

Cowan, J. and George, J.W. (1992a) How was it for you? *The New Academic,* 1(2): Spring, 20–1.

Cowan, J. and George, J.W. (1992b) Diminishing lists of questions – a technique for curriculum design and formative evaluation, *Education and Training Technology International,* 29(2): 118–23.

Cowan, J. and George, J.W. (1993) A toolkit of techniques for formative evaluation by tutors, Paper to ICDE Conference on Quality Assurance in Open and Distance Education. Cambridge: ICDE.

Cowan, J. and George, J. W. (1997) *Formative Evaluation – Bordering on Action Research.* Project Report 97/5 Edinburgh: The Open University in Scotland.

Cowan, J. George, J.W. and Pinheiro-Torres, A. (2004) Alignment of developments in higher education, *Higher Education,* 48.

Cowan, J., Joyce, J., McPherson, D. and Weedon, E.M. (1999) Self-assessment of Reflective Journalling – and its effect on the learning outcomes, Paper presented to the 4th Northumbria Assessment Conference.

Cowan, J. and Harding, A.G. (1986) A logical model for curriculum development, *British Journal of Educational Technology,* 2(17): 103–9.

Cowan, J. and McConnell, S.G. (1967) An experiment in the teaching of Materials Science, *Metals and Materials,* July.

Cowan, J. and Morton, J. (1973) MOCO – A structural game for undergraduates, *Programmed Learning and Educational Technology,* 10(4): 267–73.

Cowan, J., Morton, J. and Bolton, A. (1973) An experimental learning unit for structural engineering studies, *The Structural Engineer,* 51(9): 337–9.

Cowan, J. and Westwood, J. (2006 in press) Collaborative and reflective professional development – a pilot. Accepted for publication in *Active Learning in Higher Education,* Vol. 6.

Cross, K.P. (1986) A proposal to improve teaching, *AAHE Bulletin,* September, 1086: 9–14.

Cross, K.P. and Angelo, T.A. (1988) *Classroom Assessment Techniques.* Michigan: National Center for Research to Improve Postsecondary Teaching and Learning.

Cross, K.P. and Steadman, M.H. (1996) *Classroom Research: Implementing the Scholarship of Teaching.* San Francisco: Jossey-Bass.

Davies, I.K. (1971) *The Management of Learning.* London: McGraw-Hill.

de Chardin, Pierre Teilhard (1955), *The Phenomenon of Man.* Trans. B. Wall. London and New York: Harper Collins, p.165.

Entwistle, N.J. (1978) Knowledge structures and styles of learning; a summary of Pask's recent research, *British Journal of Educational Technology,* 48: 1–11.

Entwistle, N.J. (1992) *The Impact of Teaching on Learning Outcomes in Higher Education.* Sheffield: CVCP Universities' Staff Development and Training Unit.

Entwistle, N.J. (2000) Promoting deep learning through teaching and assessment: conceptual frameworks and educational contexts, ESRC Teaching and Learning Research Programme Conference, November.

Entwistle N.J. and Ramsden, P. (1983) *Understanding Student Learning.* London: Croom Helm.

Fordyce, D.S.E. and Cowan, J. (1985) Developing the fundamental cognitive abilities appropriate to engineering education, *Proceedings of SEFI 1985 Conference.* Madrid: SEFI.

Gardner, R., Cairns, J. and Lawton, D. (eds) (2000) *Education for Values.* London and Sterling: Kogan Page.

Garrison, D. R. and Anderson, T. (2003), *E-Learning in the 21st Century, A Framework for Research and Practice.* London: RoutledgeFalmer.

Garry, A.M. and Cowan, J. (1987) To each according to his needs, in *Aspects of Educational Technology, Vol. XX.* London: Kogan Page.

Gatlin, L. (1987) Losing control and liking it; journal in Victorian literature, in

T. Fulwiler (ed.) *The Journal Book.* Portsmouth, NH: Heinemann.

Geddes, C. and Wood, H.M. (1995) *The Evaluation of Teaching Transferable Skills in Science.* Project Report 95/1. Edinburgh: The Open University in Scotland.

George, J.W. (1983) *On the Line: Counselling and teaching by telephone.* Open University short course, P519.

George, J.W. (1992) Alverno College; a learner's perspective, *British Journal of Educational Technology,* 22(3): 194–8.

George, J. W. (2001) *Higher Education Learning Development; Final report.* Edinburgh, Open University internal paper.

George, J.W. and Cowan, J. (1999a) *Ten Years of Action Research.* Edinburgh: The Open University in Scotland.

George, J.W. and Cowan, J. (1999b) *A Handbook of Techniques for Formative Evaluation.* London: Kogan Page.

Gibbs, G. (1988) *Learning by Doing.* Sheffield: Further Education Unit.

Gibbs, G. (1992) *Improving the Quality of Student Learning.* Bristol: Technical and Education Services.

Gibbs, G. (1997) *A Teaching and Learning Strategy for Higher Education.* Bristol: Commissioned report to the Higher Education Funding Council for England.

Gibbs, G. (1999a) *Institutional Learning and Teaching Strategies: A Summary of current practice.* Bristol: Higher Education Funding Council for England, Circular 99/55.

Gibbs, G. (1999b) *Institutional Learning and Teaching Strategies; a guide to good practice.* Bristol: Commissioned report to the Higher Education Funding Council for England.

Gibbs, G. (2004) Improving university teaching and learning through institution-wide strategies, in V.M.S. Gil, I. Alarcão and H, Hooghoff, Challenges in Teaching & *Learning in Higher Education.* Aveiro, Portugal: University of Aveiro, pp.149–66.

Gibbs, G., Habeshaw, S. and Habeshaw, T. (1988) *53 Interesting Ways to Appraise Your Teaching.* Bristol: Technical and Educational Services.

Gould, N. and Taylor, I. (1996) *Reflective Learning for Social Work.* Aldershot: Arena.

Handal, G. and Lauvas, P. (1987) *Promoting Reflective Teaching.* Buckingham: SRHE and Open University Press.

Hartley, J. (1998) *Learning and Studying.* London and New York: Routledge.

Hinett, K. and Thomas, J. (1999) *Staff Guide to Self and Peer Assessment.* Oxford: Oxford Centre for Staff and Learning Development.

Hewitt, P., Lentell, H., Phillips, M. and Stevens, V. (1997) *Open Teaching Toolkit: How Do I Know I Am Doing a Good Job?* Milton Keynes: The Open University.

Heywood, J. (1989) *Assessment in Higher Education* (2nd edition). Chichester: Wiley.

Heywood, J. (1992) Student teachers as researchers of instruction, in J.H.C. Vonk and H.J. van Hielden (eds) *New Prospects for Teacher Education in Europe.* Amsterdam and Brussels: Vrije Universiteit, Amsterdam, on behalf of the Association for Teacher Education in Europe.

Heywood, J. (2000) *Assessment in Higher Education.* London and Philadelphia: Jessica Kingsley Publishers.

Heywood, J., Sharp, J.M., and Hides, M.T. (2002) *Improving Teaching in Higher Education.* Salford: University of Salford.

Hirschhorn, L. (1991) Organising Feelings Toward Authority: a Case Study of Reflection-in-Action, in Schön, D.A., (ed.) *The Reflective Turn.* New York and London: Teachers College Press, Columbia University.

Hopkins, D. (1993) *A Teacher's Guide to Classroom Research* (2nd edition). Buckingham: Open University Press.

Hutchings, P. and Wutzdorff, A. (eds) (1988) *Knowing and Doing: Learning Through Experience*. San Francisco: Jossey-Bass.

JISC (2005) imaginative-curriculum-network@jiscmail.ac.

Kagan, N., Krathwohl, D. and Miller, R. (1963) Stimulated recall in therapy using video tape: a case study, *Journal of Counseling Psychology*, 24: 150–2.

Ketteridge, S., Marshall, S. and Fry, H. *The Effective Academic*. London: Kogan Page.

King, P.M. and Kitchener, K.S. (1994) *Developing Reflective Judgment*. San Francisco: Jossey-Bass.

Kirschenbaum, H. and Henderson, V.L. (eds) (1990) *Carl Rogers Dialogues*. London: Constable.

Knight, P. (ed.) (1995) *Assessment for Learning in Higher Education*. London: Kogan Page.

Knight, P.T. (2002) *Being a Teacher in Higher Education*. Buckingham: SRHE and Open University Press.

Kolb, D.A. (1984) *Experiential Learning*. Engelwood Cliffs, NJ: Prentice-Hall.

Kolmos, A. and Kofoed, L. (2004) Development of Process Competencies by reflection and experimentation, in V.M.S. Gil, I. Alarcão, and H. Hooghoff, (eds) *Challenges in Teaching & Learning in Higher Education*. Aveiro, Portugal: University of Aveiro.

Krueger, R.A. and Casey, M.A (2000) *Focus Groups* (3rd edition). Thousand Oaks, CA, London and New Delhi: Sage Publications Ltd.

Lewin, K. (1951) *Field Theory in Social Sciences*. New York: Harper and Row.

Loacker, G. (ed.) (2000) *Self Assessment at Alverno College*. Milwaukee: Alverno College Institute.

Loacker, G., Cromwell, L. and O'Brien, K. (1986) Assessment in higher education; to serve the learner, in C. Adelman (ed.) *Assessment in Higher Education*. Washington, DC: US Office of Education.

MacLean, R. (1970) Educational Television in the Universities, *Education and Training*, 12(11).

Marton, F., Hounsell, D. and Entwistle, N.J. (eds) (1997) *The Experience of Learning* (2nd edition). Edinburgh: Scottish Academic Press.

Mason, J.H. (1984) *Learning and Doing Mathematics*. Milton Keynes: The Open University.

Mason, J.H., with Burton, L. and Stacey, K. (1982) *Thinking Mathematically*. Wokingham: Addison-Wesley.

McGill, I. and Beaty, L. (2001) *Action Learning* (2nd edition). London: Kogan Page.

McKernan, J. (1996) *Curriculum Action Research* (2nd edition). London: Kogan Page.

Megginson, D. and Whittaker, V. (2003) *Continuous Professional Development*. London: Chartered Institute of Professional Development.

Mentkowski, M. and Associates (2000) *Learning that Lasts*. San Francisco, Jossey-Bass.

Mentkowski, M. and Strait, M.J. (1983) *A Longitudinal Study of Student Change in Cognitive Development, Learning Styles and Generic Abilities in an Outcome-centered Liberal Arts Curriculum*. (NIE-G-77-0058). Milwaukee: Alverno Productions.

Milne, A.A. (1926) *Winnie-the-Pooh*. London: Methuen.

Moon, J. (1999a) *Reflection in Learning and Professional Development*. London: Kogan Page.

Moon, J. (1999b) *Learning Journals*. London: Kogan Page.

Moon, J. (2004) *A Handbook of Reflective and Experiential Learning.* London and New York: RoutledgeFalmer.

Morgan, A. (1993) *Improving your Students' Learning.* London: Kogan Page.

Open University (1978–97). *M101: Mathematics: A Foundation Course.*

Open University (1993–2005) *A295: Homer: Poetry and Society*

Parlett, M. and Hamilton, D. (1972) *Evaluation as Illumination: A New Approach to the Study of Innovatory Programmes.* Edinburgh: Centre for Research in Educational Sciences, University of Edinburgh.

Pask, G.B. (1975) *The Cybernetics of Human Learning and Performance.* London: Hutchinson.

Pavlica, K., Holman, D., and Thorpe, R. (1998) The manager as a practical author of learning. *Career Development International,* 3(7): 300–7.

Perry, W.G. (1970) *Forms of Intellectual and Ethical Development in the College Years.* New York: Holt, Rinehart and Winston.

Perry, W.G. (1988) Different worlds in the same classroom, in P. Ramsden (ed.) *Improving Learning – New Perspectives.* London: Kogan Page.

Popper, K.R. (1962) *The Structure of Scientific Discovery.* Chicago: University of Chicago Press.

Popper, K.R. (1963) *Conjectures and Refutations – The Growth of Scientific Knowledge.* London, Routledge & Kegan Paul (4th edition, 1972).

Postman, N. and Weingartner, C. (1971) *Teaching as a Subversive Activity.* Harmondsworth: Penguin.

Prosser, M. and Trigwell, K. (1999) *Understanding Learning and Teaching.* Buckingham: SRHE and Open University Press.

QAA (Quality Assurance Agency) (2001a) The framework for higher education qualifications in England, Wales and Northern Ireland (FHEQ), January.

QAA (Quality Assurance Agency) (2001b) Scottish Credit and Qualifications Framework (SCQF), January.

Race, P. (2005) *Making Learning Happen.* Thousand Oaks, CA, London and New Delhi: Sage Publications Ltd.

Rainier, T. (1980) *The New Diary.* London: Angus and Robertson.

Ramsden, P. (ed.) (1988) *Improving Learning – New Perspectives.* London: Kogan Page.

Ramsden, P. (1992) *Learning to Teach in Higher Education.* London: Routledge.

Richardson, J.T.E., Eysenck, M.W. and Warren Piper, D. (1987) *Student Learning.* Buckingham: SRHE and Open University Press.

Roethlisberger, Fritz and Dickson, William (1939) *Management and the Worker: An account of a research program conducted by the Western Electric Company, Chicago.* Cambridge, MA: Harvard University Press.

Rogers, C. (1951) *Client-centred Therapy.* Boston, MA: Houghton Mifflin.

Rogers, C. (1961) *On Becoming a Person.* Boston, MA: Houghton Mifflin.

Rogers, C. (1969) *Freedom to Learn.* Columbus, OH: Merrill.

Rogers, C.R. (1980) *A Way of Being.* Boston, MA: Houghton Mifflin Co.

Rogers, C.R. (1983) *Freedom to Learn for the 80's.* Columbus, OH: Merrill.

Rosier, N. (1998) Faxes up North, Project Report (Unnumbered). Edinburgh: The Open University in Scotland.

Rowland, S. (2000) *The Enquiring University Teacher,* Buckingham: Society for Research into Higher Education, and Open University Press.

Rowntree, D. (1977) *Assessing Students: How Shall We Know Them?* London: Harper and Row.

Royal Society for the Encouragement of Arts, Manufacture and Commerce (1980) *The Education for Capability Manifesto.* London: RSA.

Russell, T. and Munby, H. (1991) *Reframing: The Role of Experience in Developing Teachers' Professional Knowledge,* in Schön, D.A. (ed.) *The Reflective Turn.* New York and London: Teachers College Press, Columbia University.

Rust, C., Price, M. and O'Donovan, B. (2003) Improving Students' Learning by Developing their Understanding of Assessment Criteria and Processes, *Assessment and Evaluation in Higher Education,* 28(2).

Sadler, D.R. (1983) Evaluation and the improvement of academic learning, *Journal of Higher Education,* 54.

Savin-Baden, M. and Wilkie, J. (eds) (2004) *Challenging Research in Problem-Based Learning.* Buckingham: SRHE and Open University Press.

Schmeck, R.R. (ed.) (1988) *Learning Strategies and Learning Styles.* New York: Plenum Press.

Schön, D.A. (1983) *The Reflective Practitioner.* New York: Basic Books.

Schön, D.A. (1987) *Educating the Reflective Practitioner.* San Francisco: Jossey-Bass.

Schön, D.A. (ed.) (1991) *The Reflective Turn.* New York and London: Teachers College Press, Columbia University.

Skemp, R.R. (1979) *Intelligence, Learning and Action.* Chichester: Wiley.

Skemp, R.R. (1971) *The Psychology of Learning Mathematics.* Harmondsworth: Penguin.

Smyth, K. (2005) Personal communication, when asked for comments on a draft of Chapter 9 as a 'critical friend', and as an educational adviser specialising in e-learning.

Snyder, B.R. (1971) *The Hidden Curriculum.* Cambridge, MA, MIT Press

Stenhouse, L. (1975) *An Introduction to Curriculum Research and Development.* London: Heinemann.

Stenhouse, L. (1984) Artistry and teaching: the teacher as focus of research and development, in D. Hopkins and M. Wideen (eds) *Alternative Perspectives on School Improvement.* Lewes: Falmer Press.

Stice, J.E. (1987) *Developing Critical Thinking and Problem-Solving Abilities.* San Francisco: Jossey-Bass.

Taras, M. (2005) Assessment, Summative and formative – some theoretical reflections. *British Journal of Educational Studies, 53(3).*

Taylor, P.V. (1993) *The Texts of Paulo Freire.* Buckingham: Open University Press.

Thompson, J. (1992) E530/730: Resource Pack Section 2 – *Your Learning Journey.* Milton Keynes: Open University.

Tresman, S. and Edwards, D. (1993) Reflecting on practice: some illustrations, in E. Whitelegg, J. Thomas and D. Tresman. (eds) *Challenges and Opportunities for Science Education.* Milton Keynes: The Open University.

Verulum (2004) Discussions of understanding of structural behaviour, *The Structural Engineer,* 82(7): 18–19.

Verulam (2005) Discussions of understanding of structural behaviour, *The Structural Engineer,* 82(19): 32–3.

Vygotsky, L.S. (1978) *Mind in Society.* Cambridge, MA: Harvard University Press.

Weedon, E.M. (1994) *An Investigation of the Effect of Feedback to Students on TMAs.* Project report 94/5. Edinburgh: The Open University in Scotland.

Weedon, E.M. and Cowan, J. (2002) Commenting Electronically on Students' Reflective Learning Journals, in C. Rust (ed.) *Improving Student Learning, Theory and Practice Using Learning Technology.* Oxford: Oxford Centre for Staff & Learning Development.

Weedon, E.M. and Cowan, J. (2003) The Kolb Cycle, Reflection and all that . . . what is new?, in C. Rusk (ed.) *Improving Student Learning, Theory and Practice – 10 years on*. Oxford: Oxford Centre for Staff & Learning Development, pp 97-108.

Weil, S.W. and McGill, I. (1989) *Making Sense of Experiential Learning*. Buckingham: SRHE and Open University Press.

Wertsch, J.V. (1985) *Vygotsky and the Social Formation of Mind*. Cambridge, MA, and London: Harvard University Press.

Wikipedia (2005) http://en.wikipedia.org/wiki/Empathy.

Winner, L. (1998) Tech Knowledge Review. *NetFuture: Technology and Human Responsibility*, 72: 4–10.

Winter, R. (1989) *Learning from Experience*. Lewes: Falmer Press.

Woods, D.R. (1987), in J.E. Stice (ed.) *Developing Critical Thinking and Problem-Solving Abilities*. San Francisco: Jossey-Bass.

Woods, D.R. (1994) *Problem-based Learning: How to Gain the Most from PBL*. Hamilton, Ontario: McMaster University Bookstore.

Index